THE
ASTRAL
BODY

THE
ASTRAL
BODY

AND OTHER ASTRAL PHENOMENA

A. E.
POWELL

A publication supported by
THE KERN FOUNDATION

Quest Books
Theosophical Publishing House

Wheaton, Illinois ♦ Madras, India

Library of Congress Cataloging-in-Publication Data

Powell, Arthur Edward,
    The astral body and other astral phenomena

    (A Quest book)
    1. Astral projection.   2. Theosophy.   I. Title.
BP573.A7P58   1973   133.9   73-4775
ISBN 0-8356-0438-1

Printed in the United States of America

DEDICATION

*This book is dedicated with gratitude
and appreciation to all those whose
painstaking labour and researches have
provided the materials out of
which it has been
compiled*

" To know man is to know God.

" To know God is to know man.

" To study the universe is to learn both God and man ; for the universe is the expression of the Divine Thought, and the universe is mirrored in man.

" Knowledge is necessary if the SELF would become free and know Itself as Itself alone."

ANNIE BESANT.

CONTENTS

AUTHORS QUOTED

Book	Author	Edn.	Abbreviation
Ancient Wisdom . .	A. Besant . .	1897	*A W*
Astral Plane . .	C. W. Leadbeater .	1910	*A P*
Changing World . .	A. Besant . .	1909	*C W*
Clairvoyance . . .	C. W. Leadbeater .	1908	*C*
Crowd in Peace and War .	Sir Martin Conway	1915	*C P W*
Death and After . .	A. Besant . .	1901	*D A*
Dreams	C. W. Leadbeater .	1903	*D*
Hidden Side of Things, Vol. I.	C. W. Leadbeater .	1913	*H S I*
Hidden Side of Things, Vol. II.	C. W. Leadbeater .	1913	*H S II*
Inner Life, Vol. I. . .	C. W. Leadbeater .	1910	*I L I*
Inner Life, Vol. II. . .	C. W. Leadbeater .	1911	*I L II*
Introduction to Yoga .	A. Besant . .	1908	*I Y*
Invisible Helpers . .	C. W. Leadbeater .	1911	*I H*
Karma	A. Besant . .	1897	*K*
Key to Theosophy .	H. P. Blavatsky .	1893	*K T*
Law of Psychic Phenomena	T. J. Hudson .	1905	*L P P*
Life after Death . .	C. W. Leadbeater .	1912	*L A D*
London Lectures, 1907 .	A. Besant . .	1907	*L L*
Man and His Bodies . .	A. Besant . .	1900	*M B*
Man Visible and Invisible .	C. W. Leadbeater .	1902	*M V I*
Masters and the Path .	C. W. Leadbeater .	1925	*M P*
Monad	C. W. Leadbeater .	1920	*M*
Occult Chemistry . .	A. Besant and C. W. Leadbeater	1919	*O C*
Occult World . . .	A. P. Sinnett .	1906	*O W*
Other Side of Death . .	C. W. Leadbeater .	1904	*O S D*
Reincarnation . .	A. Besant . .	1898	*R*
Science of the Emotions .	Bhagavan Das .	1900	*S E*
Secret Doctrine, Vol. I. .	H. P. Blavatsky .	1905	*S D I*
Secret Doctrine, Vol. II. .	H. P. Blavatsky .	1905	*S D II*
Secret Doctrine, Vol. III. .	H. P. Blavatsky .	1897	*S D III*
Self and its Sheaths . .	A. Besant . .	1903	*S S*
Seven Principles of Man .	A. Besant . .	1904	*S P*
Seven Rays . . .	Ernest Wood .	1925	*S R*
Some Glimpses of Occultism	C. W. Leadbeater .	1909	*S G O*
Some Occult Experiences .	J. Van Manen .	1913	*S O E*
Study in Consciousness .	A. Besant . .	1904	*S C*
Textbook of Theosophy .	C. W. Leadbeater .	1914	*T B*
Theosophy and the New Psychology	A. Besant . .	1909	*T N P*
Thought Forms . .	A. Besant and C. W. Leadbeater	1905	*T F*
Thought Power: Its Control and Culture	A. Besant . .	1903	*T P*

N.B.—In a few cases, where the unsupported opinions of the compiler are given, they are indicated by the letters A.E.P.

PUBLISHER'S PREFACE

THE author's purpose in compiling the books in this series was to save students much time and labour by providing a condensed synthesis of the considerable literature on the respective subjects of each volume, coming mostly from the pens of Annie Besant and C. W. Leadbeater. The accompanying list shows the large number of books from which he drew. So far as possible, the method adopted was to explain the form side first, before the life side: to describe the objective mechanism of phenomena and then the activities of consciousness that are expressed through the mechanism. There is no attempt to prove or even justify any of the statements. Marginal references give opportunity to refer to the sources.

The works of H. P. Blavatsky were not used because the author said that the necessary research in *The Secret Doctrine* and other writings would have been too vast a task for him to undertake. He added: "The debt to H. P. Blavatsky is greater than could ever be indicated by quotations from her monumental volumes. Had she not shown the way in the first instance, later investigators might never have found the trail at all."

The present edition has been slightly abridged and edited to avoid possible misunderstanding in the changed conditions of today. The reader is asked to take note of the following points:

1. " Ego " is used in this book for the reincarnating Individuality; not, as in modern psychology, for the evanescent personality.

2. The words " atom," " atomic," " sub-atomic " and " molecule " are used in a specialized sense and do not refer to a chemical atom and molecule. So also are " ether" and " etheric ".

INTRODUCTION

THE purpose of this book is to present to the student of Theosophy a condensed synthesis of the information at present[1] available concerning the Astral Body of man, together with a description and explanation of the astral world and its phenomena. The book is thus a natural sequel of *The Etheric Double and Allied Phenomena* published in 1925.

As in the case of *The Etheric Double*, the compiler has consolidated the information obtained from a large number of books, a list of which is given, arranging the material, which covers a vast field and is exceedingly complex, as methodically as lay within his power. It is hoped that by this means present and future students of the subject will be saved much labour and research, being able not only to find the information they require presented in a comparatively small compass, but also, with the help of the marginal references, to refer, should they so desire, to the original sources of information.

In order that the book may fulfil its purpose by being kept within reasonable dimensions, the general plan followed has been to expound the principles underlying astral phenomena, omitting particular examples or instances. Lecturers and others who wish specific illustrations of the principles enunciated, will find the marginal references useful as a clue to the places where the examples they seek may be found.

Again, so far as the complexities and ramifications of the subject permit, the method has been to explain the *form* side first, before the *life* side : *i.e.*, to describe first the objective mechanism of phenomena, and then the activities of consciousness which are expressed through that mechanism. The careful student, bearing this in

[1] 1926.

mind, will thus recognise many passages, which at first glance might appear to be repetitive, in which the same phenomenon is described first from the point of view of the outer material form and then again later from the point of view of the spirit or consciousness.

It is hoped that the present volume may be followed by similar ones dealing with man's Mental and Causal bodies, thus completing the consolidation of all information so far available regarding man's constitution up to the Causal or Higher Mental level. •

There is to-day a great deal of information on these and similar subjects, but it is for the most part scattered over large numbers of books. In order, therefore, to make the whole of it available for the student, whose time for intensive study is limited, such books as the present is intended to be are (in the writer's opinion) urgently needed. " The proper study of mankind is man : " and the subject is so vast, so absorbing, and so important that everything possible should be done to make readily accessible to all who thirst for such knowledge the whole of the information which has so far been accumulated.

A. E. P.

THE ASTRAL BODY

CHAPTER I

GENERAL DESCRIPTION

BEFORE proceeding to a detailed study of the astral body, and of phenomena associated with it, it may be useful to lay before the student a brief outline of the ground it is proposed to cover, in order to give in proper perspective a view of the whole subject and of the relative dependence of its several parts.

Briefly, the astral body of man is a vehicle, to clairvoyant sight not unlike the physical body, surrounded by an aura of flashing colours, composed of matter of an order of fineness higher than that of physical matter, in which feelings, passions, desires and emotions are expressed and which acts as a bridge or medium of transmission between the physical brain and the mind, the latter operating in the still higher vehicle—the mind-body.

While every man possesses and uses an astral body, comparatively few are conscious of its existence or can control and function in it in full consciousness. In the case of large numbers of persons it is scarcely more than an inchoate mass of astral matter, the movements and activities of which are little under the control of the man himself—the Ego.[1] With others, however, the astral body is a well-developed and thoroughly organised vehicle, possessing a life of its own and conferring on its owner many and useful powers.

During the sleep of the physical body, an undeveloped man leads a dreamy, vague existence, in his relatively primitive astral body, remembering little or nothing

[1] See Publisher's Preface.

of his sleep-life when he re-awakens in his physical body.

In the case of a developed man, however, the life in the astral body, whilst the physical body is wrapped in slumber, is active, interesting and useful, and the memory of it may, under certain conditions, be brought down into the physical brain. The life of such a man ceases to be a series of days of consciousness and nights of oblivion, becoming instead a continuous life of unbroken consciousness, alternating between the physical and the astral planes or worlds.

One of the first things a man learns to do in his astral body is to travel in it, it being possible for the astral body to move, with great rapidity, and to great distances from the sleeping physical body. An understanding of this phenomenon throws much light on a large number of so-called " occult " phenomena, such as " apparitions " of many kinds, knowledge of places never visited physically, etc.

The astral body being *par excellence* the vehicle of feelings and emotions, an understanding of its composition and of the ways in which it operates is of considerable value in understanding many aspects of man's psychology, both individual and collective, and also provides a simple explanation of the mechanism of many phenomena revealed by modern psycho-analysis.

A clear understanding of the structure and nature of the astral body, of its possibilities and its limitations, is essential to a comprehension of the life into which men pass after physical death. The many kinds of " heavens," " hells " and purgatorial existences believed in by followers of innumerable religions, all fall naturally into place and become intelligible as soon as we understand the nature of the astral body and of the astral world.

A study of the astral body will be of assistance also in our understanding of many of the phenomena of the *séance* room and of certain psychic or non-physical methods of healing disease. Those who are interested in what is termed the fourth dimension will find also a confirmation of many of the theories which have been formulated by means of geometry and mathematics, in a study of astral world phenomena, as described by those who have observed them.

A study of the astral body of man thus takes us far afield and expands enormously a conception of life based solely on the physical world and the purely physical senses. As we proceed, we shall see that the physical senses, invaluable as they are, by no means represent the limit of what man's vehicles may teach him of the worlds in which he lives. The awakening into functioning activity of astral faculties reveals a new world within the old world and, when a man becomes able to read aright its significance, he will obtain such an expanded view of his own life, and all nature, as will reveal to him the almost limitless possibilities latent in man. From this, sooner or later but inevitably, there will come the impulse, and later the unshakable determination, to master these worlds, and himself, to rise superior to his earthly destiny, and to become an intelligent co-operator with what has been aptly termed the Supreme Will in Evolution.

We will now proceed to study, in detail, the astral body and many astral phenomena closely associated with it.

CHAPTER II

COMPOSITION AND STRUCTURE

M B 38.   ASTRAL matter exists in seven grades or orders of fineness, corresponding to the seven grades of physical matter, which are solid, liquid, gaseous, etheric,[1] super-etheric, sub-atomic and atomic.[1] No names for these astral states, however, having so far been devised, it is usual to describe them, either by the number of the grade or sub-plane, the finest being Number 1, the coarsest Number 7, or by the corresponding physical grade. *E.g.*, we speak of astral solid matter, meaning thereby the seventh or lowest variety : astral etheric matter, meaning the fourth from the finest : and so on.

M V I 12
M B 38.
T B 26.
    Astral matter, being much finer than physical matter, interpenetrates it. Every physical atom,[1] therefore, floats in a sea of astral matter, which surrounds it and fills every interstice in physical matter. It is of course, well known that even in the hardest substance no two atoms ever touch one another, the space between two adjacent atoms being in fact enormously larger than the atoms themselves. Orthodox physical science long ago has posited an ether[1] which interpenetrates all known substances, the densest solid as well as the most rarefied gas ; and just as this ether moves with perfect freedom between the particles of densest matter, so does astral matter interpenetrate it in turn, and moves with perfect freedom among its particles. Thus a being living in the astral world might be occupying the same space as a being living in the physical world ; yet each would be entirely unconscious of the other, and would in no way impede the free movement of the other. The student should thoroughly familiarise himself with this fundamental conception,

[1] See Publisher's Preface.

as, without grasping it clearly, it is not possible to understand large numbers of astral phenomena.

The principle of interpenetration makes it clear that the different realms of nature are not separated in space, but exist about us here and now, so that to perceive and investigate them no movement in space is necessary, but only an opening within ourselves of the senses by means of which they can be perceived.

The astral world, or plane, is thus a condition of nature, rather than a locality. *O C* 4.

It must be noted that a physical atom cannot be directly broken up into astral atoms. If the force which whirls the (approximately) fourteen thousand million " bubbles in koilon " into an ultimate physical atom be pressed back by an effort of will over the threshold of the astral plane, the atom disappears, releasing the " bubbles." The same force, working then on a higher level, expresses itself, not through one astral atom, but through a group of forty-nine such atoms. *O C App.* iii-iv.

A similar relationship, represented by the number 49, exists between the atoms of any two other contiguous planes of nature : thus an astral atom contains 49^5 or 282,475,249 " bubbles," a mental atom, 49^4 bubbles, and so on. *T B* 20-21.

There is reason to believe that electrons are astral atoms. Physicists state that a chemical atom of hydrogen contains probably from 700 to 1000 electrons. Occult research asserts that a chemical atom of hydrogen contains 882 astral atoms. This may be a coincidence, but that does not seem probable. *I L II* 265.

It should be noted that ultimate physical atoms are of two kinds, male and female : in the male, force pours in from the astral world, passes through the atom and out into the physical world : in the female, force passes in from the physical world, through the atom, and out into the astral world, thus vanishing from the physical world. *O C* 31.

Astral matter corresponds with curious accuracy to *I L I* 359-360.

the physical matter which it interpenetrates, each variety of physical matter attracting astral matter of corresponding density. Thus solid physical matter is interpenetrated by what we call solid astral matter : liquid physical by liquid astral, *i.e.*, by matter of the sixth sub-plane : and similarly with gaseous and the four grades of etheric matter, each of which is interpenetrated by the corresponding grade of astral matter.

A P 39.
S C 327–328.
Precisely as it is necessary that the physical body should contain within its constitution physical matter in all its conditions, solid, liquid, gaseous and etheric, so it is indispensable that the astral body should contain particles of all the seven astral sub-planes, though, of course, the proportions may vary greatly in different cases.

M B 41.
M V I 52.
The astral body of man thus being composed of matter of all seven grades, it is possible for him to experience all varieties of desire to the fullest possible extent, the highest as well as the lowest.

S P 19.
It is the peculiar type of response possessed by astral matter which enables the astral matter to serve as the sheath in which the Self can gain experience of *sensation*.

M V I 37.
In addition to the ordinary matter of the astral plane, that which is known as the Third Elemental Kingdom, or simply as the Elemental Essence of the astral plane, also enters largely into the composition of man's astral body, and forms what is called the " Desire-Elemental," which we shall deal with more fully in later chapters.

M V I 37–39.
Astral elemental essence consists of matter of the six lower levels of the astral plane, vivified by the Second Outpouring, from the Second Person of the Trinity. Astral matter of the highest or atomic level, similarly vivified, is known as Monadic Essence.

A W 94.
M B 43.
In an undeveloped man, the astral body is a cloudy, loosely organised, vaguely outlined mass of astral matter, with a great predominance of substances from the lower grades ; it is gross, dark in colour, and dense—often so dense that the outline of the physical

body is almost lost in it—and is thus fitted to respond
to stimuli connected with the passions and appetites. *A W* 95.
In size, it extends in all directions about ten or twelve
inches beyond the physical body.

In an average moral and intellectual man the astral *A W* 98.
body is considerably larger, extending about 18 inches *I L II* 252.
on each side of the body, its materials are more balanced
and finer in quality, the presence of the rarer kinds
giving a certain luminous quality to the whole, and
its outline is clear and definite.

In the case of a spiritually developed man the astral *A W* 101.
body is still larger in size and is composed of the finest
particles of each grade of astral matter, the higher
largely predominating.

There is so much to be said regarding the colours of
astral bodies that the subject is reserved for a separate
chapter. Here, however, it may be stated that in
undeveloped types the colours are coarse and muddy, *A W* 98.
gradually becoming more and more luminous as the
man develops emotionally, mentally and spiritually.
The very name "astral," inherited from mediæval *M V I* 22.
alchemists, signifies "starry," being intended to *M B* 37-38.
allude to the luminous appearance of astral matter.

As already said, the astral body of a man not only *M B* 42.
permeates the physical body, but also extends around
it in every direction like a cloud.

That portion of the astral body which extends *M B* 43.
beyond the limits of the physical body is usually
termed the astral "aura."

Intense feeling means a large aura. It may here *I L II* 252-
be mentioned that increased size of the aura is a pre- 253.
requisite for Initiation, and the "Qualifications"
should be visible in it. The aura naturally increases
with each Initiation. The aura of the Buddha is said
to have been three miles in radius.

The matter of the physical body having a very strong *I L I* 391-
attraction for the matter of the astral body, it follows 393.
that by far the greater portion (about 99 per cent.)
of the astral particles are compressed within the
periphery of the physical body, only the remaining

1 per cent. filling the rest of the ovoid and forming the aura.

The central portion of the astral body thus takes the exact form of the physical body and is, in fact, very solid and definite, and quite clearly distinguishable from the surrounding aura. It is usually termed the astral *counterpart* of the physical body. The exact correspondence of the astral body with the physical, however, is merely a matter of external form, and does not at all involve any similarity of function in the various organs, as we shall see more fully in the chapter on Chakrams.

C 14–15.

Not only man's physical body, but everything physical, has its corresponding order of astral matter in constant association with it, not to be separated from it except by a very considerable exertion of occult force, and even then only to be held apart from it as long as force is being definitely exerted to that end. In other words, every physical object has its astral counterpart. But as the astral particles are constantly moving among one another as easily as those of a physical liquid, there is no permanent association between any one physical particle and that amount of astral matter which happens at any given moment to be acting as its counterpart.

C 40.

Usually the astral portion of an object projects somewhat beyond the physical part of it, so that metals, stones, etc., are seen surrounded by an astral aura.

I L I 395.

If some part of a man's physical body be removed, *e.g.*, by amputation, the coherence of the living astral matter is stronger than its attraction towards the severed portion of the physical. Consequently the astral counterpart of the limb will not be carried away with the severed physical limb. Since the astral matter has acquired the habit of keeping that particular form, it will continue to retain the original shape, but will soon withdraw within the limits of the maimed form. The same phenomenon takes place in the case of a tree from which a branch has been severed.

In the case of an inanimate body, however, such as a chair or a basin, there is not the same kind of individual life to maintain cohesion. Consequently, when the physical object is broken the astral counterpart would also be divided.

Quite apart from the seven grades of matter, arranged *H S I* 43–46. in order of fineness, there is also a totally distinct classification of astral matter, according to its *type*. In Theosophical literature the degree of fineness is usually designated the *horizontal* division, and the type the *vertical* division. The types, of which there are seven, are as thoroughly intermingled as are the constituents of the atmosphere, and in every astral body there is matter of all seven types, the proportion between them showing the disposition of the man, whether he be devotional or philosophic, artistic or scientific, pragmatic or mystic.

The whole of the astral portion of our earth and of *H S I* 42–43. the physical planets, together with the purely astral *I L II* 431– planets of our System, make up collectively the astral 432. body of the Solar Logos, thus showing that the old pantheistic conception was a true one.

Similarly each of the seven types of astral matter *H S I* 46–49; is to some extent, regarded as a whole, a separate *51–52.* vehicle, and may be thought of as also the astral body *I L II* 431– of a subsidiary Deity or Minister, who is at the same *433.* *M P* 289– time an aspect of the Deity, a kind of ganglion or force-*290.* centre in Him. Hence the slightest thought, movement or alteration of any kind in the subsidiary Deity is instantly reflected in some way or other in all the matter of the corresponding type. Such psychic changes occur periodically : perhaps they correspond to in-breathing and out-breathing, or to the beating of the heart with us on the physical plane. It has been observed that the movements of the physical planets furnish a clue to the operation of the influences flowing from these changes : hence the rationale of astrological science. Hence, further, any such alteration must to some extent affect each man, in proportion to the amount of that type of matter which he

H S I 48 :
54 : 56.

possesses in his astral body. Thus, one change would affect the emotions, or the mind, or both, another might intensify nervous excitement and irritability, and so on. It is this proportion which determines in each man, animal, plant or mineral certain fundamental characteristics which never change—sometimes called his note, colour, or ray.

To pursue this interesting line of thought further would take us beyond the scope of this book, so the student is referred to *The Hidden Side of Things*, Vol. I, pp. 43-58.

H S I 47.

There are seven sub-types in each type, making forty-nine sub-types in all.

H S I 48–49.

The type or ray is permanent through the whole planetary scheme, so that an elemental essence (see p. 6) of type A will in due course ensoul minerals, plants and animals of type A, and from it will emerge also human beings of the same type.

I L I 396.
O S D 15 :
97.

The astral body slowly but constantly wears away, precisely as does the physical, but, instead of the process of eating and digesting food, the particles which fall away are replaced by others from the surrounding atmosphere. Nevertheless, the feeling of individuality is communicated to the new particles as they enter, and also the elemental essence included with each man's astral body undoubtedly feels itself a kind of entity, and acts accordingly for what it considers its own interests.

CHAPTER III

COLOURS

To clairvoyant sight one of the principal features of M V I 22-23. an astral body consists of the colours which are constantly playing through it, these colours corresponding to, and being the expression in astral matter of feelings, passions and emotions.

All known colours, and many which are at present M V I 23: 71. unknown to us, exist upon each of the higher planes of nature, but as we rise from one stage to another they become more delicate and more luminous, so that they may be described as higher octaves of colour. As it is not possible to portray these octaves physically on paper, the above facts should be borne in mind when considering the coloured illustrations of the astral body which are referred to below.

The following is a list of the principal colours and the emotions of which they are an expression:—

Black: in thick clouds: hatred and malice. M V I 81.

Red: deep red flashes, usually on a black ground: anger.

A scarlet cloud: irritability. M V I 73.

Brilliant scarlet: on the ordinary background of the aura: " noble indignation."

Lurid and sanguinary red: unmistakable, though not easy to describe: sensuality.

Brown-grey: dull, hard brown-grey: selfishness: M V I 82. one of the commonest colours in the astral body.

Brown-red: dull, almost rust-colour: avarice, usually arranged in parallel bars across the astral body.

Greenish-brown: lit up by deep red or scarlet flashes: jealousy. In the case of an ordinary man there is usually much of this colour present when he is " in love."

Grey : heavy, leaden : depression. Like the brown-red of avarice, arranged in parallel lines, conveying the impression of a cage.

Grey, livid : a hideous and frightful hue : fear.

Crimson : dull and heavy : selfish love.

Rose-colour : unselfish · love. When exceptionally brilliant, tinged with lilac : spiritual love for humanity.

M V I 83.   *Orange :* pride or ambition. Often found with
T F 33 : 49. irritability.

Yellow : intellect : varies from a deep and dull tint, through brilliant gold, to clear and luminous lemon or primrose yellow. *Dull yellow ochre* implies the direction of faculty to selfish purposes : *clear gamboge* indicates a distinctly higher type ; *primrose yellow* denotes intellect devoted to spiritual ends ; *gold* indicates pure intellect applied to philosophy or mathematics.

Green : in general, varies greatly in its significance, and needs study to be interpreted correctly : mostly
M V I 84.   it indicates adaptability. *Grey-green*, slimy in appearance : deceit and cunning. *Emerald green :* versatility, ingenuity and resourcefulness, applied unselfishly. *Pale, luminous blue-green :* deep sympathy and compassion, with the power of perfect adaptability which only they can give. *Bright apple-green* seems always to accompany strong vitality.

M V I 85.   *Blue :* dark and clear : religious feeling. It is
T F 34.   liable to be tinted by many other qualities, thus becoming any shade from indigo or a rich deep violet to muddy grey-blue. *Light-blue*, such as ultramarine or cobalt : devotion to a noble spiritual ideal. A tint of *violet* indicates a mixture of affection and devotion. *Luminous lilac-blue*, usually accompanied by sparkling golden stars : the higher spirituality, with lofty spiritual aspirations.

M V I 86.   *Ultra-violet :* higher and purer developments of psychic faculties.

Ultra-red : lower psychic faculties of one who dabbles in evil and selfish forms of magic.

I L II 134.   Joy shows itself in a general brightening and radiancy

of both mental and astral bodies, and in a peculiar
rippling of the surface of the body. Cheerfulness
shows itself in a modified bubbling form of this, and
also in a steady serenity.

Surprise is shown by a sharp constriction of the
mental body, usually communicated to both the astral
and physical bodies, accompanied by an increased
glow of the band of affection if the surprise is a pleasant
one, and by an increase of brown and grey if the surprise
is an unpleasant one. The constriction often causes
unpleasant feelings, affecting sometimes the solar plexus,
resulting in sinking and sickness, and sometimes the
heart centre, causing palpitation and even death.

It will be understood that, as human emotions are *M V I* 80.
hardly ever unmixed, so these colours are seldom
perfectly pure, but more usually mixtures. Thus the
purity of many colours is dimmed by the hard brown-
grey of selfishness, or tinged with the deep orange
of pride.

In reading the full meaning of colours, other points *M V I* 85–86.
have also to be taken into consideration : viz., the
general brilliance of the astral body : the comparative
definiteness or indefiniteness of its outline : the relative brightness of the different centres of force (see
Chapter V).

The yellow of intellect, the rose of affection, and the *M V I* 90.
blue of devotion are always found in the upper part
of the astral body : the colours of selfishness, avarice,
deceit and hatred are in the lower part : the mass of
sensual feeling floats usually between the two.

From this it follows that in the undeveloped man *I L II* 136 :
the lower portion of the ovoid tends to be larger than 252.
the upper, so that the astral body has the appearance
of an egg with the small end uppermost. In the more
developed man the reverse is the case, the small end
of the egg pointing downwards. The tendency always
is for the symmetry of the ovoid to re-assert itself by
degrees, so that such appearances are only temporary.

Each quality, expressed as a colour, has its own *M V I* 91.
special type of astral matter, and the average position

of these colours depends upon the specific gravity of the respective grades of matter. The general principle
H S II 154. is that evil or selfish qualities express themselves in the comparatively slow vibrations of coarser matter, while good and unselfish qualities play through finer matter.

M P 104–105. This being so, fortunately for us, good emotions persist even longer than evil ones, the effect of a feeling of strong love or devotion remaining in the astral body long after the occasion that caused it has been forgotten.

It is possible, though unusual, to have two rates of vibrations going on strongly in the astral body at the same time, *e.g.*, love and anger. The after-results will go on side by side, but one at a very much higher level than the other and therefore persisting longer.

I L I 389. High unselfish affection and devotion belong to the highest (atomic) astral sub-plane, and these reflect themselves in the corresponding matter of the mental plane. They thus touch the causal (higher mental) body, not the lower mental. This is an important point of which the student should take especial note. The Ego, who resides on the higher mental plane, is thus affected only by unselfish thoughts. Lower thoughts affect, not the Ego, but the permanent atoms (see p. 207).

Consequently, in the causal body there would be gaps, not bad colours, corresponding to the lower feelings and thoughts. Selfishness, for example, would show itself as the *absence* of affection or sympathy : as soon as selfishness is replaced by its opposite, the gap in the causal body would be filled up.

M V I 72. An intensification of the coarse colours of the astral body, representing base emotions, whilst finding no direct expression in the causal body, nevertheless tends somewhat to dim the luminosity of the colours representing the opposite virtues in the causal body.

M V I 90. In order to realise the appearance of the astral body, it must be borne in mind that the particles of which it is composed are always in rapid motion : in the vast majority of cases the clouds of colour melt into one another and are all the while rolling over one another, appearing and disappearing as they roll, the surface of the luminous mist resembling somewhat the surface of violently boiling water. The various colours, therefore, by no means retain the same positions, though there is a normal position towards which they tend to return.

The student is referred to the book, *Man Visible and Invisible*, by Bishop C. W. Leadbeater, for illustrations of the actual appearance of astral bodies :—

Plate VII., p. 88, Astral body of undeveloped man.
Plate X., p. 94, Astral body of average man.
Plate XXIII., p. 123, Astral body of developed man.
(Edition 1902.)

The main characteristics of the three types illustrated —undeveloped, the average man and the developed man—may be briefly summarised as follows:—

Undeveloped.—A very large proportion of sensuality: deceit, selfishness and greed are conspicuous: fierce anger is implied by smears and blots of dull scarlet : very little affection appears, and such intellect and religious feeling as exist are of the lowest possible kind. The outline is irregular and the colours blurred, thick and heavy. The whole body is evidently ill-regulated, confused and uncontrolled. *M V I 88–89.*

Average Man.—Sensuality is much less though still prominent : selfishness is also prominent and there is some capability of deceit for personal ends, though the green is beginning to divide into two distinct qualities, showing that cunning is gradually becoming adaptability. Anger is still marked : affection, intellect and devotion are more prominent and of a higher quality. The colours as a whole are more clearly defined and distinctly brighter, though none of them are perfectly clear. The outline of the body is more defined and regular. *M V I 94–95.*

Developed Man.—Undesirable qualities have almost entirely disappeared : across the top of the body there *M V I 123.* *I L I 280–281.*

is a strip of lilac, indicating spiritual aspiration : above and enveloping the head there is a cloud of the brilliant yellow of intellect : below that there is a broad belt of the blue of devotion : then across the trunk there is a still wider belt of the rose of affection, and in the lower part of the body a large amount of the green of adaptability and sympathy finds its place. The colours are bright, luminous, in clearly marked bands, the outline is well defined, and the whole astral body conveys the impression of being orderly and under perfect control.

Although we are not in this book dealing with the mental body, yet it should be mentioned that as a man develops, his astral body more and more resembles his mental body, until it becomes little more than a reflection of it in the grosser matter of the astral plane. This, of course, indicates that the man has his desires thoroughly under the control of the mind and is no longer apt to be swept away by surges of emotion. Such a man will no doubt be subject to occasional irritability, and to undesirable cravings of various sorts, but he knows enough now to repress these lower manifestations and not to yield to them.

At a still later stage the mental body itself becomes a reflection of the causal body, since the man now learns to follow solely the promptings of the higher self, and to guide his reason exclusively by them.

M V I 139.   Thus the mind body and the astral body of an Arhat would have very little characteristic colour of their own, but would be reproductions of the causal body in so far as their lower octaves could express it. They have a lovely iridescence, a sort of opalescent, mother-of-pearl effect, which is far beyond either description or representation.

I L I 281-283.
S G O 313.
M P 77.   A developed man has five rates of vibration in his astral body : an ordinary man shows at least nine rates, with a mixture of various shades in addition. Many people have 50 or 100 rates, the whole surface being broken up into a multiplicity of little whirlpools and cross-currents, all battling one against another

in mad confusion. This is the result of unnecessary emotion and worries, the ordinary person of the West being a mass of these, through which much of his strength is frittered away.

An astral body which vibrates fifty ways at once is not only ugly but also a serious annoyance. It may be compared to a physical body suffering from an aggravated form of palsy, with all its muscles jerking simultaneously in different directions. Such astral effects are contagious and affect all sensitive persons who approach, communicating a painful sense of unrest and worry. It is just because millions of people are thus unnecessarily agitated by all sorts of foolish desires and feelings that it is so difficult for a sensitive person to live in a great city or move amongst crowds. The perpetual astral disturbances may even react through the etheric double and set up nervous diseases.

The centres of inflammation in the astral body are *I L I* 284–291. to it what boils are to the physical body—not only acutely uncomfortable, but also weak spots through which vitality leaks away. They also offer practically no resistance to evil influences, and prevent good influences from being of profit. This condition is painfully common : the remedy is to eliminate worry, fear and annoyance. The student of occultism must not have personal feelings that can be affected under any circumstances whatever.

Only a young child has a white or comparatively *I L I* 206. colourless aura, the colours beginning to show only *I L II* 438. *H S II* 289. as the qualities develop. The astral body of a child is often a most beautiful object—pure and bright in its colours, free from the stains of sensuality, avarice, ill-will and selfishness. In it may also be seen lying latent the germs and tendencies brought over from his last life (see p. 211), some of them evil, some good, and thus the possibilities of the child's future life may be seen.

The yellow of intellect, found always near the head, *M V I* 123–124. is the origin of the idea of the nimbus or glory round the head of a saint, since this yellow is much the most conspicuous of the colours of the astral body, and the one most easily perceived by a person on the verge of clairvoyance. Sometimes, owing to the unusual activity of the intellect, the yellow may become visible even in physical matter, so as to be perceptible to ordinary physical sight.

We have already seen that the astral body has a certain normal arrangement, into which its various portions tend to group themselves. A sudden rush of passion or feeling, however, may temporarily force the whole, or almost the whole, of the matter in an astral body to vibrate at a certain rate, thus producing quite striking results. All the matter of the astral body is swept about as if by a violent hurricane, so that for the time being the colours become very much mixed. Coloured examples of this phenomenon are given in *Man Visible and Invisible* :—

M V I 91.
H S II 154–155.
I L II 136.

> Plate XI., p. 96, Sudden rush of Affection.
> Plate XII., p. 98, Sudden rush of Devotion.
> Plate XIII., p. 100, Intense Anger.
> Plate XIV., p. 103, Shock of Fear.

M V I 96.

In the case of a sudden wave of pure affection, when, for example, a mother snatches up her baby and covers it with kisses, the whole astral body in a moment is thrown into a violent agitation, and the original colours are for the time almost obscured.

Analysis discovers four separate effects :—

M V I 97–98.
T B 57.
I L II 136.

(1) Certain coils or vortices of vivid colour are to be seen, well-defined and solid-looking, and glowing with an intense light from within. Each of these is in reality a thought-form of intense affection, generated within the astral body, and about to be poured forth from it towards the object of the feeling. The whirling clouds of living light are indescribably lovely, though difficult to depict.

(2) The whole astral body is crossed by horizontal pulsating lines of crimson light, even more difficult to represent, by reason of the exceeding rapidity of their motion.

(3) A kind of film of rose-colour covers the surface of the whole astral body, so that all within is seen through it, as through tinted glass.

(4) A sort of crimson flush fills the entire astral body, tinging to some extent the other hues, and here and there condensing itself into irregular floating wisps, like half-formed clouds.

This display would probably last only a few seconds, and then the body would rapidly resume its normal condition, the various grades of matter sorting themselves again into their usual zones by their specific gravities. Yet every such rush of feeling adds a little to the crimson in the higher part of the oval and makes it a little easier for the astral body to respond to the next wave of affection which may come.

Similarly, a man who frequently feels high devotion soon comes to have a large area of blue in his astral body. The effects of such impulses are thus cumulative : and in addition the radiation of vivid vibrations of love and joy produce good influences on others.

With the substitution of blue for crimson, a sudden access of devotion, surging over a nun engaged in contemplation, produces an almost identical effect. *M V I* 98.

In the case of intense anger, the ordinary background of the astral body is obscured by coils or vortices of heavy, thunderous masses of sooty blackness, lit up from within by the lurid glare of active hatred. Wisps of the same dark cloud are to be seen defiling the whole astral body, while the fiery arrows of uncontrolled anger shoot among them like flashes of lightning. These terrible flashes are capable of penetrating other astral bodies like swords and thus inflicting injury upon other people. *M V I* 100-101.

In this instance, as in the others, each outburst of rage would predispose the matter of the entire astral body to respond somewhat more readily than before to these very undesirable vibrations. *M V I* 73: 102. *H S II* 155

A sudden shock of terror will in an instant suffuse the whole body with a curious livid grey mist, while horizontal lines of the same hue appear, but vibrating *M V I* 103 with such violence as to be hardly recognisable as separate lines. The result is indescribably ghastly: all light fades out for the time from the body and the whole grey mass quivers helplessly like a jelly.

T B 57.   A flood of emotion does not greatly affect the mental body, though for a time it may render it almost impossible for any activity from the mental body to come through into the physical brain, because the astral body, which acts as a bridge between the mental body and the brain, is vibrating so entirely at one rate as to be incapable of conveying any undulation which is not in harmony with it.

M V I 104.   The above are examples of the effects of sudden and temporary outbursts of feeling. There are other somewhat similar effects of a more permanent character produced by certain dispositions or types of character.

M V I 106.   Thus, when an ordinary man falls in love, the astral body is so completely transformed as to make it scarcely recognisable as belonging to the same person.

M V I 107.   Selfishness, deceit and avarice vanish, and the lowest part of the oval is filled with a large development of animal passions. The green of adaptability has been replaced by the peculiar brownish-green of jealousy, and the extreme activity of this feeling is shown by bright scarlet flashes of anger which permeate it. But the undesirable changes are more than counterbalanced by the splendid band of crimson which fills so large a part of the oval. This is, for the time, a dominant characteristic, and the whole astral body glows with its light. Under its influence the general muddiness of the ordinary astral body has disappeared, and the hues are all brilliant and clearly marked, good and bad alike. It is an intensification of the life in various directions. The blue of devotion is also distinctly improved, and even a touch of pale violet appears at the summit of the ovoid, indicating a capacity of response to a really high and unselfish ideal. The yellow of intellect, however, has entirely vanished for the time—a fact which the cynical might consider as characteristic of the condition !

The astral body of an irritable man usually shows a M V I 109. broad band of scarlet as a prominent feature, and, in addition, the whole astral body is covered with little floating flecks of scarlet, somewhat like notes of interrogation.

In the case of a miser, avarice, selfishness, deceit and M V I 110–111. adaptability are naturally intensified, but sensuality is diminished. The most remarkable change, however, is the curious series of parallel horizontal lines across the oval, giving the impression of a cage. The bars are a deep brown in colour, almost burnt sienna.

The vice of avarice seems to have the effect of completely arresting development for the time, and it is very difficult to shake off when once it has gained a firm hold.

Deep depression produces an effect in grey, instead M V I 111. of brown, very similar to that of the miser. The result is indescribably gloomy and depressing to the observer. No emotional condition is more infectious than the feeling of depression.

In the case of a non-intellectual man who is definitely M V I 113–114. religious, the astral body assumes a characteristic appearance. A touch of violet suggests the possibility of response to a high ideal. The blue of devotion is unusually well developed, but the yellow of intellect is scanty. There is a fair proportion of affection and adaptability, but more than the average of sensuality, and deceit and selfishness are also prominent. The colours are irregularly distributed, melting into one another, and the outline is vague, indicating the vagueness of the devotional man's conceptions.

Extreme sensuality and the devotional temperament are frequently seen in association : perhaps because these types of men live chiefly in their feelings, being governed by them instead of trying to control them by reason.

A great contrast is shown by a man of a scientific M V I 114–115. type. Devotion is entirely absent, sensuality is much below the average, but the intellect is developed to an abnormal degree. Affection and adaptability are small in quantity and poor in quality. A good deal of selfishness and avarice is present and also some jealousy. A huge cone of bright orange in the midst of the golden yellow of intellect indicates pride and ambition in connection with the knowledge that has been acquired. The scientific and orderly habit of mind causes the arrangement of the colours to fall into regular bands, the lines of demarcation being quite definite and clearly marked.

The student is urged to study for himself the admirable book from which the above information is taken, this being one of the most valuable of the many works produced by that great and gifted writer—Bishop C. W. Leadbeater.

K 14-15.

As we have been dealing here with colours in the astral body, it may be mentioned that the means of communication with the elementals, which are associated so closely with man's astral body, is by sounds and colours. Students may recollect obscure allusions now and again to a language of colours, and the fact that in ancient Egypt sacred manuscripts were written in colours, mistakes in copying being punished with death. To elementals, colours are as intelligible as words are to men.

CHAPTER IV

FUNCTIONS

THE functions of the astral body may be roughly grouped under three headings :—

1. To make sensation possible.
2. To serve as a bridge between mind and physical matter.
3. To act as an independent vehicle of consciousness and action.

We will deal with these three functions in sequence.

When man is analysed into " principles," *i.e.*, into modes of manifesting life, the four lower principles, sometimes termed the " Lower Quaternary," are :— A W 105. K 10-11.

Physical Body.
Etheric Body
Prâna, or Vitality.
Kâma, or Desire.

The fourth principle, Kâma, is the life manifesting in the astral body and conditioned by it : its characteristic is the attribute of feeling, which in rudimentary form is sensation, and in complex form emotion, with many grades in between these two. This is sometimes summed up as desire, that which is attracted or repelled by objects, according as they give pleasure or pain.

Kâma thus includes feelings of every kind, and might be described as the passional and emotional nature. It comprises all animal appetites, such as hunger, thirst, sexual desire : all passions, such as the lower forms of love, hatred, envy, jealousy ; it is the desire for sentient existence, for experience of material joys—" the lust of the flesh, the lust of the eyes, the pride of life." S P 17-18. A W 105.

Kâma is the brute in us, the " ape and tiger " of Tennyson, the force which most avails to keep us bound to earth and to stifle in us all higher longings by the illusions of sense. It is the most material in man's nature, and is the one that binds him fast to earthly life. " It is not molecularly constituted matter, least of all the human body, Sthûla Sharîra, that is the grossest of all our ' principles,' but verily the *middle* principle, the real animal centre ; whereas our body is but its shell, the irresponsible factor and medium through which the beast in us acts all its life " (*Secret Doctrine*, I., 280-1).

S C 305-307. Kâma or Desire is also described as a reflection or lower aspect of Âtmâ or Will, the distinction being that Will is Self-determined, whereas Desire is moved to activity by attractions to or repulsions from surrounding objects. Desire is thus Will discrowned, the captive, the slave of matter.

S R 148. Another way of regarding Kâma has been well expressed by Mr. Ernest Wood in his illuminating book *The Seven Rays :* Kâma " means all desire. And desire is the outward-turned aspect of love, the love of the *things* of the three worlds ; while love proper is love of life and love of the divine, and belongs to the higher or inward-turned self."

S C 348. For our purposes in this book desire and emotion are frequently used as practically synonymous : strictly, however, emotion is the product of desire and intellect.

A W 231. The astral body is often known as the Kâma Rûpa : and sometimes, in the older nomenclature, as the Animal Soul.

S P 18.
S S 59.
A W 89.
S C 310. Impacts from without, striking on the physical body, are conveyed as vibrations by the agency of Prâna or Vitality, but they would remain as vibrations only, merely motion on the physical plane, did not Kâma, the principle of sensation, translate the vibration into feeling. Thus pleasure and pain do not arise until the astral centre is reached. Hence Kâma joined to Prâna is spoken of as the " breath of life," the vital sentient principle spread over every particle of the body.

It appears that certain organs of the physical body
are specifically associated with the workings of Kâma :
among these are the liver and the spleen. *S P 35.*

It may be noted here that Kâma, or desire, is just
beginning to be active in the mineral kingdom, where
it expresses itself as chemical affinity. *M V I 48-
49.
S C 123-124:
128.*

In the vegetable kingdom it is, of course, much
more developed, indicating a far greater capacity of
utilising lower astral matter. Students of botany are
aware that likes and dislikes, *i.e.,* desire, are much
more prominent in the vegetable world than in the
mineral, and that many plants exhibit a great deal of
ingenuity and sagacity in attaining their ends.

Plants are quick to respond to loving care and are
distinctly affected by man's feelings towards them.
They delight in and respond to admiration : they are
also capable of individual attachments, as well as of
anger and dislike. *H S II 318-
321.*

Animals are capable to the fullest possible extent
of experiencing the lower desires, though the capacity
for the higher desires is more limited. Nevertheless
it exists, and in exceptional cases an animal is capable
of manifesting an exceedingly high quality of affection
or devotion. *M V I 49-50,*

Passing now to the second function of the astral
body—to act as a bridge between mind and physical
matter—we note that an *impact* on the physical senses
is transmitted inwards by Prâna, becomes a *sensation*
by the action of the sense-centres, which are situated in
Kâma, and is *perceived* by Manas, or Mind. Thus, without the general action through the astral body there
would be no connection between the external world
and the mind of man, no connection between physical
impacts and the perception of them by the mind. *S S 59 : 86.
M B 40.
A W 102-
103.*

Conversely, whenever we think, we set in motion
the mental matter within us ; the vibrations thus
generated are transferred to the matter of our astral
body, the astral matter affects the etheric matter,
this, in turn, acting on the dense physical matter, the
grey matter of the brain. *M V 14.*

A W 102–103.
S C 249–250.   The astral body is thus veritably a bridge between our physical and our mental life, serving as a transmitter of vibrations both from physical to mental and from mental to physical, and is, in fact, principally developed by this constant passage of vibrations to and fro.

S C 248–249.   In the course of the evolution of man's astral body, there are two distinct stages : the astral body has first to be developed to a fairly high point as a *transmitting vehicle :* then it has to be developed as an independent body, in which the man can function on the astral plane.

S P 18.   In man, the normal brain-intelligence is produced by the union of Kâma with Manas, or Mind, this *S P 35.* union being often spoken of as Kâma-Manas. Kâma-Manas is described by H. P. Blavatsky as " the rational, but earthly or physical intellect of man, encased in, and bound by, matter, and therefore subject to the influence of the latter "; this is the " lower self " which, acting on this plane of illusion, imagines itself to be the real Self or Ego, and thus falls into what Buddhist philosophy terms the " heresy of separateness."

S R 148.   Kâma-Manas, that is Manas with desire, has also been picturesquely described as Manas taking an interest in external things.

S P 35–36.   It may, in passing, be noted that a clear understanding of the fact that Kâma-Manas belongs to the human personality, and that it functions in and through the physical brain, is essential to a just grasp of the process of reincarnation, and is sufficient of itself to show how there can be no memory of previous lives so long as the consciousness cannot rise beyond the brain-mechanism, this mechanism, together with that of Kâma, being made afresh each life, and therefore having no direct touch with previous lives.

S P 34.   Manas, of itself, could not affect the molecules of the physical brain cells : but, when united to Kâma, it is able to set the physical molecules in motion, and thus produce " brain-consciousness," including the brain memory and all the functions of the human

mind, as we ordinarily know it. It is, of course, not *D A* 12.
the Higher Manas, but the Lower Manas (*i.e.*, matter
of the four lower levels of the mental plane), which
is associated with Kâma. In Western psychology,
this Kâma-Manas becomes a part of what in that
system is termed Mind. Kâma-Manas, forming the
link between the higher and lower nature in man,
is the battleground during life, and also, as we shall
see later, plays an important part in post-mortem
existence.

So close is the association of Manas and Kâma that *S S* 30 : 89.
the Hindus speak of man having five sheaths, one of *A W* 231.
which is for all manifestations of working intellect
and desire. These five are :—

1	Ânandamayakosha	the Bliss sheath	Buddhi
2	Vignânamayakosha	the Discriminating sheath	Higher Manas
3	Manomayakosha ...	the sheath of Intellect and Desire	Lower Manas and Kâma
4	Prânamayakosha...	the Vitality sheath	Prâna
5	Annamayakosha ...	the Food sheath	Dense physical body

In the division used by Manu, the prânamayakosha *S S* 69.
and the annamayakosha are classed together, and
known as the Bhûtâtman or elemental self, or body
of action.

The vignânamayakosha and the manomayakosha *S S* 70-72.
he terms the body of feeling, giving it the name Jîva :
he defines it as that body in which the Knower, the
Kshetragna, becomes sensible of pleasures and of
pains.

In their external relations, the vignânamayakosha
and the manomayakosha, especially the manomayakosha, are related to the Deva world. The Devas
are said to have " entered into " man, the reference
being to the presiding deities of the elements (see
p. 188). Those presiding deities give rise to sensations
in man, changing the contacts from without into

sensations, or the recognition of the contacts, from within, this being essentially a Deva action. Hence the link with all these lower Devas, which, when supreme control has been obtained, makes man the master in every region of the Universe.

S P 28.
Manas, or mind, being unable, as said above, to affect the gross particles of the brain, projects a part of itself, *i.e.*, lower Manas, which clothes itself with astral matter, and then with the help of etheric matter permeates the whole nervous system of the child before birth. The projection from Manas is often spoken of as its reflection, its shadow, its ray, and is known also by other allegorical names. H. P. Blavatsky writes

S P 29.
M B 77.
(*Key to Theosophy*, p. 184) : " Once imprisoned, or incarnate, their (the Manas) essence becomes dual ; that is to say, the *rays* of the eternal divine Mind, considered as individual entities, assume a two-fold attribute, which is (*a*) their essential, inherent, characteristic, heaven-aspiring mind (higher Manas), and (*b*) the human quality of thinking, of animal cogitation, rationalised owing to the superiority of the human brain, the Kâma-tending or lower Manas."

Lower Manas is thus engulfed in the quaternary, and may be regarded as clasping Kâma with one hand, whilst with the other it retains its hold on its father, the higher Manas. Whether it will be dragged down by kâma altogether and be torn away from the triad (âtmâ-buddhi-manas) to which, by its nature it belongs, or whether it will triumphantly carry back to its source the purified experiences of its earth life—that is the life-problem set and solved in each successive incarnation. This point will be considered further in the chapters on *After-Death Life*.

Kâma thus supplies the animal and passional elements ; lower Manas rationalises these and adds the intellectual faculties. In man these two principles are interwoven during life and rarely act separately.

S P 30.
Manas may be regarded as the flame, Kâma and the physical brain as the wick and fuel which feed the flame. The egos of all men, developed or undeveloped,

are of the same essence and substance : that which makes of one a great man, and of another a vulgar, silly person, is the quality and make-up of the physical body, and the ability of the brain and body to transmit and express the light of the real inner man.

In brief, Kâma-Manas is the personal self of man : *S P* 32-33 : Lower Manas gives the individualising touch that 36. makes the personality recognise itself as " I." Lower Manas is a ray from the immortal Thinker, *illuminating a personality*. It is Lower Manas which yields the last touch of delight to the senses and to the animal nature, by conferring the power of anticipation, memory and imagination.

Whilst it would be out of place in this book to *S P* 49-52. encroach too far into the domain of Manas and the mental body, yet it may help the student at this stage to add that freewill resides in Manas, Manas being the representative of Mahat, the Universal Mind. In physical man, the Lower Manas is the agent of freewill. From Manas comes the feeling of liberty, the knowledge that we can rule ourselves, that the higher nature can master the lower. To identify the consciousness with the Manas, instead of with Kâma, is thus an important step on the road to self-mastery.

The very struggle of Manas to assert itself is the best testimony that it is by nature free. It is the presence and power of the ego which enables a man to choose between desires and to overcome them. As the lower Manas rules Kâma, the lower quaternary takes its rightful position of subservience to the higher triad—âtmâ-buddhi-manas.

We may classify the principles of man in the following manner :—

1	Âtmâ Buddhi Higher Manas	} Immortal
2	Kâma-Manas	Conditionally Immortal.
3	Prâna Etheric Double Dense Body	} Mortal.

We come now to consider the third function of the astral body—as an independent vehicle of consciousness and action. The full treatment of this portion of our subject—the use, development, possibilities and limitations of the astral body on its own plane— will be dealt with step by step in most of the succeeding chapters. For the present it will suffice to enumerate very briefly the principal ways in which an astral body can be used as an independent vehicle of consciousness. These are as follows :—

1. During ordinary waking consciousness, *i.e.*, while the physical brain and senses are wide-awake, the powers of the astral senses may be brought into action. Some of these powers correspond to the senses and powers of action possessed by the physical body. They will be dealt with in the next chapter, on *Chakrams*.

2. During sleep or trance it is possible for the astral body to separate itself from the physical body and to move about and function freely on its own plane. This will be dealt with in the chapter on *Sleep-Life*.

3. It is possible so to develop the powers of the astral body that a man may consciously and deliberately, at any time that he chooses, leave the physical body and pass with unbroken consciousness into the astral body. This will be dealt with in the chapter on *Continuity of Consciousness*.

4. After physical death the consciousness withdraws itself into the astral body, and a life, varying greatly in intensity and duration, dependent upon a number of factors, may be led on the astral plane. This will be dealt with in the chapters on *After-Death Life*.

These divisions of our subject, with numerous ramifications, will constitute the major portion of the remainder of this treatise.

CHAPTER V

CHAKRAMS

THE word Chakram is Sanskrit, and means literally *I L I* 443. a wheel, or revolving disc. It is used to denote what *C* 17-18. are often called Force-Centres in man. There are such Chakrams in all man's vehicles, and they are points of connection at which force flows from one vehicle to another. They are also intimately associated with the powers or senses of the various vehicles.

The Chakrams of the etheric body are fully described in *The Etheric Double*, and the student is referred to that work, as a study of the etheric Chakrams will materially assist him to understand the astral Chakrams.

The etheric Chakrams are situated in the surface *I L I* 443- of the etheric double and are usually denoted by the 444. name of the physical organ to which they correspond. They are :—

1. Base of Spine Chakram.
2. Navel Chakram.
3. Spleen Chakram.
4. Heart Chakram.
5. Throat Chakram.
6. Between the Eyebrows Chakram.
7. Top of the Head Chakram.

There are also three lower Chakrams, but as these are used only in certain schools of " black magic,"[1] we are not concerned with them here.

The astral Chakrams, which are frequently in the *I L I* 451. interior of the etheric double, are vortices in four dimensions (see Chapter XVIII.), thus having an extension in a direction quite different from the etheric : consequently, though they correspond to the etheric Chakrams, they are by no means always coterminous with them, though some part is always coincident.

[1] "Black" has no relation to colour of skin.

I L I 452.   The astral Chakrams are given the same names as those in the etheric douɒle, and their functions are as follows :—

1. *Base of Spine Chakram.*—This is the seat of the Serpent Fire, Kundalini, a force which exists on all planes and by means of which the rest of the Chakrams are aroused.

Originally, the astral body was an almost inert mass, possessing but the vaguest consciousness, with no definite power of doing anything, and with no clear knowledge of the world surrounding it. The first thing that happened was the awakening of Kundalini at the astral level.

2. *Navel Chakram.*—Kundalini having been awakened in the first Chakram, it moved to the navel
I L I 453.   Chakram, which it vivified, thus awakening in the astral body the power of feeling—a sensitiveness to all sorts of influences, though without as yet anything like the definite comprehension that comes from seeing and hearing.

3. *Spleen Chakram.*—Kundalini then moved to the spleen Chakram, and through it vitalised the whole
H S I 64.
I L I 461 :
347.
astral body, this Chakram having as one of its functions the absorption of Prâna, the Vitality Force, which also exists on all planes.   The vivification of the spleen Chakram enables the man to travel in his astral body
I L I 453.   consciously, though with only a vague conception as yet of what he encounters on his journeys.

4. *Heart Chakram.*—This Chakram enables the man to comprehend and sympathise with the vibrations of other astral entities, so that he can instinctively understand their feelings.

5. *Throat Chakram.*—This Chakram confers the power in the astral world which corresponds to hearing in the physical world.

6. *Between the Eyebrows Chakram.*—This Chakram confers the power to perceive definitely the shape and nature of astral objects, instead of merely vaguely sensing their presence.

A P 23.   Associated with this Chakram appears also the power
C 47.

of magnifying at will the minutest physical or astral particle to any desired size, as though by a microscope. This power enables an occult investigator to perceive and study molecules, atoms, etc. The full control of this faculty, however, belongs rather to the causal body.

The power of magnification is one of the *siddhis* C 48. described in Oriental books as " the power of making oneself large or small at will." The description is apposite, because the method employed is that of using a temporary visual mechanism of inconceivable minuteness. Conversely, minification of vision may be obtained by the construction of a temporary and enormously larger visual mechanism.

The power of magnification is quite distinct from O C App. IX. the faculty of functioning on a higher plane, just as the power of an astronomer to observe planets and stars is quite a different thing from the ability to move or function amongst them.

In the Hindu sutras it is stated that meditation in I Y 24. a certain part of the tongue will confer astral sight. The statement is a " blind," the reference being to the pituitary body, situated just over this part of the tongue.

7. *Top of the Head Chakram.*—This Chakram rounds off and completes the astral life, endowing the man with the perfection of his faculties.

There appear to be two methods in which this I L 454. Chakram works.

In one type of man, the sixth and seventh Chakrams both converge upon the pituitary body, this body being for this type practically the only direct link between the physical and the higher planes.

In another type of man, however, while the sixth Chakram is still attached to the pituitary body, the seventh Chakram is bent or slanted until its vortex coincides with the pineal gland. In people of this type the pineal gland is thus vivified and made into a line of communication directly with the lower mental, without apparently passing through the intermediate astral plane in the ordinary way.

I L I 392–
393: 455–
456.
I L II 210–
212.
C 14: 16-18.
In the physical body, as we know, there are specialised organs for each sense, the eye for seeing, the ear
for hearing, and so on.   In the astral body, however,
this is not the case.

The particles of the astral body are constantly
flowing and swirling about like those of boiling water :
consequently, there are no special particles which
remain continuously in any of the Chakrams.   On
the contrary, all the particles of the astral body pass
through each of the Chakrams.

Each Chakram has the function of awakening a
certain power of response in the particles which flow
through it, one Chakram the power of sight, another
that of hearing, and so on.

Consequently, any one astral sense is not, strictly
speaking, localised or confined to any particular part
of the astral body.   It is rather the whole of the
particles of the astral body which possess the power of
response.   A man, therefore, who has developed astral
sight uses any part of the matter of his astral body in
order to see, and so can see equally well objects in
front, behind, above, below, or to either side.   Similarly
with all the other senses.   In other words, the astral
senses are equally active in all parts of the body.

II 97–99.
It is not easy to describe the substitute for language
by means of which ideas are communicated astrally.
Sound in the ordinary sense of the word is not possible
in the astral world—in fact it is not possible even in
the higher part of the physical world.   It would also
not be correct to say that the language of the astral
world is thought-transference : the most that could
be said is that it is the transference of thoughts formulated in a particular way.

In the mental world a thought is instantaneously
transmitted to the mind of another without any form
of words : therefore in the mental world language
does not in the least matter.   But astral communication lies, as it were, half-way between the thought-
transference of the mental world and the concrete
speech of the physical, and it is still necessary to

formulate the thought in words. For this exchange it is therefore necessary that the two parties should have a language in common.

The astral and etheric Chakrams are in very close *I L I* 472. correspondence; but between them, and interpenetrating them in a manner which is not readily describable, there is a sheath or web of closely woven texture, composed of a single layer of physical atoms much compressed and permeated by a special form of Prâna. The divine life which normally descends from the astral body to the physical is so attuned as to pass through this shield with perfect ease, but it is an absolute barrier to all the forces which cannot use the atomic matter of both planes. The web is a natural protection to prevent a premature opening up of communication between the planes, a development which could lead to nothing but injury.

It is this which normally prevents clear recollection *I L I* 473. of the sleep-life, and which also causes the momentary unconsciousness which always occurs at death. But for this provision the ordinary man could at any moment be brought by any astral entity under the influence of forces with which he could not possibly cope. He would be liable to constant obsession by astral entities desirous of seizing his vehicles.

The web may be injured in several ways :—

1. A great shock to the astral body, *e.g* , a sudden fright, may rend apart this delicate organism and, as it is commonly expressed, drive the man mad.

A tremendous outburst of anger may also produce *I L I* 474. the same effect, as may any other very strong emotion of an evil character which produces a kind of explosion in the astral body.

2. The use of alcohol or narcotic drugs, including tobacco. These substances contain matter which on breaking up volatilises, some of it passing from the physical to the astral plane. Even tea and coffee contain this matter, but only in infinitesimal quantities, so that only long-continued abuse of them would produce the effect.

These constituents rush through the Chakrams in the opposite direction to that for which they are intended, and in doing this repeatedly they seriously injure and finally destroy the delicate web.

This deterioration or destruction may take place in two ways, according to the type of person concerned and to the proportion of the constituents in his etheric and astral bodies.

In one type of person the rush of volatilising matter actually burns away the web, and therefore leaves the door open to all sorts of irregular forces and evil influences. Those affected in this way fall into delirium tremens, obsession or insanity.

In the other type of person, the volatile constituents, in flowing through, somehow harden the atom so that its pulsation is to a large extent checked and crippled, and it is no longer capable of being vitalised by the particular type of Prâna which welds it into a web. This results in a kind of ossification of the web, so that instead of too much coming through from one plane to another, we have very little of any kind coming through. Such subjects tend to a general deadening down of their qualities, resulting in gross materialism, brutality and animalism, in the loss of all finer feelings and of the power to control themselves.

All impressions which pass from one plane to the other are intended to come only through the atomic sub-planes, but when the deadening process takes place it infects not only other atomic matter, but even matter of the second and third sub-planes, so that the only communication between the astral and the etheric is from the lower sub-planes, upon which only unpleasant and evil influences are to be found.

The consciousness of the ordinary man cannot yet use pure atomic matter, either of the physical or astral, and therefore there is normally for him no possibility of conscious communication at will between the two planes. The proper way to obtain it is to purify the vehicles until the atomic matter in both is fully vivified, so that all communications between the two may pass by that road. In that case the web retains to the fullest degree its position and activity, and yet is no longer a barrier to the perfect communication, while it still continues to prevent close contact with the lower and undesirable sub-planes.

3. The third way in which the web may be injured *I L I* 474. is that known in spiritualistic parlance as " sitting for development."

It is quite possible, in fact very common, for a man *I L I* 456. to have his astral Chakrams well developed, so that *S C* 260. he is able to function freely on the astral plane, and yet he may recollect nothing of his astral life when he returns to waking consciousness. With this pheno-menon and its explanation we shall deal more appro-priately in the Chapter on *Dreams.*

CHAPTER VI

KUNDALINI

THE student is referred to *The Etheric Double* for a description of Kundalini with special reference to the etheric body and its Chakrams. Here we are concerned with it in connection with the astral body.

I L I 461. The three known forces which emanate from the Logos are :—

1. Fohat : which shows itself as electricity, heat, light, motion, etc.
2. Prâna : which shows itself as vitality.
3. Kundalini : also known as the Serpent Fire.

Each of these three forces exists on all planes of which we know anything. So far as is known, no one of the three is convertible into any of the others : they each remain separate and distinct.

I L I 462. Kundalini is called in *The Voice of the Silence,* " the Fiery Power," and " the World's Mother." The first, because it appears like liquid fire as it rushes through the body : and the course it should follow is a spiral one, like the coils of a serpent. It is called the World's Mother because through it our various vehicles may be vivified, so that the higher worlds may open before us in succession.

Its home in man's body is the Chakram at the base of the spine, and for the ordinary man it lies there unawakened and unsuspected during the whole of his life. It is far better for it to remain dormant until *I L I 463.* the man has made definite moral development, until his will is strong enough to control it and his thoughts pure enough to enable him to face its awakening without injury. No one should experiment with it without definite instruction from a teacher who thoroughly understands the subject, for the dangers connected with it are very real and terribly serious. Some of them are purely physical. Its uncontrolled movement often produces intense physical pain, and it may readily tear tissues and even destroy physical life. It may also do permanent injury to vehicles higher than the physical.

One very common effect of rousing it prematurely is that it rushes downwards in the body instead of upwards, and thus excites the most undesirable passions—excites them and intensifies their effects to such a degree that it becomes quite impossible for the man to resist them, because a force has been brought into play in whose presence he is quite helpless. Such men become satyrs, monsters of depravity, the force being beyond the normal human power of resistance. *I L I* 464. They may probably gain certain supernormal powers, but these will be such as will bring them into touch with a lower order of evolution, with which humanity is intended to hold no commerce, and to escape from its thraldom may take more than one incarnation.

There is a school of black magic which purposely uses this power in this way, in order that through it may be vivified those lower Chakrams which are never used by followers of the Good Law.

The premature unfoldment of Kundalini has other unpleasant possibilities. It intensifies everything in the man's nature, and it reaches the lower and evil qualities more readily than the good. In the mental body, ambition is very readily aroused, and soon swells to an incredibly inordinate degree. It would probably bring with it a great intensification of *I L I* 465. intellect, accompanied by abnormal and satanic pride, such as is quite inconceivable to the ordinary man.

An uninstructed man who finds that Kundalini has been aroused by accident should at once consult some one who fully understands these matters.

The arousing of Kundalini—the method of doing which is not publicly known—and the attempt to pass it through the Chakrams—the order of which is also deliberately concealed from the public—should never be attempted except at the express suggestion of a Master, who will watch over His pupil during the various stages of the experiment.

The most solemn warnings are given by experienced occultists against in any way attempting to arouse Kundalini, except under qualified tuition, because of the real and great dangers involved. As is said in the *Hathayogapradipika*: "It gives liberation to Yogis and bondage to fools" (III., 107).

I L I 466.

In some cases Kundalini wakes spontaneously, so that a dull glow is felt: it may even begin to move of itself, though this is rare. In this latter case it would be likely to cause great pain, as, since the passages are not prepared for it, it would have to clear its way by actually burning up a great deal of etheric dross, which is necessarily a painful process. When it thus awakes of itself or is accidentally aroused, it usually tries to rush up the interior of the spine, instead of following the spiral course into which the occultist is trained to guide it. If it be possible, the will should be set in motion to arrest its onward rush, but if that proves to be impossible, as is most likely, no alarm need be felt. It will probably rush out through the head and escape into the surrounding atmosphere, and it is likely that no harm will result beyond a slight weakening. Nothing worse than a temporary loss of consciousness need be apprehended. The worst dangers are connected, not with its upwards rush, but with its turning downwards and inwards.

I L I 467.

I L I 468.

Its principal function in connection with occult development is that by being sent through the Chakrams in the etheric body, it vivifies these Chakrams and makes them available as gates of connection between the physical and astral bodies. It is said in *The Voice of the Silence* that when Kundalini reaches the centre between the eyebrows and fully vivifies it, it confers the power of hearing the voice of the Master—which means, in this case, the voice of the ego or higher self. The reason is that when

I L I 469.

the pituitary body is brought into working order it forms a perfect link with the astral vehicle, so that through it all communications from within can be received.

In addition, all the higher Chakrams have to be awakened, in due course, and each must be made responsive to all kinds of astral influences from the various astral sub-planes. Most people cannot gain this during the present incarnation, if it is the first in which they have begun to take these matters seriously in hand. Some Indians might succeed in doing so, as their bodies are by heredity more adaptable than most others: but it is for the majority of men the work of a later Round altogether.

The conquest of Kundalini has to be repeated in each incarnation, since the vehicles are new each time, but after it has been once achieved these repetitions will be an easy matter. Its action will vary with *I L I* 470. different types of people. Some would see the higher self rather than hear its voice. Also this connection with the higher has many stages ; for the personality it means the influence of the ego : but for the ego himself it means the power of the monad : and for the monad in turn it means to become a conscious expression of the Logos.

There does not appear to be any age limit with *I L I* 471-2. regard to the arousing of Kundalini : but physical health is a necessity owing to the strain involved.

An ancient symbol was the thyrsus—that is, a staff *I L I* 130. with a pine-cone on its top. In India the same symbol is found, but instead of the staff a stick of bamboo with seven knots is used. In some modifications of the mysteries a hollow iron rod, said to contain fire, was used instead of the thyrsus. The staff, or stick, *I L I* 131. with seven knots represents the spinal cord, with its seven Chakrams. The hidden fire is, of course, Kundalini. The thyrsus was not only a symbol, but also an object of practical use. It was a very strong magnetic instrument, used by initiates to free the astral body from the physical when they passed in full consciousness to this higher life. The priest who had magnetised it laid it against the spinal cord of the candidate and gave him in that way some of his own magnetism, to help him in that difficult life and in the efforts which lay before him.

CHAPTER VII

THOUGHT-FORMS

THE mental and astral bodies are those chiefly con- *T F* 17.
cerned with the production of what are called thought-
forms. The term thought-form is not wholly accurate,
because the forms produced may be composed of mental
matter, or, in the vast majority of cases, of both astral
and mental matter.

Although in this book we are dealing primarily with
the astral, and not with the mental body, yet thought-
forms, as just said, are, in a vast majority of cases,
both astral and mental. In order, therefore, to make
the subject intelligible, it is necessary to deal very
largely with the mental as well as with the astral
aspect of the subject.

A purely intellectual and impersonal thought—such *T F* 34-35.
as one concerned with algebra or geometry—would *H S II* 164 :
be confined to mental matter. If on the other hand 256.
the thought has in it something of selfish or personal
desire, it will draw round itself astral matter in addition
to the mental. If, furthermore, the thought be of a
spiritual nature, if it be tinged with love and aspiration
or deep and unselfish feeling, then there may also
enter in some of the splendour and glory of the buddhic
plane.

Every definite thought produces two effects : first, *T F* 21.
a radiating vibration : second, a floating form. *H S II* 165.

The vibration set up in and radiating from the *T F* 18.
mental body is accompanied with a play of colour
which has been described as like that in the spray of
a waterfall as the sunlight strikes it, raised to the
n^{th} degree of colour and vivid delicacy.

This radiating vibration tends to reproduce its own *T F* 23-24.
rate of motion in any mental body on which it may *H S II* 170-
171.

T B 54–56.   impinge :   *i.e.*, to produce thoughts of the same type as those from which the vibration originated.   It should be noted that the radiating vibration carries, not the subject of the thought, but its character. Thus, the waves of thought-emotion radiating from a Hindu sitting rapt in devotion to Shri Krishna would tend to stimulate devotional feeling in any who came under its influence,. not necessarily towards Shri Krishna, but, in the case of a Christian, to the Christ, in the case of a Buddhist, to the Lord Buddha : and so on.

T F 23–24.   The power of the vibration to produce such effects depends principally upon the clearness and definiteness of the thought-emotion, as well, of course, as upon the amount of force put into it.

T F 23.   These radiating vibrations become less effective in proportion to the distance from their source, though it is probable that the variation is proportional to the cube of the distance instead of (as with gravitation and other physical forces) to the square, because of the additional (fourth) dimension involved.

H S II 257.   The distance to which a thought-wave can radiate effectively also depends upon the opposition with which it meets.   Waves in the lower types of astral matter are usually soon deflected or overwhelmed by a multitude of other vibrations at the same level, just as a soft sound is drowned in the roar of a city.

T F 18.   The second effect, that of a floating form, is caused by the mental body throwing off a vibrating portion of itself shaped by the nature of the thought, which gathers round itself matter of the corresponding order of fineness from the surrounding elemental essence (see page 6) of the mental plane.   This is a thought-form pure and simple, being composed of mental matter only.

L A D 55.   If made of the finer kinds of matter, it will be of great power and energy, and may be used as a most potent agent when directed by a strong and steady will.

T F 18–19,
25.   When the man directs his energy towards external objects of desire, or is occupied with passional or

emotional activities, a similar process takes place in his astral body : a portion of it is thrown off and gathers round itself elemental essence of the astral plane. Such thought-desire forms are caused by Kâma-Manas, the mind under the dominion of the animal nature, Manas dominated by Kâma.

Such a thought-desire form has for its body the elemental essence, and for its animating soul, as it were, the desire or passion which threw it forth. Both these thought-desire forms, and also purely mental thought-forms, are called *artificial elementals.* *T F.* 20. The vast majority of ordinary thought-forms are of the former type, as few thoughts of ordinary men and women are untinged with desire, passion or emotion.

Both mental and astral elemental essence, which *T F* 25. possess a half-intelligent life of their own, respond *A P* 88. very readily to the influence of human thought and desire : consequently every impulse sent out, either from a man's mental body or from his astral body, is immediately clothed in a temporary vehicle of elemental essence. These artificial elementals thus become for *T F* 18. the time a kind of living creature, entities of intense activity animated by the one idea that generated them. They are, in fact, often mistaken by untrained psychics or clairvoyants for real living entities.

Thus, when a man thinks of a concrete object—a *T B* 50-51. book, house, landscape, etc.—he builds a tiny image of the object in the matter of his mental body. This image floats in the upper part of that body, usually in front of the face of the man, and at about the level of the eyes. It remains there as long as the man is contemplating the object, and usually for a little time afterwards, the length of life depending upon the intensity and the clearness of the thought. The form is quite objective and can be seen by another person possessed of mental sight. If a man thinks of another person he creates a tiny portrait in just the same way.

Thought-forms have been usefully compared to a *T F* 26. Leyden jar (a vessel charged with static electricity), *S G O* 246.

the jar itself corresponding to the elemental essence and the electric charge to the thought-emotion. And just as a Leyden jar when it touches another object discharges its stored electricity into that object, so does an artificial elemental, when it strikes a mental or astral body, discharge its stored mental and emotional energy into that body.

T F 31.

The principles which underlie the production of all thought-emotion forms are :—

    1. *Colour* is determined by the *quality* of the thought or emotion.

    2. *Form* is determined by the *nature* of the thought or emotion.

    3. *Clearness of Outline* is determined by the *definiteness* of the thought or emotion.

K 16–17.

The life-period of a thought-form depends upon (1) its initial intensity ; (2) the nutriment afterwards supplied to it by a repetition of the thought, either by the generator or by others. Its life may be continually reinforced by this repetition, a thought which is brooded over acquiring great stability of form. So again thought-forms of similar character are attracted to and mutually strengthen each other, making a form of great energy and intensity.

A P 90.

Furthermore, such a thought-form appears to possess instinctive desire to prolong its life, and will react on its creator, tending to evoke from him renewal of the feeling which created it. It will react in a similar, though not so perfect, manner on any others with whom it may come into contact.

T P 32.

The colours in which thought-forms express themselves are identical with the colours found in the aura, vide pp. 11–12.

T F 34.

The brilliance and depth of the colours are usually a measure of the strength and the activity of the feeling.

For our present purpose we may classify thought-forms into three kinds : (1) those connected solely with their originator : (2) those connected with another person : (3) those not definitely personal.

If a man's thought is about himself, or based on a
personal feeling, as the vast majority of thoughts are,
the form will hover in the immediate neighbourhood
of its generator.   At any time, then, when he is in a
passive condition, his thoughts and feelings not being
specifically occupied, his own thought-form will return
to him and discharge itself upon him.   In addition,
each man also serves as a magnet to draw towards
himself the thought-forms of others similar to his own,
thus attracting towards himself reinforcements of
energy from outside.   People who are becoming sensitive have sometimes imagined, in such cases, that
they have been tempted by the " devil," whereas it is
their own thought-desire forms which are the case of
the " temptation."   Long brooding over the same
subject may create a thought-form of tremendous
power.   Such a form may last for many years and
have for a time all the appearance and powers of a
real living entity.   Most men move through life
enclosed literally within a cage of their own building,
surrounded by masses of forms created by their
habitual thoughts.   One important effect of this is
that each man looks out upon the world *through* his
own thought-forms, and thus sees everything tinged
by them.

Thus a man's own thought-forms re-act upon him,
tending to reproduce themselves and thus setting up
definite habits of thought and feeling, which may be
helpful if of a lofty character, but are often cramping
and a hindrance to growth, obscuring the mental
vision and facilitating the formation of prejudice and
fixed moods or attitudes which may develop into
definite vices.

As a Master has written : " Man is continually
peopling his current in space with a world of his own,
crowded with the offspring of his fancies, desires,
impulses and passions."   These thought-forms remain
in his aura, increasing in number and intensity, until
certain kinds of them so dominate his mental and
emotional life that the man rather answers to their

Marginal references:

T F 26.
H S II 96 :
174-175.
I L II 145-
146.
K 18-19.
T B 53.
A P 88-89.

T F 27.

K 17.
T B 52.
H S II 101,

O W III.

impulse than decides anew : thus are habits, the outer expression of his stored-up force, created, and thus is character built.

T B 52. Moreover, as each man leaves behind him a trail of thought-forms, it follows that as we go along a street we are walking amidst a sea of other men's thoughts. If a man leaves his mind blank for a time, these thoughts of others drift through it : if one happens to attract his attention, his mind seizes upon it, makes it its own, strengthening it by the addition of its force, and then casts it out again to affect somebody else. A man, therefore, is not responsible for a thought which floats into his mind, but he *is* responsible if he takes it up, dwells upon it, and then sends it out again strengthened.

M V I 99.
T F 45. An example of thought-forms is that of the shapeless clouds of heavy blue which may often be seen rolling along like wreaths of dense smoke over the heads of the congregation of a church. In churches where the level of spirituality is a low one, the minds of the men may create rows of figures, representing their calculations of business deals or speculations, while the minds of the women may create pictures of millinery, jewellery, etc.

R 22. Hypnotism provides another example of thought-forms. The operator may make a thought-form and project it on to blank paper, where it may become visible to his hypnotised subject : or he may make the form so objective that the subject will see and feel it as though it were an actual physical object. The literature of hypnotism is full of such examples.

T F 38–40.
H S II 96 :
173.
I L II 145 :
152.
A W 78–80.
K 18.
T B 52–54.
A P 89–91.
If the thought-form is directed towards another person, it will go to that person. Either of two effects may then result. (1) If in the aura of the person concerned there is material capable of responding sympathetically to the vibration of the thought-form, then the thought-form will remain near the person, or even in his aura, and, as opportunity serves, automatically discharge itself, thus tending to strengthen in the person that particular rate of vibration. If the person

at whom a thought-form is aimed happens to be busy, or already engaged in some definite train of thought, the thought-form, being unable to discharge itself into the man's mental body, which is already vibrating at a certain determinate rate, hangs in the vicinity until the man's mental body is sufficiently at rest to permit its entrance, when it immediately discharges itself.

In doing this it will display what appears like a very considerable amount of intelligence and adaptability, though really it is a force acting along the line of least resistance—pressing steadily in one direction all the time, and taking advantage of any channel that it can find.   Such elementals can, of course, be strengthened and their life-period extended by repetition of the same thought.

(2) If, on the other hand, there is in the person's aura no matter capable of response, then the thought-form cannot affect it at all.   It will therefore rebound from it, with a force proportional to the energy with which it impinged upon it, and return to and strike its creator.

Thus, for example, the thought of the desire for drink could not enter the body of a purely temperate man.   It would strike upon his astral body, but it could not penetrate and it would then return to the sender.

The old saying that "Curses (to which might be added blessings) come home to roost" conveys this truth and explains cases where, as many have known, evil thoughts directed to a good and highly-advanced man affect such a man not at all, but re-act, sometimes with terrible and devastating effect, on their creator. Hence also the obvious corollary that a pure heart and mind are the best protection against inimical assaults of feeling and thought.

On the other hand, a thought-form of love and of desire to protect, strongly directed to some beloved object, acts as a shielding and protecting agent : it will seek all opportunities to serve and defend, will

L A D 58.
T F 38–39.
H W 79.
K 18.

strengthen friendly forces and weaken unfriendly ones, that impinge on the aura. It may protect its object from impurity, irritability, fear, etc.

A P 92.

Friendly thoughts and earnest good wishes thus create and maintain what is practically a " guardian angel " always at the side of the person thought of, no matter where he may be. Many a mother's thoughts and prayers, for example, have given assistance and protection to her child. They may often be seen by clairvoyants, and in rare cases they may even materialise and become physically visible.

T B 51.

It is thus apparent that a thought of love sent from one person to another involves the actual transference of a certain amount both of force and of matter from the sender to the recipient.

If the thought is sufficiently strong, distance makes absolutely no difference to it : but a weak and diffused thought is not effective outside a limited area.

T F 36.
O S D 166.

A variant of our first group consists of those cases where a man thinks strongly of himself in a distant place. The form thus created contains a large proportion of mental matter, takes the image of the thinker, and is at first small and compressed. It draws around itself a considerable amount of astral matter and usually expands to life size before it appears at its destination. Such forms are often seen by clairvoyants, and not infrequently are mistaken for the man's astral body or even for the man himself.

O S D 166.

When this takes place, the thought or desire must be sufficiently strong to do one of three things : (1) To call up by mesmeric influence the image of the thinker in the mind of the person to whom he wishes to appear : (2) by the same power to stimulate for the moment that person's psychic faculties so that he is able to see the astral visitor ; (3) to produce a temporary materialisation which will be physically visible.

A P 105.
O S D 155.

Apparitions at the time of death, which are by no means uncommon, are very often really the astral form of the dying man : but they may also be thought-forms called into being by his earnest wish to see some friend before he passes on. In some instances the visitor is perceived just after the moment of death, instead of just before : but for various reasons this form of apparition is far less frequent than the other.

A family ghost may be (1) a thought-form, (2) an unusually vivid impression in the astral light, or (3) a genuine earth-bound ancestor still haunting some particular place. *A P 100.*

In this connection, it may be added that wherever any intense passion has been felt, such as terror, pain, sorrow, hatred, etc., so powerful an impression is made on the astral light that persons with but a faint glimmer of psychic faculty may be impressed by it. A slight temporary increase of sensibility would enable a man to visualise the entire scene : hence many stories of haunted places, and of the unpleasant influences of such spots as Tyburn Tree, the Chamber of Horrors at Madame Tussaud's, etc. *A P 106. C 161. O S D 290.*

Apparitions at the spot where a crime was committed are usually thought-forms projected by the criminal who, whether living or dead, but most especially when dead, is perpetually thinking over again and again the circumstances of his action. Since these thoughts are naturally specially vivid in his mind on the anniversary of the crime, it may happen that the thought-form is strong enough to materialise itself so as to be visible to physical sight, thus accounting for many cases where the manifestation is periodical. *A P 105*

Similarly, a jewel, which has been the cause of many crimes, may retain the impressions of the passions prompting the crimes, with unimpaired clearness, for many thousands of years, and continue to radiate them. *H S II 68.*

A thought of phenomenal energy and concentration, whether it be a blessing or a curse, calls into being an elemental which is practically a living storage-battery with a kind of clockwork attachment. It can be arranged to discharge itself regularly at a certain hour daily, or upon a certain anniversary, or its discharge may be contingent upon certain occurrences. Many instances of this class of elemental are on record, *O S D 241. A P 93-95.*

particularly in the Highlands of Scotland, where physical warnings occur before the death of a member of the family.   In these cases it is usually the powerful thought-form of an ancestor which gives the warning, according to the intention with which it was charged.

A sufficiently strong wish—a concentrated effort of intense love or envenomed hate—would create such an entity once for all, an entity which would then be quite disconnected from its creator, and would carry on its appointed work entirely irrespective of later intentions and desire on his part.   Mere repentance could not recall it or prevent its action any more than repentance could stop a bullet once discharged.   Its power could be to a considerable extent neutralised only by sending after it thoughts of a contrary tendency.

A P 91.   Occasionally an elemental of this class, being unable to expend its force either upon its object or its creator, may become a kind of wandering demon, and be attracted by any person who harbours similar feelings. If sufficiently powerful, it may even seize upon and inhabit a passing shell (see page 171), in which it is able to husband its resources more carefully.   In this form it may manifest through a medium, and, by masquerading as a well-known friend, may obtain influence over people upon whom it would otherwise have little hold.

A P 96-97.
S G O 217.   Such elementals, whether formed consciously or unconsciously, which have become wandering demons, invariably seek to prolong their life, either by feeding like vampires upon the vitality of human beings, or by influencing them to make offerings to them. Among simple primitive tribes they have frequently succeeded in getting themselves recognised as village or family gods.   The less objectionable types may be content with offerings of rice and cooked foods : the lowest and most loathsome class demand blood-sacrifices.   Both varieties exist to-day in India, and in greater numbers in Africa.

By drawing mainly upon the vitality of their devotees, and also upon the nourishment they can obtain from the offerings, they may prolong their existence for years, or even centuries. They may even perform occasional phenomena of a mild type in order to stimulate the faith and zeal of their followers, and they invariably make themselves unpleasant in some way or other if the sacrifices are neglected.

The black magicians of Atlantis—the " lords of the dark face "—seem to have specialised in this type of artificial elementals, some of which, it is hinted, may have kept themselves in existence even to this day. The terrible Indian goddess, Kâli, may well be a relic of this type. *A P 98.*

The vast majority of thought-forms are simply copies or images of people or other material objects. They are formed first within the mental body and then pass outwards and remain suspended before the man. This applies to anything about which one may be thinking : persons, houses, landscapes, or anything else. *T F 36–37, 45.*

A painter, for example, builds out of the matter of his mental body a conception of his future picture, projects it into space in front of him, keeps it before his " mind's eye," and copies it. This thought- and emotion-form persists and may be regarded as the unseen counterpart of the picture, radiating out its own vibrations and affecting all who come within its influence. *T F 36.* *H S II 59–60.*

Similarly a novelist builds in mental matter images of his characters, and then, by his will, moves these puppets from one position or grouping to another, so that the plot of the story is literally acted out before him. *T F 37.*

A curious effect arises in such a case. A playful nature-spirit (see Chapter XX) may ensoul the images and cause them to do things other than those which the author intended them to do. More frequently a dead writer may perceive the images, and, being still interested in the craft of writing, may mould the characters and influence their actions according to his *T F 37.* *H S I 161.*

own ideas. The actual writer thus often finds his plots working themselves out according to a plan quite different from his original conception.

H S II 34-35, 36-37.
O S D 82.
In reading a book, it is possible for a genuine student, with attention fully concentrated, to get into touch with the original thought-form which represents the author's conception as he wrote. Through the thought-form the author himself may even be reached, and additional information thus obtained, or light gained on difficult points.

There are in the mental and astral worlds many renderings of well-known stories, each nation usually having its special presentation, with the characters dressed in its own particular national garb. There thus exist excellent and life-like thought-forms of people like Sherlock Holmes, Captain Kettle, Robinson Crusoe, Shakespeare's characters, etc.

I L II 161-165.
O S D 82.
In fact, there are on the astral plane vast numbers of thought-forms of a comparatively permanent character, often the result of the cumulative work of generations of people. Many of these refer to alleged religious history, and the sight of them by sensitive people is responsible for many quite genuine accounts given by untrained seers and seeresses. Any great historical event, having been constantly thought of, and vividly imaged by large numbers of people, exists as a definite thought-form on the mental plane, and wherever there is any strong emotion connected with it, it is materialised also in astral matter and consequently can be seen by a clairvoyant.

The above applies equally, of course, to scenes and situations in fiction, drama, etc.

A W 81-83.
T P 37-38.
K 20-21.
Considered in the mass, it is easy to realise the tremendous effect that these thought-forms or artificial elementals have in producing national and race-feelings, and thus in biasing and prejudicing the mind : for thought-forms of a similar kind have a tendency to aggregate together and form a kind of collective entity. We see everything through this atmosphere, every thought is more or less refracted by it, and our own

astral bodies are vibrating in accord with it. As most people are receptive rather than initiative in their nature, they act almost as automatic reproducers of the thoughts which reach them, and thus the national atmosphere is continually intensified. This fact obviously explains many of the phenomena of crowd-consciousness (see Chapter XXV).

The influence of these aggregated thought-forms *K 21 : 75.* extends still further. Thought-forms of a destructive type act as a disruptive agent and often precipitate havoc on the physical plane, causing " accidents," natural convulsions, storms, earthquakes, floods, or crime, disease, social upheavals and wars.

It is possible also for dead people and other non- *O S D 83–84.* human entities, such as mischievous nature-spirits, (see p. 181) for example, to enter and vivify these thought-images. The trained seer has to learn to distinguish the thought-form, even when vivified, from the living being, and prominent facts of the astral world from the temporary moulds into which they are cast.

Our third class of thought-emotion forms consists *T F 37–38.* of those which are not directly connected with any natural object, and which therefore express themselves in forms entirely their own, displaying their inherent qualities in the matter which they draw around themselves. In this group, therefore, we have a glimpse of the forms natural to the astral and mental planes. Thought-forms of this class almost invariably manifest themselves on the astral plane, as the vast majority of them are expressions of feeling as well as of thought.

Such a form simply floats detached in the atmos- *T F 27.* phere, all the time radiating vibrations similar to those originally sent forth by its creator. If it does not come into contact with any other mental body, the radiation gradually exhausts its store of energy and the form then falls to pieces ; but if it succeeds in awakening sympathetic vibrations in any mental body near at hand, an attraction is set up, and the thought-form is usually absorbed by that mental body.

T F 27.
H S II 250
From the above we see that the influence of a thought-*form* is less far-reaching than that of a thought-*vibration*, but it acts with much greater precision. A thought-vibration reproduces thoughts of an order *similar* to that which gave it birth. A thought-form reproduces the *same* thought. The radiations may affect thousands and stir in them thoughts of the same level as the original, though none of them may be identical with it. The thought-form can affect only very few, but in those few cases it will reproduce exactly the initiatory idea.

For pictorial, coloured illustrations of many kinds of thought and emotion forms, the student is referred to the classic work on the subject : *Thought-Forms*, by Annie Besant and C. W. Leadbeater. This whole chapter, indeed, is largely a condensed summary of the principles enunciated in that work.

T F 40–41 :
44 : 49 : 55.
T F 42.
T F 43.
T F 42.
Vague thoughts or feelings show themselves as vague clouds. Definite thoughts or feelings create clearly defined forms. Thus a form of definite affection directed to a particular individual shapes itself not unlike a projectile : a thought of protective affection becomes somewhat like a bird, with a central portion of yellow and two wing-shaped projections of rose-pink : a thought of universal love becomes a rose-pink sun with rays in every direction.

T F 43–44 :
51, 52, 56,
57, 61, 62.
Thoughts in which selfishness or greed are prominent usually take a hooked form, the hooks in some cases actually clawing round the object desired.

T F 46–48.
H S I 246–248.
I L I 7.
H S II 261–262.
As a general principle, the energy of a selfish thought moves in a closed curve, and thus inevitably returns and expends itself upon its own level. An absolutely unselfish thought or feeling, however, rushes forth in an open curve, and thus does *not* return, in the ordinary sense, but pierces through into the plane above, because only in that higher condition, with its additional dimension, can it find room for its expansion. But, in thus breaking through, such a thought or feeling opens a door, as we might say symbolically, of dimension equivalent to its diameter, and thus provides a

channel through which the higher planes can pour themselves into the lower—often with wonderful results, as in the case of prayer, both for the thinker and for others.

Herein lies the highest and best part of the belief in answers to prayer. On the higher planes there is an infinite flood of force always ready and waiting to be poured through when a channel is offered. A thought of perfectly unselfish devotion provides such a channel, the grandest and noblest part of such a thought ascending to the Logos Himself. The response from Him is a descent of the divine life, resulting in a great strengthening and uplifting of the maker of the channel, and the spreading all about him of a powerful and beneficent influence, which flows through the reservoir that exists on the higher planes for the helping of mankind. It is this adding to the reservoir of spiritual force which is the truth in the catholic idea of works of supererogation. The Nirmânakâyas are especially associated with this great reservoir of force. *T F 46-48. I L I 5-8. H S II 261-262.*

Meditation upon a Master makes a link with Him, which shows itself to clairvoyant vision as a kind of line of light. The Master always subconsciously feels the impinging of such a line, and sends out along it in response a steady stream of magnetism which continues to play long after the meditation is over. Regularity in such meditation is a very important factor. *I L I 69-70. H S II 45-46. M P 73.*

A thought of definite, well-sustained devotion may assume a form closely resembling a flower, whilst devotional aspiration will create a blue cone, the apex pointing upwards. *T F 48. T F. 46.*

Such thought-forms of devotion are often exceedingly beautiful, varying much in outline, but characterised by curved upward-pointing petals like azure flames. It is possible that the flower-like characteristic of devotion forms may have led to the custom of offering flowers in religious worship, the flowers suggesting the forms visible to astral sight. *L A D 57.*

T F 50–51
T F 53.
T F 52.
T F 54.

Intense curiosity, or desire to know, takes the form of a yellow snake: explosive anger or irritation, of a splash of red and orange: sustained anger, of a sharp, red stiletto: spiteful jealousy shows itself as a brownish snake.

T F 66–73:
74–75.
L A D 57.

Forms produced by people who have mind and emotion well under control and definitely trained in meditation, are clear, symmetrical objects of great beauty, often taking well-known geometrical forms, such as triangles, two triangles interlaced, five-pointed stars, hexagons, crosses, and so on, these indicating thoughts concerned with cosmic order, or metaphysical concepts.

H S II 259,
265.

The power of the united thought of a number of people is always far more than the sum of their separate thoughts: it would be more nearly represented by their product.

T F 75–76.
H S I 268–
273.

Music also produces forms which are perhaps not technically thought-forms—unless we take them, as we well may, as the result of the thought of the composer, expressed by the skill of the musician through his instrument.

These music forms will vary according to the type of music, the kind of instrument which plays it, and the skill and merits of the performer. The same piece of music will, if accurately played, always build the same form, but that form will, when played on a church organ or by an orchestra, be enormously larger than, as well as of different texture from, that produced when played upon a piano. There will also be a difference in texture between the result of a piece of music played upon a violin and the same piece executed upon a flute. There is also a wide difference between the radiant beauty of the form produced by a true artist, perfect in expression and execution, and the relatively dull effect produced by a wooden and mechanical player.

T F 77.
H S I 271.

Music forms may remain as coherent erections for a considerable time—an hour or two at least—and during all that time they are radiating their characteristic vibrations in every direction, just as thought-forms do.

In *Thought-Forms* three coloured examples are given, of music forms built by music of Mendelssohn, of Gounod, and of Wagner respectively. *T F* 77: 80. *T F* 82. *H S I* 269.

The forms which are built vary much with different composers. An overture by Wagner makes a magnificent whole, as though he built with mountains of flame for stones. One of Bach's fugues builds up an ordered form, bold yet precise, rugged but symmetrical, with parallel rivulets of silver and gold or ruby running through it, marking the successive appearances of the *motif*. One of Mendelssohn's Lieber ohne Worte makes an airy erection, like a castle of filigree work in frosted silver.

These forms, created by the performers of the music, are quite distinct from the thought-forms made by the composer himself, which often persist for many years, even for centuries, if he is so far understood and appreciated that his original conception is strengthened by the thoughts of his admirers. Similar edifices are constructed by a poet's idea of his epic, or a writer's conception of his subject. Sometimes crowds of nature-spirits (see p 181) may be seen admiring the music-forms and bathing in the waves of influence which they send forth. *H S I* 270–271.

In studying pictorial representations of thought-forms it is important to bear in mind that thought-forms are four-dimensional objects. It is therefore a practical impossibility to describe them adequately in words which pertain to our ordinary three-dimensional experiences, still less to portray them in two-dimensional pictures on paper. Students of the fourth dimension will realise that the most that can be done is to represent a section of the four-dimensional forms. *T F* 16-17.

T F 48-49

It is a remarkable, and possibly deeply significant fact, that many of the higher types of thought-forms assume shapes closely resembling vegetable and animal forms. We thus have at least a presumption that the forces of nature work along lines somewhat similar to those along which thought and emotion work. Since the whole universe is a mighty thought-form called into existence by the Logos, it may well be that tiny parts of it also result from the thought-forms of minor entities engaged in the same creative work. This conception naturally recalls the Hindu belief that there are 330,000,000 Devas.

T F 29–30.　　It is also worthy of notice that, whilst some of the thought-forms are so complicated and so exquisitely fashioned as to be beyond the power of the human hand to reproduce, yet they may be very closely approximated by mechanical means. The instrument, known as a Harmonograph, consists of a fine point guided in its path by several pendulums, each of which has its own independent swing, all of these being welded into one composite movement, which is communicated to the pointer, and which the pointer registers on a suitable surface.

T F 28　　Other, though simpler forms, resemble the sand figures produced by the well-known Chladni's sound plate or by the Eidophone (vide *Eidophone Voice Figures*, by Margaret Watts Hughes).

H S I 274–275.　　Scales and arpeggios throw out lasso-like loops and curves : a song with a chorus produces a number of beads strung on a silver thread of melody : in a glee or part-song intertwining threads of different colours and textures are produced. A processional hymn builds a series of precise rectangular forms, like the links of a chain or the carriages of a railway train. An Anglican chant makes glittering fragments, quite different from the glowing uniformity of the Gregorian tone, which is not unlike the effect of Sanskrit verses chanted by an Indian pandit.

H S I 277–278　　Military music produces a long stream of rhythmically vibrating forms, the regular beat of these undulations tending to strengthen those of the astral bodies of the soldiers, the impact of a succession of steady and powerful oscillations supplying for the time the place of the will-force which, through fatigue, may have been slackened.

A thunderstorm creates a flaming band of colour, *H S I 279-280.*
a crash making a form suggestive of an exploding
bomb, or an irregular sphere with spikes projecting
from it. Sea-waves breaking on the shore create
wavy, parallel lines of changing colour, becoming
mountain ranges in a storm. Wind in the leaves of a
forest covers it with iridescent network, rising and
falling with gentle wave-like movement.

The song of birds shows as curving lines and loops
of light, from the golden globes of the campanero to
the amorphous and coarsely-coloured mass of the
scream of a parrot or macaw. The roar of a lion is
also visible in higher matter and it is possible that
some wild creatures are able to see it clairvoyantly,
thus adding to their terror. A purring cat surrounds *H S I 280-282.*
itself with concentric rosy cloud-films: a barking
dog shoots forth well-defined sharp-pointed projectiles
not unlike a rifle bullet, which pierce the astral bodies
of people and seriously disturb them. The bay of a
bloodhound throws off beads like footballs, slower in
motion and less liable to injure. The colour of these
projectiles is usually red or brown, varying with the
emotion of the animal and the key of his voice.

The lowing of a cow produces blunt-ended clumsy
shapes like logs of wood. A flock of sheep makes a
many-pointed yet amorphous cloud not unlike a dust-
cloud. The cooing of a pair of doves makes graceful
curved forms like the letter S reversed.

Turning to human sounds, an angry ejaculation *H S I 282-283.*
throws itself forth like a scarlet spear: a stream of
silly chatter produces an intricate network of hard
brown-grey metallic lines, forming an almost perfect
barrier against any higher or more beautiful thoughts
and feelings. The astral body of a garrulous person
is a striking object-lesson on the folly of unnecessary,
useless and unpleasant speech.

A child's laughter bubbles forth in rosy curves: *H S I 283-284.*
the guffaw of an empty-minded person causes an *M P 105-106.*
explosive effect in an irregular mass, usually brown
or dirty green. A sneer throws out a shapeless pro-

jectile of dull red, usually flecked with brownish-green and bristling with sharp points.

The cachinations of the self-conscious produce the appearance and colour of a pool of boiling mud. Nervous giggles create a sea-weed-like tangle of brown and dull yellow lines, and have a very bad effect upon the astral body. A jolly, kindly laugh billows out in rounded forms of gold and green. A soft and musical whistle produces an effect not unlike that of a small flute, but sharper and more metallic. Tuneless whistling sends out small piercing projectiles of dirty brown.

M P 108. Fidgetiness or fussiness produces in the aura tremulous vibrations, so that no thought or feeling can pass in or out without distortion, even good thought that is being sent out taking with it a shiver that practically neutralises it. Accuracy in thought is essential, but it should be attained not by hurry or fuss but by perfect calmness.

H S I 284-286. The strident screech of a railway engine makes a far more penetrating and powerful projectile than even the bark of a dog, producing upon the astral body an effect comparable to that of a sword thrust upon the physical body. An astral wound heals in a few minutes, but the shock to the astral organism disappears by no means so readily.

The firing of a gun produces a serious effect upon astral currents and astral bodies. Rifle or pistol fire throws out a stream of small needles.

H S II 57. Repeated noises affect the mental and astral bodies precisely as blows affect the physical body. In the physical body the result would be pain : in the astral body it means irritability : in the mental body a feeling of fatigue and inability to think clearly.

H S I 286-287. It is abundantly clear that all loud, sharp or sudden sounds should, as far as possible, be avoided by any one who wishes to keep his astral and mental vehicles in good order. Especially disastrous is the effect, *e.g.*, of the ceaseless noise and roar of a city upon the plastic astral and mental bodies of children.

All the sounds of nature blend themselves into one tone, called by the Chinese the "Great Tone," or KUNG. This also has its form, a synthesis of all forms, vast and changeful as the sea, representing the note of our earth in the music of the spheres. This is said by some writers to be the note F of our scale. *H S I 287. S D III 463–464.*

It is, of course, possible to destroy a thought-form, and this is sometimes done, for example, where a person after death is pursued by a malignant thought-form, created probably by the hate of those whom the person had injured whilst in the physical world. Although such a thought-form may appear almost as a living creature—an instance is given where it resembled a huge distorted gorilla—it is simply a temporary creation of evil passion and in no sense an evolving entity, so that to dissipate it is simply like destroying a Leyden jar, and is not in any sense a criminal action. *O S D 73.*

Most men recognise that acts which injure others are definitely and obviously wrong, but few recognise that it is also wrong to feel jealousy, hatred, ambition, etc., even though such feelings are not expressed in speech or deed. An examination of the conditions of life after death (Chapters XIII–XV) reveals that such feelings injure the man who harbours them, and cause him acute suffering after death. *L A D 12. O S D 61.*

A study of thought-forms thus brings home to the earnest student the tremendous possibilities of such creations, and the responsibility attaching to a right use of them. Thoughts are not only things, but exceedingly puissant things. Every one is generating them unceasingly night and day. Often it is not possible to render physical aid to those in need, but there is no case in which help may not be given by thought, or in which it can fail to produce a definite result. No one need hesitate to use this power to the full: provided always that it be employed for unselfish purposes, and for furthering the divine scheme of evolution. *T F 73-74. H S II 191–192.*

CHAPTER VIII

PHYSICAL LIFE

IN Chapter II we considered, in general outline, the composition and structure of the astral body. We shall now proceed to study it, in greater detail, as it exists and is used during the ordinary *waking* consciousness of the physical body.

The factors which determine the nature and quality of the astral body during physical life may be roughly grouped as follows :—

1. The physical life.
2. The emotional life.
3. The mental life.

M B 44.
S P 35.
H S II 8.
S G O 280.

1. *The Physical Life.*—We have already seen (p. 8) that every particle of the physical body has its corresponding astral " counterpart." Consequently, as the solids, liquids, gases and ethers of which the physical is composed may be coarse or refined, gross or delicate, so will be the nature of the corresponding astral envelopes. A physical body nourished on impure food will produce a correspondingly impure astral body, whilst a physical body fed on clean food and drink will help to purify the astral vehicle.

H S II 9.
S G O 280.

The astral body being the vehicle of emotion, passion and sensation, it follows that an astral body of the grosser type will be chiefly amenable to the grosser varieties of passion and emotion : whereas a finer astral body will more readily vibrate to more refined emotions and aspirations.

L L 15.
I Y 125.

It is impossible to make the physical body coarse and at the same time to organise the astral and mental bodies for finer purposes : neither is it possible to have a pure physical body with impure mental and astral bodies. All three bodies are thus interdependent.

Not only the physical body, but also the higher *S G O* 280–282. bodies also, are affected by the food which is eaten. Carnivorous diet is fatal to anything like real occult development, and those who adopt it are throwing serious and unnecessary difficulties in their own way, for flesh food intensifies all the undesirable elements and passions of the lower planes.

In the ancient Mysteries were men of the utmost *T N P* 128–129. purity and they were invariably vegetarian. The Râja Yogi takes especial pains to purify the physical body by an elaborate system of food, drink, sleep, etc., and insists on foods which are *sâtvic*, or " rhythmic." A whole system relating to foodstuffs is built up to help in the preparation of the body for use by the higher consciousness. Flesh foods are *rajâsic*, *I Y* 126. *i.e.*, they come under the quality of activity, being *C W* 124. stimulants, and built up to express animal desires and activities. They are utterly unsuited to the finer type of nervous organisation. The yogi therefore cannot afford to use these for the higher processes of thought.

Foods on the way to decay, such as game, venison, etc., as well as alcohol, are *tamâsic*, or heavy, and also to be avoided.

Foods which tend to growth, such as grain and fruits, are *sâtvic*, or rhythmic, being the most highly vitalised and suitable for building up a body sensitive and at the same time strong.

Certain other substances also affect the physical *I L I* 497–8. and astral bodies detrimentally. Thus tobacco per- *H S II* 20–21. meates the physical body with impure particles, causing emanations so material that they are frequently perceptible to the sense of smell. Astrally, tobacco not only introduces impurity, but tends also to deaden the sensibility of the body : " soothing the nerves," as it is called. While this may, in conditions of modern life, be sometimes less harmful than leaving the nerves " unsoothed," it is certainly undesirable for an occultist, who needs the capacity of answering instantly to all possible vibrations, combined, of course, with perfect control.

I L I 499.
H S II 10.
Similarly, there is no doubt whatever that from the point of view of both astral and mental bodies the use of alcohol is always an evil.

C W 124.
Bodies fed on flesh and alcohol are liable to be thrown out of health by opening up of the higher consciousness : and nervous diseases are partly due to the fact that the human consciousness is trying to express itself through bodies clogged with flesh products and poisoned with alcohol.   In particular, the pituitary body is very readily poisoned by even a
C W 123 : 197.
very small amount of alcohol, and its highest evolution is thereby checked.   It is the poisoning of the pituitary body with alcohol that leads to the abnormal and irrational vision associated with delirium tremens.

I L I 499–
500.
H S II 7–8 :
11–12.
S G O 282 :
283.
I Y 128.
In addition to the direct coarsening of the physical and astral bodies, meat, tobacco and alcohol are open also to the serious objection that they tend to attract undesirable astral entities which take pleasure in the scent of blood and spirits : they surge around the person, impressing their thoughts upon him, forcing their impressions on his astral body, so that the person may have a kind of shell of objectionable entities hanging on to his aura.   Principally for this reason, in the Yoga of the Right Hand Path meat and wine are absolutely forbidden.

M B 45.
These entities consist of artificial elementals, given birth to by the thoughts and desires of men, and also of depraved men imprisoned in their astral bodies, known as elementaries (see p. 145).   The elementals are attracted towards people whose astral bodies contain matter congenial to their nature, while the elementaries naturally seek to indulge in vices such as they themselves encouraged while in physical bodies.

H S II 22–
23.
Nearly all drugs—such as opium, cocaine, the theine in tea, caffeine in coffee, etc.—produce a deleterious effect upon the higher vehicles.   Occasionally they are, of course, almost a necessity, in certain diseases : but an occultist should use them as sparingly as possible.

One who knows how to do it can remove the evil effect of opium (which may have been used to relieve

great pain) from the astral and mental bodies after it
has done its work on the physical.

Dirt of all kinds is also more objectionable in the *H S II* 23-
higher worlds even than in the physical, and attracts 25.
a low class of nature-spirits (see p. 181). The occultist
therefore needs to be stringent in all matters of cleanli- *H S II* 204.
ness. Especial attention should be paid to the hands
and feet, because through these extremities emanations
flow out so readily.

Physical noises, such as prevail in cities, jar the *M P* 100-
nerves and thus cause irritation and fatigue : the 101.
effect is accentuated by the pressure of so many astral
bodies vibrating at different rates, and all excited
and disturbed by trifles. Although such irritation is
superficial, and may pass out of the mind in ten
minutes, yet an effect may be produced in the astral
body lasting for forty-eight hours. Hence it is difficult, whilst living in modern cities, to avoid irritability,
especially for one whose bodies are more highly strung
and sensitive than those of the ordinary man.

In general, it may be said that everything which *H S II* 30.
promotes the health of the physical body also reacts
favourably upon the higher vehicles.

Travel is another of the many factors which affect *H S I* 110-
the astral body, by bringing to bear on the traveller 111.
a change of etheric and astral influences connected
with each place or district. Ocean, mountain, forest,
waterfall, each has its own special type of life, astral
and etheric as well as visible, and therefore its own
set of influences. Many of these unseen entities are
pouring out vitality, and in any case their effect on
etheric, astral and mental bodies is likely to be healthy
and desirable in the long run, though a change may be
somewhat tiring at the time. Hence an occasional
change from town to country is beneficial on the
ground of emotional as well as physical health.

The astral body may also be affected by such objects *H S II* 69-
as talismans. The methods of making them have 72.
already been described in *The Etheric Double*, pp. 113-9. *M P* 126.
We shall here deal only with their general effects.

When an object is strongly charged with magnetism for a particular purpose by a competent person, it becomes a talisman, and when properly made continues to radiate this magnetism with unimpaired strength for many years.

It may be used for many purposes. Thus, for example, a talisman may be charged with thoughts of purity, which will express themselves as definite rates of vibration in astral and mental matter. These vibratory rates, being directly contrary to thoughts of impurity, will tend to neutralise or overpower any impure thoughts which may arise. In many cases the impure thought is a casual one that has been picked up and is not therefore a thing of great power in itself. The talisman, on the other hand, has been intentionally and strongly charged, so that when the two streams of thought meet, there is not the slightest doubt that the thoughts connected with the talisman will vanquish the others.

In addition, the initial conflict between the opposing sets of thoughts will attract the man's attention, and thus give him time to recollect himself, so that he will not be taken off his guard, as so frequently happens.

H S II 72-77.

Another example would be that of a talisman charged with faith and courage. This would operate in two ways. First, the vibrations radiating from the talisman would oppose feelings of fear as soon as they arose, and thus prevent them from accumulating and strengthening one another, as they often do, until they become irresistible. The effect has been compared to that of a gyroscope which, once set in motion in one direction, strongly resists being turned into another direction.

Secondly, the talisman works indirectly upon the mind of the wearer : as soon as he feels the beginnings of fear, he will probably recollect the talisman, and call up the reserve strength of his own will to resist the undesirable feeling.

A third possibility of a talisman is that of its being linked with the person who made it. In the event of the wearer being in desperate circumstances, he may call upon the maker and evoke a response from him. The maker may or may not be physically conscious of the appeal, but in any case his ego will be conscious and will respond by reinforcing the vibrations of the talisman.

Certain articles are to a large extent natural amulets or talismans. All precious stones are such, each having a distinct influence which can be utilised in two ways: (1) the influence attracts to it elemental essence of a certain kind, and thoughts and desires which naturally express themselves through that essence ; (2) these natural peculiarities make it a fit vehicle for magnetism which is intended to work along the same line as those thoughts and emotions. Thus, for example, for an amulet of purity, a stone should be chosen whose natural undulations are inharmonious to the key in which impure thoughts express themselves. *H S II 78-80.*

Although the particles of the stone are physical, yet, being in a key identical at this level with the key of purity on higher levels, they will, even without the stone being magnetised, check impure thought or feeling by virtue of the overtones. Furthermore, the stone can readily be charged at astral and mental levels with the undulations of pure thought and feeling which are set in the same key.

Other examples are (1) the rudraksha berry, frequently used for necklaces in India, which is especially suitable for magnetisation where sustained holy thought or meditation is required, and where all disturbing influences are to be kept away ; (2) the beads of the tulsi plant, whose influence is somewhat different. *H S II 80.*

Objects which produce strong scents are natural talismans. Thus the gums chosen for incense give out radiations favourable to spiritual and devotional thought, and do not harmonise with any form of disturbance or worry. Mediæval witches sometimes combined the ingredients of incense so as to produce the opposite effect, and it is also done to-day in Luciferian ceremonies. It is generally desirable to avoid coarse *H S II 80-81.*

and heavy scents, such as that of musk or of satchet powder, as many of them are akin to sensual feelings.

H S II 81-82. An object not intentionally charged may sometimes have the force of a talisman : e.g., a present from a friend, worn on the person, such as a ring or chain, or even a letter

H S II 82-86. An object, such as a watch, habitually carried in the pocket, becomes charged with magnetism and is able, if given away, to produce decided effects on the recipient. Coins and money notes are usually charged with mixed magnetism, feeling and thought, and may, therefore, radiate a disturbing and irritating effect.

H S II 97. A man's thoughts and feelings thus affect not only himself and other people, but also impregnate the inanimate objects round him, even walls and furniture. He thus unconsciously magnetises these physical objects, so that they have the power of suggesting similar thoughts and feelings to other people within range of their influence.

(2) *The Emotional Life.*—It is scarcely necessary to insist that the quality of the astral body is largely determined by the kind of feelings and emotions which constantly play through it.

I L I 376. A man is using his astral body, whether he be conscious of the fact or not, whenever he expresses an emotion, just as he is using his mental body whenever he thinks, or his physical body whenever he performs physical work. This, of course, is quite a different thing from utilising his astral body as an *independent* vehicle through which his consciousness can be fully expressed, a matter which we shall have to consider later, in due course.

M V I 177. The astral body, as we have seen, is the field of manifestion of desire, the mirror in which every feeling is instantly reflected, in which even every thought which has in it anything that touches the personal self must express itself. From the material of the astral body bodily form is given to the dark " elementals " (see p. 45), which men create and set in motion by evil wishes and malicious feelings : from it also are

bodied forth the beneficent elementals called into life
by good wishes, gratitude and love.

The astral body grows by use, just as every other
body does, and it also has its own habits, built up and
fixed by constant repetition of similar acts.   The astral   D A 39.
body during physical life being the recipient of and
respondent to stimuli both from the physical body and
from the lower mental, it tends to repeat automatically
vibrations to which it is accustomed ; just as the hand
may repeat a familiar gesture, so may the astral body
repeat a familiar feeling or thought.

All the activities that we call evil, whether selfish   I L I 425-
thoughts (mental) or selfish emotions (astral), invari-   427.
ably show themselves as vibrations of the coarser
matter of those planes, whilst good and unselfish
thought or emotion sets in vibrations the higher types of
matter.   As finer matter is more easily moved than
coarse, it follows that a given amount of force spent
in good thought or feeling produces perhaps a hundred
times as much result as the same amount of force sent
out into coarser matter.   If this were not so, it is
obvious that the ordinary man could never make any
progress at all.

The effect of 10 per cent. of force directed to good
ends enormously outweighs that of 90 per cent.
devoted to selfish purposes, and so on the whole such
a man makes an appreciable advance from life to life.
A man who has even 1 per cent. of good makes a slight
advance.   A man whose account balances exactly, so
that he neither advances nor retrogresses, must live
a distinctly evil life : whilst in order to go downwards
in evil a person must be an unusually consistent villain.

Thus even people who are doing nothing consciously   I L I 261-
towards their evolution, and who let everything go as   262.
it will, are nevertheless gradually evolving, because of   M V I 74-75.
the irresistible force of the Logos which is steadily   T B 47.
pressing them onwards.   But they are moving so
slowly that it will take them millions of years of
incarnation and trouble and uselessness to gain even
a step.

The method by which progress is made certain is simple and ingenious. As we have seen, evil qualities are vibrations of the coarser matter of the respective planes, while good qualities are expressed through the higher grades of matter. From this follow two remarkable results.

It must be borne in mind that each sub-plane of the astral body has a special relationship to the corresponding sub-plane of the mental body ; thus the four lower astral sub-planes correspond to the four kinds of matter in the mental body, while the three higher astral sub-planes correspond to the three kinds of matter in the causal body.

Hence the lower astral vibrations can find no matter in the causal body capable of responding to them, and so the higher qualities alone can be built into the causal body. Thence it emerges that any good which a man develops in himself is permanently recorded by a change in his causal body, while the evil which he does, feels, or thinks cannot possibly touch the real ego, but can cause disturbance and trouble only to the mental body, which is renewed for each fresh incarnation. The result of evil is stored in the astral and mental permanent atoms : the man, therefore, has still to face it all over and over again, until he has vanquished it, and finally rooted from his vehicles all tendency to respond to it   That is evidently a very different matter from taking it into the ego and making it really a part of himself.

M B 42. Astral matter responds more rapidly than physical to every impulse from the world of mind, and consequently the astral body of a man, being made of astral matter, shares this readiness to respond to the impact of thought, and thrills in answer to every thought that strikes it, whether the thoughts come from without, *i.e.*, from the minds of other men, or from within, from the mind of its owner.

M B 44. An astral body, therefore, which is made by its owner to respond habitually to evil thoughts acts as a magnet to similar thought- and emotion-forms in

its vicinity, whereas a pure astral body acts on such
thoughts with repulsive energy, and attracts to itself
thought- and emotion-forms of matter and vibrations
congruous with its own.

For it must be borne in mind that the astral world
is full of thoughts and emotions of other men, and
that these exert a ceaseless pressure, constantly bom-
barding every astral body and setting up in it vibrations similar to their own.

I L I 47.
H S I 102.

In addition, there are nature-spirits (see p. 181)
of a low order, which enjoy the coarse vibrations of
anger and hatred, and throw themselves into any
current of such nature, thus intensifying the undulations and adding fresh life to them.   People yielding
themselves to coarse feelings can depend on being
constantly surrounded by such carrion-crows of the
astral world who jostle one another in eager anticipation of an outburst of passion.

H S I 102:
129–130.

Many of the moods to which most people are subject, in greater or lesser degree, are due to outside
astral influences.   Whilst depression, for example, may
be due to a purely physical cause, such as indigestion,
a chill, fatigue, etc., even more frequently it is caused
by the presence of an astral entity who is himself
depressed and is hovering around either in search of
sympathy or in the hope of drawing from the subject
the vitality which he lacks.

I L I 267–
268 : 386.
H S II 99.

Furthermore, a man who, for example, is beside
himself with rage, temporarily loses hold of his astral
body, the desire-elemental (see p. 6) becoming
supreme.   Under such circumstances the man may
be seized upon and obsessed either by a dead
man of similar nature or by some evil artificial
elemental.

M V I 011–
102.
L I I 487–
488.

The student should sternly and especially disregard
depression, which is a great barrier to progress, and
at least should endeavour to let no one else know that
he is oppressed by it.   It indicates that he is thinking
more of himself than of the Master, and it makes it
more difficult for the Master's influence to act upon

I L I .267–
268 : 70.
H S II 99–
100.
I L II 152.

him. Depression causes much suffering to sensitive people, and is responsible for much of the terror of children at night. The inner life of an aspirant ought not to be one of continual emotional oscillation.

Above all things, the aspirant should learn not to worry. Contentment is not incompatible with aspiration. Optimism is justified by the certainty of the ultimate triumph of good, though it is true that if we take into account only the physical plane it is not easy to maintain that position.

H S I 362-370.

Under the stress of very powerful emotions, if a man lets himself go too far, he may die, become insane, or be obsessed. Such obsession need not necessarily be what we call evil, though the truth is that all obsession is injurious.

An illustration of this phenomenon may be taken from " conversion " at a religious revival. On such occasions some men get worked up into a condition of such tremendous emotional excitement that they swing beyond the degree of safety : they may then be obsessed by a departed preacher of the same religious persuasion, and thus two souls may temporarily work through one body. The tremendous energy of these hysterical excesses is contagious and may spread rapidly through a crowd.

An astral disturbance is set up of the nature of a gigantic whirlpool. Towards this pour astral entities whose one desire is for sensation : these are all kinds of nature-spirits (see p. 181) who delight in and bathe in the vibrations of wild excitement, of whatever character, be it religious or sexual, just as children play in the surf. They supply and reinforce the energy so recklessly expended. The dominant idea being usually the selfish one of saving one's own soul, the astral matter is of a coarse kind, and the nature-spirits are also of a primitive type.

The emotional effect of a religious revival is thus very powerful. In some cases a man may be genuinely and permanently benefited by his " conversion," but the serious student of occultism should avoid such excesses of emotional excitement, which for many people are apt to be dangerous. " Excitement is alien to the spiritual life."

There are, of course, many causes of insanity : it may be due to defects in one or more of the vehicles —physical, etheric, astral, mental. In one variety it is caused by a want of accurate adjustment between the astral particles and the particles of either the etheric or the mental body. Such a case would not recover sanity until he reached the heaven-world, *i.e.*, until he had left his astral body and passed into his mental body. This type of insanity is rare. *I L I* 482–483.

The effect on the astral body caused by astral vibrations of another astral body has long been recognised in the East, and is one of the reasons why it is such an immense advantage to a pupil to live in close proximity to one more highly evolved than himself. An Indian teacher not only may prescribe for his pupil special kinds of exercises or study, in order to purify, strengthen and develop the astral body, but also by keeping the pupil in his neighbourhood physically seeks by this close association to harmonise and attune the pupil's vehicles to his own. Such a teacher has already calmed his own vehicles and accustomed them to vibrate at a few carefully selected rates instead of in a hundred promiscuous frenzies. These few rates of vibration are very strong and steady, and day and night, whether he is sleeping or waking, they play unceasingly upon the vehicles of the pupil, and gradually raise him to his teacher's key. *I L I* 46–48. *H S I* 102–105.

For similar reasons, an Indian who wishes to live the higher life, retires to the jungle, as a man of other races withdraws from the world and lives as a hermit. He thus has at least breathing space, and rest from the endless conflict caused by the 'perpetual battering on his vehicles of other people's feelings and thoughts, and can find time to think coherently. The calm influences of Nature are also to a certain extent helpful. *I L I* 47–48.

Somewhat analagous are the effects produced on animals which are closely associated with human beings. *M V I* 61. *H S I* 157.

The devotion of an animal for the master whom he loves, and his mental efforts to understand his master's wishes and to please him, enormously develop the animal's intellect and his power of devotion and affection. But in addition to this, the constant play of the man's vehicles on those of the animal greatly assist the process, and thus prepare the way for the animal to individualise and become a human entity.

H S I 469–472. *M B* 87.
It is possible, by an effort of will, to make a shell of astral matter on the periphery of the astral aura. This may be done for three purposes : (1) to keep out emotional vibrations, such as anger, envy or hatred, intentionally directed at one by another ; (2) to keep out casual vibrations of low type which may be floating in the astral world and impinge upon one's aura ; (3) to protect the astral body during meditation. Such shells do not usually last for long, but need to be frequently renewed if required for any length of time.

Such a shell would, of course, keep vibrations *in* as well as *out*. The student should therefore make the shell only of the coarsest astral matter, as he will not wish to keep away, or to prevent from passing outwards, vibrations in the higher types of astral matter.

H S I 476.
As a general principle, it may be said that to use a shell for oneself is to some extent a confession of weakness, as if one is all one should be, no artificial protection of this kind would be needed. On the other hand, shells may often be used with advantage to help other people who need protection.

A P 39-40. *O S D* 87–99.
It will be recollected (see p. 6) that a man's astral body consists not only of ordinary astral matter, but also of a quantity of elemental essence. During the man's life this elemental essence is segregated from the ocean of · similar matter around, and practically becomes for that time what may be described as a kind of artificial elemental (see p. 45), *i.e.*, a kind of semi-intelligent separate entity known as the Desire-Elemental. The Desire-Elemental follows the course

of its own evolution downwards into matter without any reference to (or, indeed, any knowledge of) the convenience or intention of the Ego to whom it happens to be attached. Its interests are thus diametrically opposed to those of the man, as it is seeking ever stronger and coarser vibrations. Hence the perpetual struggle described by St. Paul as "the law in the members warring against the law of the mind." Furthermore, finding that association with the mental matter of the man's mind-body brings to it more vivid vibrations, it endeavours to stir up the mental matter into sympathy with it, and to induce the man to believe that *he* desires the sensations which it desires.

Consequently, it becomes a sort of tempter. Nevertheless the desire-elemental is not an evil entity : in fact it is not an evolving entity at all, having no power of reincarnation : it is only the essence of which it is composed which is evolving. Nor has this shadowy being any evil designs upon the man, for it knows nothing whatever of the man of whom, for the time, it forms a part. It is thus in no way a fiend to be regarded with horror, but is as much a part of the divine life as the man himself, though at a different stage of its unfoldment.

It is a mistake to imagine that by refusing to gratify *I L I* 405. the desire-elemental with coarse vibrations, a man is *O S D* 101. thereby checking its evolution : for this is not the case. By controlling the passions and developing the higher qualities, a man drops the lower and helps to evolve the higher types of essence : the lower kinds of vibrations can be supplied by an animal, at some later time, even better than by a man, whereas no one but a man can evolve the higher type of essence.

All through life a man should definitely fight against *I L I* 404. the desire-elemental and its tendency to seek for the lower, coarser physical vibrations, recognising quite clearly that its consciousness, its likes and dislikes, are not his own. He has himself created it and should not become a slave to it, but learn to control it and realise himself as apart from it.

This matter will be further considered in Chapter XII.

(3) *The Mental Life.*—Our third and last factor which affects the astral body during ordinary waking consciousness is the mental life. The mental activities have the most far-reaching effects on the astral body for two reasons :—

(1) Because lower mental matter, Manas, is so inextricably linked with astral matter, Kâma, that it is almost impossible for most people to utilise one without the other : *i.e.*, few people can think without at the same time feeling, or feel without at the same time, to some extent, thinking.

L L 9-10.   (2) Because the organisation and control of the astral body rest with the mind. This is an example of the general principle that each body is built up by consciousness working in the plane next above it. Without the creative power of thought the astral body cannot be organised.

M B 98 : 68.   Every impulse sent by the mind to the physical body has to pass through the astral body, and produces an effect on it also. Further, as astral matter is far more responsive to thought-vibrations than is physical, the effect of mental vibrations on it is proportionately greater than on the physical body. Consequently a controlled, trained and developed mind tends also *D* 16.   to bring the astral body under control and to develop it. When, however, the mind is not actively controlling the astral body, the latter, being peculiarly susceptible to the influence of passing thought-currents, is perpetually receiving these stimuli from without, and eagerly responding to them.

So far, we have dealt with the general effects produced on the astral body, during ordinary life, by the nature of the physical, emotional and mental life. We have now to deal, but in general outline only, with the use of the special faculties of the astral body itself, during the waking consciousness.

The nature of these faculties, and their connection with the various Chakrams in the astral body, we have already described in Chapter V. By means of

the powers of astral matter itself, developed through
the agency of the Chakrams, a man is enabled not *M V I* 16.
only to receive vibrations from etheric matter, transmitted through the astral body to his mind, but also
to receive impressions direct from the surrounding
matter of the astral world, these, of course, being also
similarly transmitted through the mental body to the
real man within.

But in order to receive impressions in this manner
direct from the astral world, the man must learn to
focus his consciousness in his astral body, instead of,
as is usually the case, in his physical brain.

In the lower types of men, Kâma, or desire, is still *M V I* 53.
emphatically the most prominent feature, though the   *M* 18 : 34.
mental development has also proceeded to some
extent. The consciousness of such men is centred in
the lower part of the astral body, their life being
governed by sensations connected with the physical
plane. That is the reason why the astral body forms *L A D* 55.
the most prominent part of the aura in the undeveloped
man.

The ordinary average man is also still living almost *M V I* 53.
entirely in his sensations, although the higher astral
is coming into play: but still, for him, the prominent
question which guides his conduct is not what is right
or reasonable to do, but simply what he himself desires
to do. The more cultured and developed are beginning to govern desire by reason: that is to say, the *M V I* 54.
centre of consciousness is gradually transferring itself
from the higher astral to the lower mental. Slowly as
the man progresses it moves up further still, and the
man begins to be dominated by principle rather than
by interest and desire.

The student will recollect that humanity is still *I L I* 36.
in the Fourth Round, which should naturally be   *L L* 138.
devoted to the development of desire and emotion ;
yet we are engaged in the unfolding of intellect, which
is to be the special characteristic of the Fifth Round.
That this is so is due to the immense stimulus given
to our evolution by the descent of the Lords of the

Flame from Venus, and by the work of the Adepts, who have preserved for us that influence and steadily sacrificed themselves in order that we might make the better progress.

M V I 54. In spite of the fact that, in the vast majority of cases the centre of consciousness is located in the astral body, most men are quite unaware of the fact, knowing nothing at all about the astral body or its uses. They have behind them the traditions and customs of a long series of lives in which the astral faculties have not been used ; yet all the time those faculties have been gradually and slowly growing inside a shell, somewhat as a chick grows inside the egg. Hence a very large number of people have astral faculties, of which they are entirely unconscious, in reality very near the surface, so to speak, and it is probable that in the near future, as these matters become more widely known and understood, in great numbers of cases these latent faculties will break through, and astral powers will then become far more common than they are to-day.

The shell spoken of above is composed of a great mass of self-centred thought in which the ordinary man is almost hopelessly entombed. This applies also, perhaps with even greater force, to the sleep life, with which we shall deal in the next chapter.

l L I 441. We spoke above of focussing the consciousness in the astral body. The consciousness of man can be focussed in only one vehicle at a time, though he may be simultaneously conscious through the others in a vague way. A simple analogy may be taken from ordinary physical sight. If the finger be held up before the face, the eyes can be so focussed as to see the finger perfectly : at the same time the distant background can also be seen, though imperfectly, because it is out of focus. In a moment the focus can be changed so that the background is seen perfectly, but the finger, now out of focus, only dimly and vaguely.

Precisely in the same way, if a man who has developed astral and mental consciousness focusses himself in the physical brain, as in ordinary life, he will see perfectly the physical bodies of people, and at the same time he will see their astral and mental bodies, but only somewhat dimly. In far less than a moment he can change the focus of his consciousness so that he sees the astral fully and perfectly : but in that case he will see the mental and physical bodies also, but not in full detail. The same thing is true of the mental sight and of the sight of higher planes. *I L I* 442.

Thus in the case of a highly developed man, whose *M V I* 65. consciousness has already developed even beyond the causal (higher mental) body, so that he is able to function freely on the buddhic plane, and has also a measure of consciousness upon the âtmic plane, the centre of consciousness lies between the higher mental and the buddhic plane. The higher mental and the higher astral are in him much more developed than their lower parts, and though he still retains his physical body, he holds it merely for the convenience of working in it, and not in any way because his thoughts and desires are fixed there. Such a man has transcended all Kâma which could bind him to incarnation, and his physical body is therefore retained in order *M V I* 66. that it may serve as an instrument for the forces of the higher planes to reach down even to the physical plane.

CHAPTER IX

SLEEP-LIFE

I L I 488–489.
THE real cause of sleep would appear to be that the bodies grow tired of one another. In the case of the physical body, not only every muscular exertion, but also every feeling and thought, produce certain slight chemical changes. A healthy body is always trying to counteract these changes, but it never quite succeeds whilst the body is awake. Consequently with every thought, feeling or action there is a slight, almost imperceptible loss, the cumulative effect of which eventually leaves the physical body too exhausted to be capable of further thought or work. In some cases

H S I 73–74.
even a few moments of sleep will be sufficient for recuperation, this being effected by the physical elemental.

I L I 488–489 : 396–397.
L A D 45.
In the case of the astral body, it very soon becomes tired of the heavy labour of moving the particles of the physical brain, and needs a considerable period of separation from it to enable it to gather strength to resume the irksome task.

On its own plane, however, the astral body is practically incapable of fatigue, since it has been known to work incessantly for twenty-five years without showing signs of exhaustion.

I L I 397.
Although excessive and long-continued emotion tires a man very quickly in ordinary life, it is not the astral body which becomes fatigued, but the physical organism through which the emotion is expressed or experienced.

L A D 45.
Similarly with the mental body. When we speak of mental fatigue, it is in reality a misnomer, for it is

I L I 398.
M 31.
the brain, not the mind, that is tired. There is no such thing as fatigue of the *mind*.

When a man leaves his body in sleep (or in death), *I L I* 360–361.
the pressure of the surrounding astral matter—which
really means the force of gravity on the astral plane—
immediately forces other astral matter into the astrally
empty space.   Such a temporary astral counterpart
is an exact copy, so far as arrangement is concerned,
of the physical body, but nevertheless it has no real
connection with it, and could never be used as a vehicle.
It is merely a fortuitous concurrence of particles,
drawn from any astral matter of a suitable kind that
happens to be at hand.   When the true astral body
returns, it pushes out this other astral matter without
the slightest opposition.

This is clearly one reason why extreme care should
be exercised as to the surroundings in which a man
sleeps : for, if those surroundings are evil, astral
matter of an objectionable type may fill the physical
body while the man's astral body is absent, leaving
behind influences which cannot but react unpleasantly
upon the real man when he returns.

When a man " goes to sleep," his higher principles *M B* 48–49.
in their astral vehicle withdraw from the physical body, *D* 24.
A W 98.
the dense body and the etheric body remaining by
themselves on the bed, the astral body floating in the *L A D* 45.
air above them.   In sleep, then, a man is simply using
his astral body instead of his physical : it is only the
physical body that is asleep, not necessarily the man
himself.

Usually the astral body, thus withdrawn from *I L I* 393–394.
the physical, will retain the form of the physical *A P* 33–34.
body, so that the person is readily recognisable
to any one who knows him physically.   This is
due to the fact that the attraction between the
astral and the physical particles, continued all through
physical life, sets up a habit or momentum in the
astral matter, which continues even while it is
temporarily withdrawn from the sleeping physical
body.

For this reason, the astral body of a man who is *I L I* 398.
asleep will consist of a central portion, corresponding

to the physical body, relatively very dense, and a
surrounding aura, relatively much rarer.

L A D 45.
I H 34.
A very undeveloped man may be nearly as much
asleep as his physical body, because he is capable
of very little definite consciousness in his astral
body. He is also unable to move away from the
immediate neighbourhood of the sleeping physical
body, and if an attempt were made to draw him away
in his astral body, he would probably awake in his
physical body in terror.

M B 49 : 100.
D 32.
I L I 399.
A P 34.
I H 34.
A W 98.
His astral body is a somewhat shapeless mass, a
floating wreath of mist, roughly ovoid in shape, but
very irregular and indefinite in outline : the features
and shape of the inner form (the dense astral counter-
part of the physical body) are also vague, blurred and
indistinct, but always recognisable.

A man of this primitive type has been using his
astral body, during waking consciousness, sending
mind currents through the astral to the physical brain.
But when, during sleep, the physical brain is inactive,
the astral body, being undeveloped, is incapable of
receiving impressions on its own account, and so the
man is practically unconscious, being unable to
express himself clearly through the poorly organised
astral body. The centres of sensation in it may be
affected by passing thought-forms, and he may
answer in it to stimuli that rouse the lower nature.
But the whole effect given to the observer is one of
sleepiness and vagueness, the astral body lacking all
definite activity and floating idly, inchoate, above the
sleeping physical form.

A P 32.
In a quite unevolved person, therefore, the higher
principles, *i.e.*, the man himself, are almost as much
asleep as the physical body.

In some cases the astral body is less lethargic, and
floats dreamily about on the various astral currents,
occasionally recognising other people in a similar condition, and meeting with experiences of all sorts,
pleasant and unpleasant, the memory of which, hopelessly confused and often travestied into a grotesque

caricature of what really happened (see Chapter **X** on *Dreams*) will cause the man to think next morning what a remarkable dream he has had.

In the case of a more evolved man, there is a very great difference. The inner form is much more distinct and definite—a closer reproduction of the man's physical appearance. Instead of the surrounding mist-wreath, there is a sharply defined ovoid form preserving its shape unaffected amidst all the varied currents which are always swirling around it on the astral plane. *I L I* 399. *D* 33. *A P* 34. *I H* 34.

A man of this type is by no means unconscious in his astral body, but is quite actively thinking. Nevertheless, he may be taking very little more notice of his surroundings than undeveloped man. Not because he is incapable of seeing, but because he is so wrapped up in his own thought that he does not see, though he could do so if he chose. Whatever may have been the thoughts engaging his mind during the past day, he usually continues them when he falls asleep, and he is thus surrounded by so dense a wall of his own making that he observes practically nothing of what is going on outside. Occasionally a violent impact from without, or even some strong desire of his own from within, may tear aside this curtain of mist and permit him to receive some definite impression. But even then the fog would close in again almost immediately, and he would dream on unobservantly as before. *L A D* 46. *I H* 100. *A W* 100– 101.

In the case of a still more developed man, when the physical body goes to sleep, the astral body slips out of it, and the man is then in full consciousness. The astral body is clearly outlined and definitely organised, bearing the likeness of the man, and the man is able to use it as a vehicle, a vehicle far more convenient than the physical body. *M B* 49–50. *D* 33. *A W* 101– 102.

The receptivity of the astral body has increased, until it is instantly responsive to all the vibrations of its plane, the fine as well as the coarser : but in the astral body of a very highly developed person there would, of course, be practically no matter left capable of responding to coarse vibrations.

Such a man is wide awake, is working far more actively, more accurately, and with greater power of comprehension, than when he was confined in the denser physical vehicle. In addition, he can move about freely and with immense rapidity to any distance, without causing the least disturbance to the sleeping physical body.

D 34-35. He may meet and exchange ideas with friends, either incarnate or discarnate, who happen to be equally awake on the astral plane. He may meet people more evolved than himself, and receive from them warning or instruction : or he may be able to confer benefits on those who know less than himself. He may come into contact with non-human entities of various kinds (see Chapters XX and XXI on *Astral Entities*) : he will be subject to all kinds of astral influences, good or evil, strengthening or terrifying.

H S II 238. He may form friendships with people from other parts of the world : he may give or listen to lectures : if he is a student, he may meet other students and, with the additional faculties which the astral world gives, he may be able to solve problems which presented difficulties in the physical world.

H S II 237. A physician, for example, during the sleep of the body, may visit cases in which he is especially interested. He may thus acquire new information, which may come through as a kind of intuition to his waking consciousness.

S P 19. In a highly evolved man, the astral body, being thoroughly organised and vitalised, becomes as much the vehicle of consciousness on the astral plane as the physical body is on the physical plane.

M 39-41.
I L II 85.
T B 71. The astral world being the very home of passion and emotion, those who yield themselves to an emotion can experience it with a vigour and a keenness mercifully unknown on earth. Whilst in the physical body most of the efficiency of an emotion is exhausted in transmission to the physical plane, but in the astral

world the whole of the force is available in its own world. Hence it is possible in the astral world to feel far more intense affection or devotion than is possible in the physical world : similarly an intensity of suffering is possible in the astral world which is unimaginable in ordinary physical life.

An advantage of this state of affairs is that in the astral world all pain and suffering are voluntary and absolutely under control, hence life there is much easier, for the man who understands. To control physical pain by the mind is possible, but exceedingly difficult : but in the astral world any one can in a moment drive away the suffering caused by a strong emotion. The man has only to exert his will, when the passion straightway disappears. This assertion sounds startling : but it is nevertheless true, such being the power of will and mind over matter.

To have attained full consciousness in the astral body is to have already made a considerable amount of progress : when a man has also bridged over the chasm between astral and physical consciousness, day and night no longer exist for him, since he leads a life unbroken in its continuity. For such a man, even death, as ordinarily conceived, has ceased to exist, since he carries that unbroken consciousness not only through night and day, but also through the portals of death itself, and up to the end of his life upon the astral plane, as we shall see later when we come to deal with the after-death life. *I L I* 376–377.

Travelling in the astral body is not instantaneous : but it is so swift that space and time may be said to be practically conquered : for although a man is passing through space, it is passed through so rapidly that its power to divide is nearly non-existent. In two or three minutes a man might move round the world. *M B* iii–112. *M* 14 : 39.

Any fairly advanced and cultured man has already consciousness fully developed in the astral body, and is perfectly capable of employing it as a vehicle, though in many cases he does not do so, because he *M V I* 54. *I H* 34. *H S II* 167. *C* 25. *O S D* 28–29.

has not made the definite effort which is at first necessary, until the habit becomes established.

I L II 87.
O S D 29.
The difficulty with the ordinary person is not that the astral body cannot act, but that for thousands of years that body has been accustomed to being set in motion only by impressions received through the physical vehicle, so that men do not realise that the astral body can work on its own plane and on its own account, and that the will can act upon it directly. People remain " unawake " astrally because they get into the habit of waiting for the familiar physical vibrations to call out their astral activity. Hence

A P 32.
they may be said to be awake *on* the astral plane, but not in the least *to* the plane, and consequently they are conscious of their surroundings only very vaguely, if at all.

A P 32–33.
When a man becomes a pupil of one of the Masters, he is usually at once shaken out of his somnolent condition on the astral plane, fully awakened to the realities around him on that plane, and set to learn from them and to work among them, so that his hours of sleep are no longer a blank, but are filled with active and useful occupation, without in the least interfering with the healthy repose of the tired physical body.

M V I 57.
I H 100.
I L II 87 :
90–92.
In Chapter XXVIII on *Invisible Helpers* we shall deal more fully with carefully planned and organised work in the astral body : here it may be stated that even before that stage is reached, a great deal of useful work may be and is constantly being done. A man who falls asleep with the definite intention in his mind of doing a certain piece of work will assuredly go and attempt to carry out his intention as soon as he is freed from his physical body in sleep. But, when the work is completed, it is likely that the fog of his own self-centred thoughts will close round him once more, unless he has accustomed himself to initiate fresh lines of action when functioning apart from the physical brain. In some cases, of course, the work chosen is such as to occupy the whole of the time

spent in sleep, so that such a man would be exerting *M B* 36.
himself to the fullest extent possible, so far as his astral
development permits.

Every one should determine each night to do some- *I L II* 92–93.
thing useful on the astral plane : to comfort some one
in trouble : to use the will to pour strength into a
friend who is weak or ill : to calm some one who is
excited or hysterical : or to perform some similar
service.

Some measure of success is absolutely certain, and
if the helper observes closely, he will often receive
indications in the physical world of definite results
achieved.

There are four ways in which a man may be *L A D* 46–47.
" awakened " to self-conscious activity in his astral *I H* 35.
body.

(1) By the ordinary course of evolution, which,
though slow, is sure.

(2) By the man himself, having learnt the facts of
the case, making the requisite steady and persistent
effort to clear away the mist from within and gradually
overcome the inertia to which he is accustomed. In
order to do this the man should resolve before going
to sleep to try when he leaves the body to awaken
himself and see something or do some useful work.
This, of course, is merely hastening the natural process
of evolution. It is desirable that the man should first
have developed common sense and moral qualities :
this for two reasons : first, lest he may misuse such
powers as he may acquire ; second, lest he be overwhelmed by fear in the presence of forces which he
can neither understand nor control.

(3) By some accident, or by unlawful use of magical
ceremonies, he may so rend the veil that it can never
wholly be closed again. Instances of this are to be
found in *A Bewitched Life*, by H. P. Blavatsky, and
in *Zanoni*, by Lord Lytton.

(4) A friend may act from without upon the closed *L A D* 46–47.
shell surrounding the man and gradually arouse the *I H* 35.
man to higher possibilities. This, however, would

never be done unless the friend were quite sure that the man to be awakened possessed the courage, devotion, and other qualifications necessary for useful work.

M V I 56–57.   But the need of helpers on the astral plane is so great that every aspirant may be certain that there will not be a day's delay in arousing him as soon as he is seen to be ready.

I H 67–68.   It may be added that when even a child has been awakened on the astral plane, the development of the astral body would proceed so rapidly that he would very soon be in a position upon that plane but little inferior to that of the awakened adult, and would, of course, be much in advance, so far as usefulness is concerned, of the wisest man who was as yet unawakened.

But unless the ego expressing himself through the child-body possessed the necessary qualification of a determined yet loving disposition, and had clearly manifested it in his previous lives, no occultist would take the very serious responsibility of awakening him on the astral plane. When it is possible to arouse children in this way, they often prove most efficient workers on the astral plane, and throw themselves into this work with a whole-souled devotion which is beautiful to see.

I H 35.   Also, while it is comparatively easy to waken a man on the astral plane, it is practically impossible, except by a most undesirable use of mesmeric influence, to put him to sleep again.

I L II 55 : 84–85 : 105.   Sleeping and waking life are thus seen to be in reality but one : during sleep we are aware of that fact, and have the continuous memory of both, *i.e.*, astral memory includes the physical, though, of course, the physical memory by no means always includes the memory of astral experiences.

I L I 492–493.   The phenomenon of sleep-walking (somnambulism) may apparently be produced in several distinct ways.

(1) The ego may be able to act more directly upon the physical body during the absence of the mental and

astral vehicles : in cases of this nature a man might be able, for example, to write poetry, paint pictures, etc., which would be far beyond his ordinary powers when awake.

(2) The physical body may be working automatically, and by force of habit, uncontrolled by the man himself. Instances of this occur where servants rise in the middle of the night and light a fire or attend to other household duties to which they are accustomed : or where the sleeping physical body carries out to some extent the idea dominant in the mind before falling to sleep.

(3) An outside entity, incarnate or discarnate, may seize the body of a sleeping man and use it for his own ends. This would be most likely to happen with a person who was mediumistic, *i.e.*, whose bodies are more loosely joined together than usual and therefore more readily separable.

With normal people, however, the fact that the *I L I* 487. astral body leaves the physical body during sleep does *not* open the way to obsession, because the ego always maintains a close connection with his body and he would quickly be recalled to it by any attempt that might be made upon it.

(4) A directly opposite condition may also produce a similar result. When the principles or bodies fit more tightly than usual, the man, instead of visiting a distant place in his astral body only, would take his physical body along as well, because he is not wholly dissociated from it.

(5) Somnambulism is probably also connected with the complex problem of the various layers of consciousness in man, which under normal circumstances are unable to manifest themselves.

Closely akin to sleep-life is the condition of trance, *S P* 47. which is but the sleep state, artificially or abnormally *S C* 225. induced. Mediums and sensitives readily pass out of the physical body into the astral body, usually unconsciously. The astral body can then exercise its functions, such as that of travelling to a distant place, gathering impressions there from surrounding objects and bringing them back to the physical body.   In the case of a medium the astral body can describe these impressions by means of the entranced physical body : but, as a rule, when the medium comes out of the trance, the brain does not retain the impressions thus made on it, no trace being left in the physical memory of the experiences acquired.   Occasionally, but rarely, the astral body is able to make a lasting impression on the brain, so that the medium is able to recollect the knowledge acquired during trance.

CHAPTER X

DREAMS

CONSCIOUSNESS and activity in the astral body are one thing : the memory in the brain of that astral consciousness and activity are a totally different matter. The existence or the absence of physical memory in no way affects the consciousness on the astral plane, nor the ability to function in the astral body with perfect ease and freedom. It is, in fact, not only possible, but also by no means uncommon, for a man to function freely and usefully in his astral body during the sleep of the physical body, and yet to return to the physical body without the slightest memory of the astral work upon which he has been engaged. L A D 6.
O S D 30.

M B 52.

The break in consciousness between the astral and the physical life is due either to undevelopment of the astral body, or to the want of an adequate etheric bridge between the astral and the dense physical matter of the bodies. M B 50 . 100.

This bridge consists of the closely-woven web of atomic matter, through which the vibrations have to pass, and which causes a moment of unconsciousness, like a veil, between sleeping and waking. I L II 116.

The only way in which memory of the astral life can be brought through into the physical brain is by sufficient development of the astral body and by an awakening of the etheric Chakrams, one function of which is to bring forces from the astral to the etheric. In addition, there must be active functioning of the pituitary body, which focusses the astral vibrations. I L I 456.
I L I 451.
S C 260–261.

Sometimes, on awakening, there is a feeling that something has been experienced of which no memory remains. The feeling indicates that there has been M B 50–51.
I L II 105.

astral consciousness, though the brain is insufficiently receptive to receive the record. At other times the man in his astral body may succeed in making a momentary impression on the etheric double and the dense body, resulting in a vivid memory of the astral life. This is sometimes done deliberately when something occurs which the man feels that he ought to remember on the physical plane. Such a memory usually vanishes quickly and cannot be recovered : efforts to recover the memory, by setting up strong vibrations in the physical brain, still further overpower the more delicate astral vibrations, and consequently render success even more impossible.

I L II 105.   There are some events, too, which make such a vivid impression upon the astral body that they become impressed upon the physical brain by a kind of repercussion (see page 242).

M B 51.   In other cases, a man may succeed in impressing new knowledge on the physical brain, without being able to convey also the memory of where or how that knowledge was gained. Instances of this, common to most people, occur where solutions of problems, previously insoluble, suddenly arise in the consciousness, or where light is suddenly thrown on to questions previously obscure. Such cases may be taken to indicate that progress is being made with the organisation and functioning of the astral body, although the physical body is still only partially receptive.

In cases where the physical brain does respond, there are vivid, reasonable and coherent dreams, such as occur to many people from time to time.

I L II 114–116.   Few people, when in the astral body, care whether the physical brain remembers or not, and nine out of ten much dislike returning to the body. In coming back to the physical body from the astral world there is a feeling of great constraint, as though one were being enveloped in a thick, heavy cloak. The joy of life on the astral plane is so great that physical life in comparison with it seems no life at all. Many regard the daily return to the physical body as men often do their daily journey to the office. They do not positively dislike it, but they would not do it unless they were compelled.

Eventually, in the case of highly developed and advanced persons, the etheric bridge between the astral and the physical worlds is constructed, and then there is perfect continuity of consciousness between the astral and the physical lives. For such people life ceases to be composed of days of remembrance and nights of oblivion, and becomes instead a continuous whole, year after year, of unbroken consciousness. *M B 53.*

Occasionally, a man who has normally no memory of his astral life, may unintentionally, through an accident or illness, or intentionally by certain definite practices, bridge over the gap between astral and physical consciousness, so that from that time onwards his astral consciousness will be continuous, and his memory of his sleep life will therefore be perfect. But, of course, before this could take place, he must already have developed full consciousness in the astral body. It is merely the rending of the veil between the astral and physical that is sudden, not the development of the astral body. *I L I 377– 388.*

The dream life may be considerably modified as a direct result of mental growth. Every impulse sent by the mind to the physical brain has to pass through the astral body, and, as astral matter is far more responsive to thought-vibrations than is physical matter, it follows that the effects produced on the astral body are correspondingly greater. Thus, when a man has acquired mental control, *i.e.*, has learned to dominate the brain, to concentrate, and to think as and when he likes, a corresponding change will take place in his astral life ; and, if he brings the memory of that life through into the physical brain, his dreams will become vivid, well-sustained, rational, even instructive. *M B 98–99.*

In general, the more the physical brain is trained to answer to the vibrations of the mental body, the more is the bridging of the gulf between waking and sleeping *M B 105.*

consciousness facilitated. The brain should become more and more the obedient instrument of the man, acting under impulses from his will.

I L I 491-492.

The dreaming of ordinary events does not interfere with astral work, because the dreaming takes place in the physical brain, while the real man is away attending to other matters. It does not really matter what the physical brain does, so long as it keeps itself free from undesirable thoughts

Once a dream is started, its course cannot usually be changed : but the dream-life can be controlled indirectly to a considerable extent. It is especially important that the last thought on sinking to sleep should be a noble and elevating one, as this strikes the keynote which largely determines the nature of the dreams which follow. An evil or impure thought attracts evil and impure influences and creatures, which react on the mind and astral body and tend to awaken low and earthly desires.

On the other hand, if a man falls asleep with his thoughts fixed on high and holy things, he will automatically draw round him elementals created by similar efforts of others, and consequently his dreams will be lofty and pure.

As we are dealing in this book mainly with the astral body, and phenomena closely associated with it, it is not necessary to attempt to deal exhaustively with the somewhat large subject of dream consciousness. Nevertheless, in order to show the proper setting of the part which the astral body plays in the dream life, it will be useful to give a very brief outline of the main factors operative in producing dreams. For a detailed study of the whole matter the student is referred to that excellent textbook, *Dreams*, by C. W. Leadbeater, from which the following facts are extracted.

D 49-50.

The factors concerned in the production of dreams are :—

1. The *lower physical brain*, with its infantile semiconsciousness, and its habit of expressing every stimulus in pictorial form.

2. The *etheric part of the brain*, through which sweeps a ceaseless procession of disconnected pictures.

3. The *astral body*, palpitating with the wild surgings of desire and emotion.

4. The *ego* (in the causal body) who may be in any state of consciousness, from almost complete insensibility to perfect command of his faculties.

When a man goes to sleep, his ego withdraws further *D 50.* within himself, and leaves his various bodies more free than usual to go their own way. These separate bodies : (1) are much more susceptible of impressions from without than at other times ; and (2) have a very rudimentary consciousness of their own. Consequently there is ample reason for the production of dreams, as well as for confused recollections in the physical brain of the experiences of the other bodies during sleep.

Such confused dreams may thus be due to : (1) a *D 58-59.* series of disconnected pictures and impossible transformations produced by the senseless automatic action of the lower physical brain ; (2) a stream of casual thought which has been pouring through the etheric part of the brain ; (3) the ever-restless tide of earthly desire, playing through the astral body and probably stimulated by astral influences ; (4) an imperfect attempt at dramatisation by an undeveloped ego ; (5) a mingling of several or all of these influences.

We will briefly describe the principal elements in each of these kinds of dreams.

1. *Physical Brain Dreams.*—When in sleep the ego, *D 24-25.* for the time, resigns control of the brain, the physical body still has a certain dim consciousness of its own : and in addition there is also the aggregate consciousness of the individual cells of the physical body. The grasp of the physical consciousness over the brain is far feebler than that of the ego over the brain, and consequently purely physical changes are capable of affecting the brain to a very much greater extent. Examples of such physical changes are : irregularity in the circulation of the blood, indigestion, heat and cold, etc.

D 26.
M B 30.
 The dim, physical consciousness possesses certain peculiarities : (1) it is to a great extent automatic ; (2) it seems unable to grasp an idea except in the form in which it is itself an actor : consequently all stimuli, whether from within or from without, are immediately translated into perceptual images ; (3) it is incapable of grasping abstract ideas or memories, as such, but at once transforms them into imaginary percepts : (4) every local direction of thought becomes for it an actual spatial transportation, *i.e.*, a passing thought of China would transport the consciousness instantly in imagination to China ; (5) it has no power of judging the sequence, value or objective truth of the pictures that appear before it ; it takes them all just as it sees them, and never feels surprised at anything which may happen, however incongruous or absurd ; (6) it is subject to the principle of association of ideas, and consequently images, unconnected except by the fact that they represent events which happened near to one another in time, are apt to be thrown together in inextricable confusion ; (7) it is singularly sensitive to the slightest external influences, such as sounds or touches, and (8) it magnifies and distorts them to an almost incredible degree.

D 29.
 The physical brain thus is capable of creating sufficient confusion and exaggeration to account for many, but by no means all, dream phenomena.

D 29–30.
 2. *Etheric Brain Dreams.*—The etheric brain is even more sensitive during the sleep of the body than it is during ordinary waking consciousness to influences from outside. Whilst the mind is actively engaged, the brain thereby being fully employed, it is practically impervious to the continual impingement of thought from without. But the moment the brain is left

D 30–31.
 idle, the stream of inconsequent chaos begins to pour through it. In the vast majority of people, the thoughts which flow through their brains are in reality not their own thoughts at all, but fragments cast off by other people. Consequently, in sleep life especially, any passing thought which finds something

congruous to itself in the brain of a sleeper, is seized upon by that brain and appropriated, thus starting a whole train of ideas : eventually these fade away and the disconnected, purposeless stream begins flowing through the brain again.

A point to notice is that, since in the present state *D* 31-32. of the world's evolution there are likely to be more evil thoughts than good ones floating around, a man with an uncontrolled brain is open to all sorts of temptation which mind and brain control might have spared him.

Even when these thought-currents are shut out, by *D* 32 : 62. the deliberate effort of another person, from the etheric brain of a sleeper, that brain does not remain completely passive, but begins slowly and dreamily to evolve pictures for itself from its store of past memories.

3. *Astral Dreams.*—These are simply recollection in the physical brain of the life and activities of the astral body during the sleep of the physical body, to which reference has already been made in the preceding pages. In the case of a fairly well-developed person, *D* 33. the astral body can travel without discomfort to considerable distances from its physical body : can bring back more or less definite impressions of places which it may have visited, or of people whom it may have met. In every case the astral body, as already said, is ever intensely impressionable by any thought or suggestion involving desire or emotion, though the nature of the desires which most readily awaken a response in it will, of course, depend on the development of the person and the purity or otherwise of his astral body.

The astral body is at all times susceptible to the *D* 16-17. influences of passing thought-currents, and, when the mind is not actively controlling it, it is perpetually receiving these stimuli from without, and eagerly responding to them. During sleep it is even more readily influenced. Consequently, a man who has, for example, entirely destroyed a physical desire, which he may previously have possessed for lacohol, so that in waking life he may feel even a definite repulsion for it, may yet frequently dream that he is drinking, and in that dream experience the pleasure of its influence. During the day, the desire of the astral body would be under the control of the will, but when the astral body was liberated in sleep, it escaped to some extent from the domination of the ego, and, responding probably to outside astral influence, its old habit reasserted itself. This class of dream is probably common to many who are making definite attempts to bring their desire-nature under the control of the will.

S C 332–333.   It may also happen that a man may have been a drunkard in a past life and still possesses in his astral body some matter drawn thereinto by the vibrations caused in the permanent atom by the drunkenness. Although this matter is not vivified in this life, yet in dreams, the control of the ego being weak, the matter may respond to drink-vibrations from without and the man dreams that he drinks. Such dreams, once understood, need not cause distress: nevertheless they should be regarded as a warning that there is still present the possibility of the drink-craving being re-awakened.

D 33.   *Ego Dreams.*—Much as the nature of the astral body changes as it develops, still greater is the change of the ego, or real man, that inhabits it. Where the astral body is nothing but a floating wreath of mist, the ego *D*. 34.   is also almost as much asleep as his physical body, being blind to the influences of his own higher plane : and even if some idea belonging to it should manage to reach him, since he has little or no control over his lower bodies, he will be unable to impress the experience on the physical brain.

Sleepers may be at any stage from that of complete oblivion up to that of full astral consciousness. And it must be recollected, as already said, that even though there may be many important experiences on the higher planes, the ego may nevertheless be unable to impress them upon the brain, so that there is either no physical memory at all, or only a most confused memory.

The principal characteristics of the consciousness D 35-40. and experiences of the ego, whether or not they be remembered in the brain, are as follows :—

(1) The ego's measure of time and space are so entirely different from that which he uses in waking life that it is almost as though neither time nor space existed for him. Many instances are known where in a few moments of time, as we measure it, the ego may have experiences which appear to last for many years, event after event happening in full and circumstantial detail.

(2) The ego possesses the faculty, or the habit, of D 40-42. instantaneous dramatisation. Thus a physical sound I L II 107. or a touch may reach the ego, not through the usual nerve mechanism, but directly, a fraction of a second before even it reaches the physical brain. That fraction of a second is sufficient for the ego to construct a kind of drama or series of scenes leading up to and culminating in the event which awakens the physical body. The brain confuses the subjective dream and the objective event, and therefore imagines itself to have actually lived through the events of the dream.

This habit, however, seems to be peculiar to the ego which, so far as spirituality is concerned, is still comparatively undeveloped. As the ego develops spiritually, he rises beyond these graceful sports of his childhood. The man who has attained continuous consciousness is so fully occupied with higher plane work that he devotes no energy to this dramatisation, and consequently this class of dream ceases for him.

(3) The ego possesses also to some extent the faculty D 42-48. of prevision, being sometimes able to see in advance events which are going to happen, or rather which may happen unless steps are taken to prevent them, and to impress the same on the physical brain. Many instances are recorded of such prophetic or warning dreams. In some cases the warning may be heeded, the necessary steps taken, and the foreseen result either modified or entirely avoided.

D 48-49.

(4) The ego, when out of the body during sleep, appears to think in symbols : an idea, which down here would require many words to be expressed, is perfectly conveyed to him by a single symbolical image. If such a symbolic thought is impressed upon the brain, and remembered in waking consciousness, the mind may itself translate it into words : on the other hand it may come through merely as a symbol, untranslated, and so may cause confusion. In dreams of this nature, it seems that each person usually has a system of symbology of his own : thus water may signify approaching trouble : pearls may be a sign of tears : and so forth.

D 66-67.

If a man wishes to have useful dreams, *i.e.*, to be able to reap in his waking consciousness the benefit of what his ego may learn during sleep, there are certain steps he should take to bring about this result.

First, it is essential that he should form the habit of sustained and concentrated thought during ordinary waking life. A man who has absolute control of his thoughts will always know exactly what he is thinking about, and why ; he will also find that the brain, thus trained to listen to the promptings of the ego, will remain quiescent when not in use, and will decline to receive or respond to casual currents from the surrounding ocean of thought. The man will thus be more likely to receive influences from the higher planes, where insight is keener and judgment truer than they can ever be on the physical plane.

It should scarcely be necessary to add that the man should also be complete master of at least his lower passions.

By a very elementary act of magic, a man may shut out from his etheric brain the rush of thoughts which impinge upon it from without. To this end, he should, when lying down to sleep, picture his aura, and will strongly that its outer surface shall become a shell to protect him from outside influences. The auric matter will obey his thought, and form the shell. This step is of appreciable value towards the desired end.

The great importance of fixing the last thought, *D* 68. before falling to sleep, on high and noble things, has already been mentioned; it should be practised regularly by those who wish to bring their dreams under control.

It may be useful here to add the Hindu terms for *I Y* 16. the four states of consciousness:

Jâgrat is the ordinary waking consciousness.

Svapna is the dream consciousness, working in the astral body, and able to impress its experiences upon the brain.

Sushupti is the consciousness working in the mental body, and not able to impress its experiences on the brain.

Turiya is a state of trance, the consciousness working in the buddhic vehicle, being so far separated from the brain that it cannot readily be recalled by outer means.

These terms, however, are used relatively, and vary according to the context. Thus, in one interpretation of *jâgrat*, the physical and astral planes are combined, *A P* 110. the seven sub-divisions corresponding to the four conditions of physical matter, and the three broad divisions of astral matter mentioned on page 148.

For further elucidation the student is referred to *An Introduction to Yoga*, by A. Besant, page 16, *et seq.*, and also to *A Study in Consciousness*, where waking *S C* 219. consciousness is defined as that part of the total consciousness which is working through the outermost vehicle.

CHAPTER XI

CONTINUITY OF CONSCIOUSNESS

M B 103–104. As we have seen, for a man to pass in unbroken consciousness from one vehicle to another, *e.g.*, from the physical to the astral, or *vice versâ*, it is requisite that the links between the bodies should be developed. Most men are not conscious of these links, and the links are not actively vivified, being in a condition similar to that of rudimentary organs in the physical body. They have to be developed by use, and are made to function by the man fixing his attention upon them and using his will. The will sets free and guides kundalini, but unless the preliminary purification of the vehicles is first thoroughly accomplished, kundalini is a destructive instead of a vivifying energy. Hence the insistence, by all occult teachers, on the necessity of purification before true yoga is practised.

M B 105. When a man has rendered himself fit to be helped in vivifying the links, such assistance will inevitably come to him as a matter of course, from those who are ever seeking opportunities to aid the earnest and unselfish aspirant. Then, one day, the man will find himself slipping out of the physical body while he is wide awake, and without any break in consciousness he discovers himself to be free. With practice the passage from vehicle to vehicle becomes familiar and easy. The development of the links bridges the gulf between physical and astral consciousness, so that there is perfect continuity of consciousness.

A P 13. The student thus has not only to learn to see correctly on the astral plane, but also to translate accurately the memory of what he has seen from the astral to the physical brain : and to assist him in this he is trained to carry his consciousness without break from the physical plane to the astral and mental and back again, for until that can be done there is always a possibility that his recollections may be partially lost or distorted during the blank intervals which separate his periods of consciousness on the various planes. When the power of bringing over the consciousness is perfectly acquired, the pupil will have the advantage of the use of all the astral faculties, not only while out of the body during sleep or trance, but also while fully awake in ordinary physical life.

In order that the physical waking consciousness *S C* 218. should include astral consciousness it is necessary that the pituitary body should be further evolved, and that the fourth spirillae in the atoms should be perfected.

In addition to the method of moving the conscious- *I L I* 147– ness from one sub-plane to another, *of the same plane,* 148. from, *e.g.*, the *astral* atomic to the lowest sub-plane of the *mental*, there is also another line of connection which may be called the atomic short-cut.

If we picture the atomic sub-planes of astral, mental, etc., as lying side by side along a rod, the other sub-planes may be pictured as hanging from the rod in loops, as though a piece of string were wound loosely round the rod. Obviously, then, to pass from one atomic sub-plane to another one could move by a short cut along the rod, or down and up again through the hanging loops which symbolise the lower sub-planes.

The normal processes of our thinking come steadily *S C* 261–262. down through the sub-planes : but flashes of genius, illuminative ideas, come through the atomic sub-planes only.

There is also a third possibility connected with the relation of our planes with the cosmic planes, but this is too abstruse to be dealt with in a work which purports to deal only with the astral plane and its phenomena.

Merely to obtain continuity of consciousness between *M B* 106. the physical and the astral planes is, of course, quite insufficient in itself to restore memory of past lives. For this a much higher development is required, into the nature of which it is not necessary to enter here.

M B 54-55.   A man who has thus acquired complete mastery over the astral body may, of course, leave the physical body, not only during sleep, but at any time he chooses, and go to a distant place, etc.

S P 47.   Mediums and sensitives project their astral bodies unconsciously, when they go into trance : but usually on coming out of trance there is no brain-memory of the experiences acquired. Trained students are able to project the astral body consciously and to travel to great distances from the physical body, bringing back with them full and detailed memory of all the impressions they have gained.

S P 48.   An astral body thus projected may be seen by persons who are sensitive or who may chance to be temporarily in an abnormal nervous condition. There *C 74.* are on record many cases of such astral visitations by a *O S D 155.* dying person near the time of death, the approach of dissolution having loosened the principles so as to make the phenomenon possible for people who were unable at any other time to perform the feat. (See also page 50 for a similar phenomenon produced by a *thought-form.*) The astral body is also set free in many cases of disease. Inactivity of the physical body is a condition of such astral journeys.

A man may, if he knows how to set about it, slightly densify his astral body by drawing into it, from the surrounding atmosphere, particles of physical matter, and thus " materialise " sufficiently to become physically visible. This is the explanation of many cases of " apparitions," where a person, physically absent, has been seen by friends with their ordinary physical sight.

CHAPTER XII

DEATH AND THE DESIRE-ELEMENTAL

AT death, the consciousness withdraws from the dense *D A* 17. physical body into the etheric double for a short time, usually a few hours, and then passes into the astral body.

Death thus consists of a process of unrobing or unsheathing. The ego, the immortal part of man, shakes off from itself, one after the other, its outer casings . first the dense physical : then the etheric double : then even the astral body, as we shall see later.

In almost every case the actual passing-away appears *O S D* 45. to be perfectly painless, even after a long illness involving terrible suffering. The peaceful look on the face of the dead is strong evidence in favour of this statement, and it is also borne out by the direct testimony of most of those who have been questioned on the point immediately after death.

At the actual moment of death, even when death is *K T* 100. sudden, a man sees the whole of his past life mar- *A W* 110- shalled before him, in its minutest detail. In a moment 111. he sees the whole chain of causes which have been at work during his life ; he sees and now understands himself as he really is, unadorned by flattery or self-deception. He reads his life, remaining as a spectator, looking down upon the arena he is quitting.

The condition of consciousness *immediately* after the *D A* 29. moment of death is usually a dreamy and peaceful one. *I L II* 91. There will also be a certain period of unconsciousness, *O S D* 37 : which may last only for a moment, though often it is a 212. few minutes, or several hours, and sometimes even days or weeks.

The natural attraction between the astral counter- *I L I* 393- part and the physical body is such that, after death, 394. *O S D* 87.

the astral counterpart, from force of habit, retains its accustomed form : consequently a man's physical appearance will still be preserved after death almost unchanged. Almost—because in view of the fact that astral matter is very readily moulded by thought, a man who habitually thinks of himself after death as younger than he actually was at the time of death will probably assume a somewhat younger appearance.

I L I 402.
I L II 102–103.
O S D 95–99.
T B 66.

Very soon after death, in most cases, an important change takes place in the structure of the astral body, owing to the action of the desire elemental.

Much of the matter of the astral body is composed of elemental essence (see page 6) : this essence is living, though not intelligent : and for the time it is cut off from the general mass of astral essence. Blindly, instinctively, and without reason it seeks its own ends and shows great ingenuity in obtaining its desires and in furthering its evolution.

Evolution for it is a descent into matter, its aim being to become a mineral monad. Its object in life, therefore, is to get as near to the physical plane as it can, and to experience as many of the coarser vibrations as possible. It neither does nor could know anything of the man in whose astral body it is for the time living.

I L I 403.

It desires to preserve its separate life, and feels that it can do so only by means of its connection with the man : it is conscious of the man's lower mind, and realises that the more mental matter it can entangle with itself the longer will be its astral life.

On the death of the physical body, knowing that the term of its separated life is limited, and that the man's astral death will more or less quickly follow, in order to make the man's astral body last as long as possible, it rearranges its matter in concentric rings or shells, the coarsest outside. From the point of view of the desire elemental this is good policy, because the coarsest matter can hold together longest and best stand friction.

I L I 406.
I L II 50–51.
O S D 102.
A W 113.
T B 68.

A W 113.

The re-arranged astral body is called the *Yâtanâ*, or suffering body : in the case of a very evil man in whose astral body there is a preponderance of the coarsest matter, it is called the *Dhruvam* or strong body.

The re-arrangement of the astral body takes place over the surface of the counterpart of the physical body, not over the surface of the ovoid which surrounds it. *I L II* 103.

The effect is to prevent the free and full circulation of astral matter which usually takes place in the astral body. In addition, the man is able to respond only to those vibrations which are received by the outermost layer of his astral body. The man is thus shut up, as it were, in a box of astral matter, being able to see and hear things of the lowest and coarsest plane only. *I L I* 406. *I L. II* 50-51. *O S D* 103.

Although living in the midst of high influences and beautiful thought-forms, he would be almost entirely unconscious of their existence, because the particles of his astral body which could respond to those vibrations are shut in where they cannot be reached. *I L II* 47.

Consequently, also, being able to sense only the coarsest matter in the astral bodies of other people, and being entirely unconscious of his limitations, he would assume that the person he was looking at possessed only the unsatisfactory characteristics which he would be able to perceive.

Since he can see and feel only what is lowest and coarsest, the men around him appear to be monsters of vice. Under these circumstances it is little wonder that he considers the astral world a hell. *T B* 70.

The re-arrangement of the astral body by the desire-elemental does not in any way affect the recognisability of the form within the ovoid, though the natural changes which take place tend on the whole to make the form grow somewhat fainter and more spiritual in appearance as time passes on—for reasons which will presently be made clear. *I L I* 399-400.

In course of time, the outermost shell or ring disintegrates: the man then becomes able to respond to the vibrations of the next higher level of the astral plane, and thus "rises to the next sub-plane": and so *M B* 57. *I L II* 48-50.

on from one sub-plane to another. His stay on each sub-plane will, of course, correspond to the amount and activity of the matter in his astral body belonging to that sub-plane.

A P 17–18 :   When we speak of a man "rising" from one sub-
42.   plane to another, he need not necessarily move in space at all : he rather transfers his consciousness from one level to another. In the case of a man with a rearranged astral body, the focus of his consciousness shifts from the outer shell to the one next within it. The man thus gradually becomes unresponsive to the vibrations of one order of matter and answers instead to those of a higher order. Thus one world with its scenery and its inhabitants would seem to fade slowly away from his view, while another world would dawn upon him.

I L II 48–49.   As the shell usually disintegrates gradually, the man
O S D 60–61:   thus finds the counterparts of physical objects growing
103.   dimmer and dimmer, while thought-forms become more and more vivid to him. If during this process he meets another man at intervals, he will imagine that that man's character is steadily improving, merely because he is himself becoming able to appreciate the higher vibrations of that character. The re-arrangement of the astral body, in fact, constantly interferes with a man's true and full vision of his friends at all stages of their astral life.

I L I 407.   This process of re-arrangement of the astral body,
I L II 51:   which takes place with most people, can be prevented
102.   by the man setting his will to oppose it : in fact, anyone
O S D 105–   who understands the conditions of the astral plane
106.   should altogether decline to permit the re-arrangement of the astral body by the desire-elemental. The particles of the astral body will then be kept intermingled, as in life, and in consequence, instead of being confined to one astral sub-plane at a time, the man will be free of all the sub-planes, according to the constitution of his astral body.

I L II 103.   The elemental, being afraid in its curious semi-
O S D 106.   conscious way, will endeavour to transfer its fear to the

man who is jolting him out of the re-arrangement, in order to deter him from doing so.   Hence one reason why it is so useful to have knowledge of these matters before death.

If the re-arrangement, or shelling, has already occurred, it is still possible for the condition to be broken up by someone who wishes to help the man, and for the man to be thus set free to work on the whole astral plane, instead of being confined to one level.

I L I 365-366.
I L II 51.
O S D 105.

CHAPTER XIII

AFTER-DEATH LIFE : PRINCIPLES

L A D 5.
H S II 279-
280.
C 45.
O S D 33 :
52.

IT cannot be too strongly insisted that it is not found that any sudden change takes place in man at death : on the contrary, he remains after death exactly what he was before, except that he no longer has a physical body. He has the same intellect, the same disposition, the same virtues and vices ; the loss of the physical body no more makes him a different man than would the removal of an overcoat. Moreover, the conditions in which he finds himself are those which his own thoughts and desires have already created for him. There is no reward or punishment from outside, but only the actual result of what he has himself done, and said, and thought, while living in the physical world.

A P 9.
O S D 12-13.

As we proceed with our description of the astral life after death, it will be recognised that the true facts correspond with considerable accuracy with the Catholic conception of purgatory, and the Hades or underworld of the Greeks.

A P 45.

The poetic idea of death as a universal leveller is a mere absurdity born of ignorance, for, as a matter of fact, in the vast majority of cases, the loss of the physical body makes no difference whatever in the character or intellect of the person, and there are therefore as many different varieties of intelligence among the so-called dead as among the living.

This is the first and the most prominent fact to appreciate : that after death there is no strange new life, but a continuation, under certain changed conditions, of the present physical plane life.

I L II 26-28.

So much is this the case that when a man first arrives on the astral plane after physical death he by no means always knows that he is dead : and even when he does realise what has happened to him he does not always at first understand how the astral world differs from the physical.

In some cases people consider the very fact that they are still conscious an absolute proof that they have not died : and this in spite of the much-vaunted belief in the immortality of the soul. *A P 45. I H 84.*

If a man has never heard of astral plane life before, he is likely to be more or less disturbed by the totally unexpected conditions in which he finds himself. Finally, he accepts these conditions, which he does not understand, thinking them necessary and inevitable. *I L I 405. I H 75. L A D 7-9.*

Looking out upon the new worlds, at the first glance he would probably see very little difference, and he would suppose himself to be looking upon the same world as before. As we have seen, each degree of astral matter is attracted by the corresponding degree of physical matter. If, therefore, we imagined the physical world to be struck out of existence, without any other change being made, we should still have a perfect replica of it in astral matter. Consequently a man on the astral plane would still see the walls, furniture, people, etc., to which he was accustomed, outlined as clearly as ever by the densest type of astral matter. If, however, he examined such objects closely he would perceive that all the particles were visibly in rapid motion, instead of only invisibly as on the physical plane. But, as few men observe closely, a man who dies often does not know at first that any change has come over him. Thus many, especially in Western countries, find it difficult to believe that they are dead, simply because they still see, hear, feel and think. Realisation of what has happened will probably dawn gradually, as the man discovers that though he can see his friends he cannot always communicate with them. Sometimes he speaks to them, and they do not seem to hear : he tries to touch them, and finds that he can make no impression upon them. Even then, for some time he may persuade himself that he is dreaming, for at other times, when his friends are *M B 38-39. L A D 7-9. T B 73.*

asleep, they are perfectly conscious of him and talk with him as of old.

By degrees the man begins to realise the differences between his present life and that which he lived in the physical world. For example, he soon finds that for him all pain and fatigue have passed away. He also finds that in the astral world desires and thoughts express themselves in visible forms, though these are composed mostly of the finer matter of the plane. As his life proceeds, these become more and more prominent.

L A D 10.

Moreover, though a man on the astral plane cannot usually see the physical bodies of his friends, yet he can and does see their astral bodies, and consequently knows their feelings and emotions. He will not necessarily be able to follow in detail the events of their physical life : but he would at once be aware of such feelings as love or hate, jealousy or envy, as these would be expressed through the astral bodies of his friends.

L A D 43.
I L II 88 : 6.

Thus, although the living often suppose themselves to have " lost " the dead, the dead are never for a moment under the impression that they have lost the living.

T B 73.

A man, in fact, living in his astral body after death is more readily and deeply influenced by the feelings of his friends in the physical world than when he was on earth, because he has no physical body to deaden his perceptions.

I L II 88.

A man on the astral plane does not usually see the whole astral counterpart of an object, but the portion of it which belongs to the particular sub-plane upon which he is at the time.

I L II 10-11.

Moreover, a man by no means always recognises with any certainty the astral counterpart of a physical body even when he sees it. He usually requires considerable experience before he can clearly identify objects, and any attempt that he makes to deal with them is liable to be vague and uncertain. Examples of this are often seen in haunted houses, where stone-throwing, or vague, clumsy movements of physical matter take place.

Frequently, not realising that he is free from the *I L II* 26-27. necessity to work for a living, to eat, sleep, etc., a man after death may continue to prepare and consume meals, created entirely by his imagination, or even to build for himself a house in which to live. A case is recorded of a man who built for himself a house, stone by stone, each stone being separately created by his own thought. He might, of course, with the same amount of effort have created the whole house at once. He was eventually led to see, that as the stones had no weight, the conditions were different from those obtaining in physical life, and so he was induced to investigate further.

Similarly, a man new to the conditions of astral life *I L II* 196. may continue to enter and depart from a room by a door or window, not realising that he can pass through the wall just as easily. For the same reason he may walk upon the earth when he might just as well float through the air.

A man who has already during earth life acquainted *I L II* 3-4. himself, by reading or otherwise, with the general conditions of astral life, naturally finds himself after death on ground more or less familiar, and consequently he should not be at a loss to know what to do with himself.

Even an intelligent appreciation of occult teaching *O S D* 42. on this subject, as experience has shown, is of enormous advantage to a man after death, while it is a considerable advantage for a man merely to have heard of the conditions of astral life, even though he may have regarded such teachings as one of many hypotheses, and may not have followed them up further. In *I L II* 3-4. the case of others, not so fortunately situated as to their knowledge of the astral world, their best plan is to take stock of their position, endeavour to see the nature of the life before them, and how they can make the best use of it. In addition, they would do well to consult some experienced friend.

D A 24-25:
27 : 30.
A W 74:
107-108.

The conditions of life referred to above constitute Kâmaloka, literally the place or world of Kâma or desire : the Limbus of scholastic theology. In general terms Kâmaloka is a region peopled by intelligent and semi-intelligent entities. It is crowded with many types and forms of living things, as diverse from each other as a blade of grass is different from a tiger, a tiger is different from a man, there being of course, many other entities living there besides deceased human beings (see Chapters XIX-XXI). It interpenetrates the physical world, and is interpenetrated by it, but, as the states of matter in the two worlds differ, they co-exist without the entities of either world being conscious of those of the other. Only under abnormal circumstances can consciousness of each other's presence arise among the inhabitants of the two worlds.

Kâmaloka is thus not divided off as a distinct locality, but is separated off from the rest of the astral plane by the conditions of consciousness of the entities who belong to it, these entities being human beings, who have shaken off the dense and etheric bodies, but who have not yet disentangled themselves from Kâma, *i.e.*, the passional and emotional nature. This state is also called Pretaloka, a preta being a human being who has lost his physical body, but is still encumbered with the vesture of his animal nature.

The Kâmalokic condition is found on each subdivision of the astral plane.

L A D 49.
A P 46.
I H 75-76.
O S D 83.

Many who die are at first in a condition of considerable uneasiness, and others of positive terror. When they encounter the thought-forms which they and their kind have for centuries been making—thoughts of a personal devil, an angry and cruel deity, and eternal punishment—they are often reduced to a pitiable state of fear, and may spend long periods of acute mental suffering before they can free themselves from the fatal influence of such foolish and utterly false conceptions.

I H 76-77.
O S D 14-16.

It ought, however, in fairness to be mentioned that

it is only among what are called Protestant communities that this terrible evil assumes its most aggravated form. The great Roman Catholic Church, with its doctrine of purgatory, approaches much more nearly to a true conception of the astral plane, and its devout members, at any rate, realise that the state in which they find themselves shortly after death is merely a temporary one, and that it is their business to endeavour to raise themselves out of it as soon as may be by intense spiritual aspiration, while they accept any suffering which may come to them as necessary for the wearing away of the imperfections in their character, before they can pass to higher and brighter spheres.

Thus we see that although men should have been taught by their religion what to expect, and how to live on the astral plane, in most cases this has not been done. Consequently a good deal of explanation is needed regarding the new world in which they find themselves. But, after death, exactly as before it, there are few who attain to an intelligent appreciation of the fact of evolution and who, by understanding something of their position, know how to make the best of it. To-day, large numbers of people, both "living" and "dead," are engaged in looking after and helping those who have died in ignorance of the real nature of the after-death life (*vide* Chapter XXVIII on *Invisible Helpers*). Unfortunately, however, on the astral plane, as on the physical, the ignorant are rarely ready to profit by the advice or example of the wise.

To a man who has, before he dies physically, already *I L II* 28. acquainted himself with the real conditions of life on *T B* 76. the astral plane, one of the most pleasant characteristics of that life is its restfulness and complete freedom from those imperious necessities, such as eating and drinking, which burden physical life. On the astral plane a man is really free, free to do whatever he likes, and to spend his time as he chooses.

As already indicated, a man who has died physically, *L A D* 10. is steadily withdrawing into himself. The whole cycle of life and death may be likened to an ellipse, of which only the lowest portion passes into the physical world. During the first portion of the cycle, the ego is putting himself forth into matter : the central point of the curve should be a middle point in physical life, when the force of the ego has expended its outward rush and turns to begin the long process of withdrawal.

O S D 89. Thus each physical incarnation may be regarded as a putting of the ego, whose habitat is the higher part of the mental plane, outwards into the lower planes. The ego puts the soul out, as though it were an investment, and expects his investment to draw back added experience, which will have developed new qualities within him.

L A D 11. The portion of the life after death spent on the astral plane is therefore definitely in the period of withdrawal back towards the ego. During the latter part of the physical life the man's thoughts and interests should be less and less directed towards merely physical matters : similarly, during the astral life, he should pay less and less attention to the lower astral matter, out of which counterparts of physical objects are composed, and occupy himself with the higher matter, out of which desire- and thought-forms are made. It is not so much that he has changed his location in space (though this is partially true, see Chapter XIV), as that he has moved the centre of his interest. Hence the counterpart of the physical world which he has left gradually fades from his view, and his life becomes more and more a life in the world of thought. His desires and emotions still persist, and consequently, owing to the readiness with which astral matter obeys his desires and thoughts, the forms surrounding him will be very largely the expression of his own feelings, the nature of which mainly determines whether his life is one of happiness or of discomfort.

S P 41. Although we are not in this book dealing with that portion of the life after death which is spent in the "heaven-world," *i.e.*, on the mental plane, nevertheless, in order to understand fully what is happening to the

astral body on the astral plane, it is desirable to bear
in mind that the astral life is largely an intermediate
stage in the whole cycle of life and death, a preparation
for the life on the mental plane.

As we have seen, soon after physical death, the
astral body is set free : expressed from the point of
view of consciousness, Kâma-Manas is set free. From
this, that portion of lower-manas, which is not inextricably entangled with Kâma, gradually frees itself,
taking with it such of its experiences as are fit for
assimilation by the higher mental body.

Meanwhile, that portion of the lower manas which _S P_ 42.
still remains entangled with Kâma, gives to the astral
body a somewhat confused consciousness, a broken
memory of the events of the life just closed. If the
emotions and passions were strong, and the mental
element weak, then the astral body will be strongly
energised, and will persist for a considerable time on
the astral plane. It will also show a considerable
amount of consciousness, due to the mental matter
entangled with it. If, on the other hand, the earth
life just closed was charactarised by mentality and
purity rather than by passion, the astral body will be
poorly energised, will be but a pale simulacrum of the
man, and will disintegrate and perish comparatively
rapidly.

CHAPTER XIV

THE AFTER-DEATH LIFE: PARTICULARS

I L II 14-15. IN considering the conditions of a man's astral life, there are two prominent factors to be taken into account: (1) The length of *time* which he spends on any particular sub-plane: (2) The amount of his *consciousness* upon it.

The length of *time* depends upon the amount of matter belonging to that sub-plane which he has built into his astral body during physical life. He will necessarily remain upon that sub-plane until the matter corresponding to it has dropped out of his astral body.

I L II 18-19.
I H 78.
During physical life, as we have already seen, the quality of the astral body which he builds for himself is directly determined by his passions, desires and emotions, and indirectly by his thoughts, as well as by his physical habits—food, drink, cleanliness, continence, etc. A coarse and gross astral body, resulting from a coarse and gross life, will cause the man to be responsive only to lower astral vibrations, so that after death he will find himself bound to the astral plane during the long and slow process of the disintegration of the astral body.

On the other hand, a refined astral body, created by a pure and refined life, will make the man unresponsive to the low and coarse vibrations of the astral world, and responsive only to its higher influences: consequently he will experience much less trouble in his post-mortem life, and his evolution will proceed rapidly and easily.

I L II 14-15.
The amount of *consciousness* depends upon the degree to which he has vivified and used the matter of the particular sub-plane in his physical life.

If during earth-life the animal nature was indulged *S P* 20–21. and allowed to run riot, if the intellectual and spiritual *I H* 78. parts were neglected or stifled, then the astral or desire body will persist for a long time after physical death.

If, on the other hand, desire has been conquered and bridled during earth life, if it has been purified and trained into subservience to the higher nature, then there will be little to energise the astral body, and it will quickly disintegrate and dissolve away.

The average man, however, has by no means freed *A P* 39. himself from all lower desires before death, and consequently it takes a long period of more or less fully conscious life on the various sub-planes of the astral plane to allow the forces which he has generated to work themselves out, and thus release the higher ego.

The general principle is that when the astral body *A P* 41. has exhausted its attractions to one level, the greater part of its grosser particles fall away, and it finds itself in affinity with a somewhat higher state of existence. Its specific gravity, as it were, is constantly decreasing, and so it steadily rises from the dense to the lighter strata, pausing only when it is exactly balanced for a time.

To be upon any given sub-plane in the astral world *I L II* 211– is to have developed sensitiveness of those particles in 212. the astral body which belong to that sub-plane. To have perfect vision on the astral plane means to have developed sensitiveness in all particles of the astral body, so that all the sub-planes are simultaneously visible.

A man who has led a good and pure life, whose *A P* 38. strongest feelings and aspirations have been unselfish and spiritual, will have no attraction to the astral plane, and will, if entirely left alone, find little to keep him upon it, or to awaken him into activity even during the comparatively short period of his stay. His earthly passions having been subdued during *A P* 39. physical life, and the force of his will having been directed into higher channels, there is but little energy of lower desire to be worked out on the astral plane. Consequently his stay there will be very short, and most probably he will have little more than a dreamy half-consciousness, until he sinks into the sleep during which his higher principles finally free themselves from the astral body, and enter upon the blissful life of the heaven-world.

D A 30.   Expressed more technically, during physical life Manas has purified Kâma with which it was interwoven, so that after death all that is left of Kâma is a mere residuum, easily shaken off by the withdrawing ego.   Such a man therefore would have little consciousness on the astral plane.

I L II 14–15.
A P 44–45.
A W 113–
118.

It is quite possible that a man might, as a result of his previous incarnations, possess a good deal of coarse astral matter in his astral body.   Even if he has been so brought up, and has so conducted his life, that he has not vivified that coarse matter, and although much of it may have dropped out and been replaced by finer materials, yet there may be quite a good deal left. Consequently the man would have to remain on a low level of the astral plane for some time, until in fact the coarse matter had all dropped out.   But, as the coarse matter would not be vivified, he would have little consciousness and would practically sleep through the period of his sojourn there.

M B 58.
A P 41–42.

There is a point known as the critical point between every pair of sub-states of matter : ice may be raised to a point at which the least increment of heat will change it into liquid : water may be raised to a point at which the least increment of heat will change it into vapour.   And so each sub-state of astral matter may be carried to a point of fineness at which any additional refinement would transform it into the next higher sub-state.   If a man has done this for every sub-state of matter in his astral body, so that it is purified to the last possible degree of delicacy, then the first touch of disintegrating force shatters its cohesion and resolves it into its original condition, leaving him free at once to pass on to the next sub-plane. His passage through the astral plane will thus be of inconceivable rapidity, and he will flash through the plane practically instantaneously to the higher state of the heaven-world.

Every person after death has to pass through all the *A P* 39. sub-planes of the astral plane, on his way to the heaven-world. But whether or not he is conscious on any or all of them, and to what extent, will depend upon the factors enumerated.

For these reasons, it is clear that the amount of *A P* 38. consciousness a man may possess on the astral plane, and the time he may spend there in his passage to the heaven-world, may vary within very wide limits. There are some who pass only a few hours or days on the astral plane : others remain there for many years, or even centuries.

For an ordinary person 20 or 30 years on the astral *H S I* 442 plane after death is a fair average. An exceptional 434. case is that of Queen Elizabeth, who had so intense a love of her country that she has only quite recently passed into the heaven-world, having spent the time since her death in endeavouring, until recently almost without success, to impress upon her successors her ideas of what ought to be done for England.

Another notable example was that of Queen Victoria, *O S D* 72. who passed very rapidly through the astral plane and into the heaven-world, her swift passage being undoubtedly due to the millions of loving and grateful thought-forms which were sent to her, as well as to her inherent goodness.

The general question of the interval between earth-lives is complicated. It is possible here to touch briefly only on the astral portion of those intervals. For further details the student is referred to *The Inner Life*, Vol. II., pages 458-474.

Three principal factors have to be taken into *I L II* 461. account :—

(1) The class of ego.
(2) The mode of individualisation.
(3) The length and nature of the last **earth-life**.

I L II 471-472. Generally speaking, a man who dies young will have a shorter interval than one who dies in old age, but is likely to have a proportionately longer astral life, because most of the strong emotions which work themselves out in astral life are generated in the earlier part of the physical life.

H S I 444. It must be recollected that in the astral world our ordinary methods of time-measurement scarcely apply : even in physical life anxiety or pain will stretch a few hours almost indefinitely, and on the astral plane this characteristic is exaggerated a hundred-fold.

T B 75. A man on the astral plane can measure time only by his sensations. From a distortion of this fact has come the false idea of eternal damnation.

I L II 18-19.
I H 78. We have thus seen that both (1) the time spent, and (2) the amount of consciousness experienced, on each level of the astral plane depend very largely upon the kind of life the man has led in the physical world. Another factor of great importance is the man's attitude of mind after physical death.

I L II 24. The astral life may be directed by the will, just as the physical life may be. A man with little will-power or initiative is, in the astral as in the physical world, very much the creature of the surroundings which he has made for himself. A determined man, on the other hand, can always make the best of his conditions and live his own life in spite of them.

A man, therefore, does not rid himself of evil tendencies in the astral world, unless he definitely works to that end. Unless he makes definite efforts, he will necessarily suffer from his inability to satisfy such cravings as can be gratified only by means of a physical body. In process of time the desires will wear themselves out and die down simply because of the impossibility of their fulfilment.

I L II. 25. The process, however, may be greatly expedited as soon as the man realises the necessity of ridding himself of the evil desires which detain him, and makes the requisite effort. A man who is ignorant of the true state of affairs usually broods over his desires, thus lengthening their life, and clings desperately to the gross particles of astral matter as long as he can, because the sensations connected with them seem nearest to the physical life for which he still craves. The proper procedure for him, of course, is to kill out earthly desires and to withdraw into himself as quickly as possible.

Even a merely intellectual knowledge of the conditions. of astral life, and, in fact, of Theosophical truths in general, is of inestimable value to a man in the after-death life. *I L II.* 25–26.

It is of the utmost importance that after physical death a man should recognise quite clearly that he is withdrawing steadily towards the ego, and that consequently he should disengage his thoughts as far as may be from things physical and fix his attention upon spiritual matters which will occupy him when, in due time, he passes from the astral plane into the mental or heaven-world. *I L II* 19–21. *I H* 78–80. *O S D* 60.

By adopting this attitude he will greatly facilitate the natural disintegration of the astral body instead of unnecessarily and uselessly delaying himself upon the lower levels of the astral plane.

Many people, unfortunately, refuse to turn their thoughts upwards, but cling to earthly matters with desperate tenacity. As time passes on, they gradually, in the normal course of evolution, lose touch with the lower worlds : but by fighting every step of the way they cause themselves much unnecessary suffering and seriously delay their upward progress.

In this ignorant opposition to the natural course of things the possession of a physical corpse is of assistance to a man, the corpse serving as a kind of fulcrum on the physical plane. The best remedy for this tendency is cremation, which destroys the link with the physical plane.

A few typical examples of astral after-death life will best illustrate the nature and rationale of that life. *L A D* 12. *O S D* 14–15 : 62.

An ordinary colourless man, neither specially good nor specially bad, is of course in no way changed by *A W* 122–123.

death, but remains colourless. Consequently, he will
have no special suffering and no special joy : in fact,
he may find life somewhat dull, because, having culti-
vated no particular interests during his physical life,
he has none in his astral life.

If during his physical life he had no ideas beyond
gossip, sport, business or dress, he will naturally, when
these are no longer possible, be likely to find time hang
heavily on his hands.

A man, however, who has had strong desires of a
low type, who has been, for example, a drunkard or a
sensualist, will be in far worse case. Not only will
his cravings and desires remain with him (it will be
recollected that the centres of sensation are situated,
not in the physical body, but in Kâma, see page 24),
but they will be stronger than ever, because their full
force is expressed in astral matter, none of it being
absorbed in setting in motion the heavy physical particles.

O S D 66.　　Being in the lowest and most depraved condition of
astral life, such a man seems often to be still sufficiently
near to the physical to be sensitive to certain odours,
though the titillation produced is only sufficient still
further to excite his mad desires and to tantilise him
to the verge of frenzy.

L A D 12–13.　　But, as he no longer possesses a physical body,
through which alone his cravings can be allayed, he
has no possibility of gratifying his terrible thirsts.
Hence the innumerable traditions of the fires of purgatory, found in nearly every religion, which are no inapt
symbols for the torturing conditions described. Such
a condition may last for quite a long time, since it
passes away only by gradually wearing itself out.

The rationale and automatic justice of the whole
process is clear : the man has created his conditions
himself, by his own actions, and determined the exact
degree of their power and duration. Furthermore, it
is the only way in which he can get rid of his vices.
For, if he were to be reincarnated immediately, he
would start his next life precisely as he finished the

preceding one : *i.e.*, a slave to his passions and appetites : and the possibility of his ever becoming master of himself would be immeasurably reduced.   But, as things are, his cravings having worn themselves out, he will be able to commence his next incarnation without the burden of them : and his ego, having had so severe a lesson, is likely to make every possible effort to restrain its lower vehicles from again making a similar mistake.

A confirmed drunkard will sometimes be able to draw round himself a veil of etheric matter, and thus partially materialise himself.   He can then draw in the odour of the alcohol, but he does not smell it in the same sense as we do.   Hence he is anxious to force others into the condition of drunkenness, so that he may be able partially to enter their physical bodies and obsess them, through their bodies being once more able to experience directly the tastes and other sensations for which he craves. *I L II* 6. *A P* 42. *O S D* 66.

Obsession may be permanent or temporary.   As just mentioned, a dead sensualist may seize upon any vehicle he can steal in order to gratify his coarse desires.   At other times a man may obsess someone as a calculated act of revenge : a case is recorded where a man obsessed the daughter of his enemy. *I L I* 479–480.

Obsession can be best prevented or resisted by an exercise of will-power.   When it occurs it is almost always because the victim has in the first place voluntarily yielded himself to the invading influence, and his first step therefore is to reverse the act of submission.   The mind should be set steadily against the obsession in determined resistance, realising strongly that the human will is stronger than any evil influence. *I L I* 484. *O S D* 403.

Such obsession is of course utterly unnatural and in the highest degree harmful to both parties.

The effect of excessive tobacco-smoking on the astral body after death is remarkable.   The poison so fills the astral body that it stiffens under its influence and is unable to work properly or to move freely.   For the time, the man is as though paralysed— *H S II* 21.

able to speak, yet debarred from movement, and almost entirely cut off from higher influences. When the poisoned part of his astral body wears away, he emerges from this unpleasant predicament.

I L I 396.
O S D 15.

The astral body changes its particles, just as does the physical body, but there is nothing to correspond to eating and digesting food. The astral particles which fall away are replaced by others from the surrounding atmosphere. The *purely physical* cravings of hunger and thirst no longer exist there: but the *desire* of the glutton to gratify the sensation of taste, and the *desire* of the drunkard for the feelings which follow the absorption of alcohol, being both astral, still persist: and, as already stated, they may cause great suffering owing to the absence of the physical body through which alone they could be satisfied.

L A D 13-14.
I L I 125-128.
O S D 65: 70.

Many myths and traditions exist, exemplifying the conditions described. One of them is that of Tantalus, who suffered from raging thirst, yet was doomed to see the water recede just as it was about to touch his lips. Another, typifying ambition, is that of Sisyphus, condemned to roll a heavy rock up a mountain, only to see it roll down again. The rock represents ambitious plans which such a man continues to form, only to realise that he has no physical body with which to carry them out. Eventually he wears out his selfish ambition, realises that he need not roll his rock, and lets it rest in peace at the bottom of the hill.

I L I 126-127.

Another story was that of Tityus, a man who was tied to a rock, his liver being gnawed by vultures, and growing again as fast as it was eaten. This symbolised a man tortured by the gnawings of remorse for sins committed on earth.

O S D 52.
T B 76.

The worst that the ordinary man of the world usually provides for himself after death is a useless and unutterably wearisome existence, void of all rational interests—the natural sequel of a life wasted in self-indulgence, triviality and gossip here on earth.

T B 76.

The only things for which he craves are no longer possible to him, for in the astral world there is no

business to be done, and, though he may have as much
companionship as he wishes, society is now for him
a very different matter, because all the pretensions
upon which it is usually based in this world are no
longer possible.

Man thus makes for himself both his own purgatory   T B 64–65.
and his own heaven, and these are not places but states
of consciousness. Hell does not exist : it is only a
figment of the theological imagination. Neither purgatory nor heaven can ever be eternal, for a finite
cause cannot produce an infinite result.

Nevertheless, the conditions of the worst type of   A W 123–
man after death are perhaps best described by the word   124.
" hell," though they are *not* everlasting. Thus, for
example, it sometimes happens that a murderer is
followed about by his victim, never being able to escape
from his haunting presence. The victim (unless himself of a very base type) is wrapped in unconsciousness,
and this very unconsciousness seems to add a new
horror to the mechanical pursuit.

Such conditions are not produced arbitrarily, but   A W 124–
are the inevitable result of causes set in operation by   125.
each person. Nature's lessons are sharp, but in the
long run they are merciful, for they lead to the evolution
of the soul, being strictly corrective and salutary.

For most people the state after death is much   T B 76.
happier than life upon earth. The first feeling of
which the dead man is usually conscious is one of the
most wonderful and delightful freedom ; he has
nothing to worry about, and no duties rest upon him,
except those which he chooses to impose upon himself.

Regarded from this point of view, it is clear that
there is ample justification for the assertion that people
physically " alive," buried and cramped as they are in
physical bodies, are in the true sense far less " alive "
than those usually termed dead. The so-called dead
are much more free and, being less hampered by
material conditions, are able to work far more effectively and to cover a wider field of activity.

A man who, not having permitted the re-arrangement   T B 83.

of his astral body, is free of the entire astral world, does not find it inconveniently crowded, because the astral world is much larger than the surface of the physical earth, while its population is somewhat smaller, the average life of humanity in the astral world being shorter than the average in the physical.

In addition to the dead, there are also, of course, on the astral plane about one-third of the living, who have temporarily left the physical body during sleep.

T B 71.　Although the whole astral plane is open to any of its inhabitants who have not permitted the re-arrangement of their astral bodies, yet the great majority remain near the surface of the earth.

L A D 14–15.　Passing to a higher type of man, we may consider
O S D 76–78.　one who has some interests of a rational nature, *e.g.*, music, literature, science, etc. The need to spend a large proportion of each day in " earning a living " no longer existing, the man is free to do precisely what he likes, so long as it is capable of realisation without physical matter. In the astral life it is possible not only to listen to the grandest music but to hear far more of it than before, because there are in the astral world other and fuller harmonies than the relatively dull physical ears can hear. For the artist, all the loveliness of the higher astral world is open for his enjoyment. A man can readily and rapidly move from place to place and see the wonders of Nature, obviously far more easily than he could ever do on the physical plane. If he is a historian or a scientist, the libraries and the laboratories of the world are at his disposal : his comprehension of natural processes will be far fuller than ever before, because he can now see the inner as well as the outer workings, and many of the causes where previously he saw only the effects. In all these cases his delight is greatly enhanced, because no fatigue is possible (see p. 82).

A philanthropist can pursue his beneficent work more vigorously than ever before and under better conditions than in the physical world. There are thousands whom he can help, and with greater certainty of conferring real benefit.

It is quite possible for any person upon the astral *I L II* 101-
plane after death to set himself to study, and to 102.
acquire entirely new ideas. Thus, people may learn
of Theosophy for the first time in the astral world. A
case is on record even of a person learning music there,
though this is unusual.

In general, life on the astral plane is more active *A W* 73.
than on the physical plane, astral matter being more
highly vitalised than physical matter, and form being
more plastic. The possibilities on the astral plane, *O S D* 52–53.
both of enjoyment and of progress, are in every way 132–133.
much greater than those on the physical plane. But
the possibilities are of a higher class, and it needs a
certain amount of intelligence to take advantage of
them. A man who has whilst on earth devoted the
whole of his thought and energy solely to material
things, is little likely to be able to adapt himself to
more advanced conditions, as his semi-atrophied mind
will not be strong enough to grasp the wider possibilities of the grander life.

A man whose life and interests are of a higher type
may be able to do more good in a few years of astral
existence than ever he could have done in the longest
physical life.

Astral pleasures being so much greater than those *I L II* 117.
of the physical world, there is danger of people being
turned aside by them from the path of progress. But
even the delights of the astral life do not present a
serious danger to those who have realised a little of
something higher. After death a man should try to
pass through the astral levels as speedily as possible,
consistently with usefulness, and not yield to their
refined pleasures any more than to those of the
physical.

Any developed man is in every way quite as active *I L II* 65.
during astral life after death as during his physical
life : he can unquestionably help or hinder his own
progress and that of others quite as much after death
as before, and consequently he is all the time generating
karma of the greatest importance.

In fact, the consciousness of a man living entirely *I L II* 71.

in the astral world is usually much more definite than it has been during his sleep astral life, and he is correspondingly better able to think and act with determination, so that his opportunities of making good or bad karma are the greater.

I L II 519- 520. It may be said in general that a man can make karma wherever his consciousness is developed, or wherever he can act or choose. Thus actions done on the astral plane may bear karmic fruit in the next earth life.

I L II 7–8. *A P 42.* On the lowest astral sub-plane a man, having other things to occupy his attention, concerns himself little with what takes place in the physical world, except when he haunts vile resorts.

On the next sub-plane, the sixth, are found men who, whilst alive, centred their desires and thoughts chiefly in mere worldly affairs. Consequently, they still hover about the persons and places with which they were most closely associated while on earth, and may be conscious of many things in connection with these. They never, however, see physical matter itself, but always the astral counterpart of it.

I L II 11. *H S II 29.* Thus, for example, a theatre full of people has its astral counterpart, which is visible to astral entities. They would not, however, be able to see, as we see them, either the costumes or the expressions of the actors, and the emotions of the players, being not real but simulated, would make no impression on the astral plane.

I L II 27. Those on the sixth sub-plane, which is on the surface of the earth, find themselves surrounded by the astral counterparts of physically existing mountains, trees, lakes, etc.

I L II 7–8. On the next two sub-planes, the fifth and fourth, this consciousness of physical affairs is also possible, though in rapidly diminishing degree.

On the next two sub-planes, the third and second, contact with the physical plane could be obtained only by a special effort to communicate through a medium.

From the highest, the first sub-plane, even communication through a medium would be very difficult.

Those living on the higher sub-planes usually provide   *I L II* 27.
themselves with whatever scenes they desire. Thus in
one portion of the astral world men surround themselves
with landscapes of their own creation : others accept
ready-made the landscapes which have already been
constructed by others. (A description of the various
levels or sub-planes will be given in Chapter XVI.)

In some cases men construct for themselves the   *I L II* 27–28.
weird scenes described in their various religious scrip-
tures, manufacturing clumsy attempts at jewels growing on trees, seas of glass mingled with fire, creatures
full of eyes within, and deities with a hundred heads
and arms.

In what the Spiritualists call the Summerland, people   *I L I* 355–
of the same race and the same religion tend to keep   356.
together after death just as they do during life, so that   *A W* 131–
there is a kind of network of summerlands over the   132.
countries to which belong the persons who have created   *T B* 82–83.
them, communities being formed, differing as widely
from each other as do similar communities on earth.
This is due not only to natural affinity but also to the
fact that barriers of language still exist on the astral
plane.

This principle applies, in fact, to the astral plane in   *O S D* 20.
general. Thus, at spiritualistic *séances* in Ceylon, it
was found that the communicating entities were
Buddhists, and that beyond the grave they had found
their religious preconceptions confirmed, exactly as had
the members of various Christian sects in Europe.
Men find on the astral plane not only their own thought-   *O S D* 81.
forms, but those made by others—these, in some cases,
being the product of generations of thought from
thousands of people, all following along the same lines.

It is not uncommon for parents to endeavour to   *H S I* 435.
impress their wishes on their children, *e.g.*, with regard   *O S D* 79.
to some particular alliance on which their heart is set.
Such an influence is insidious, an ordinary man being
likely to take the steady pressure for his own sub-
conscious desire.

In many cases the dead have constituted themselves
guardian angels to the living, mothers often protecting

their sons, husbands their widows, and so on, for many years.

H S I 435-436. In other cases a dead writer or musical composer may impress his ideas upon a writer or composer in the physical world, so that many books credited to the living are really the work of the dead. The person who actually executes the writing may be conscious of the influence, or may be entirely unconscious of it.

M 109-110. One leading novelist has stated that his stories come to him he knows not whence—that they are in reality written not by him, but through him. He recognises the state of affairs : there are probably many others in the same case who are quite unconscious of it.

H S II 237. A doctor who dies often continues after death to take an interest in his patients, endeavouring to cure them from the other side, or to suggest to his successor methods of treatment which, with his newly-acquired astral faculties, he sees would be useful.

I L II 8-9. Whilst most ordinary "good" people, who die natural deaths, are unlikely to be conscious of anything physical at all, as they sweep through all the lower stages before awakening to astral consciousness, yet some, even of these, may be drawn back into touch with the physical world by great anxiety about someone left behind.

I L II 9-10.
O S D 104. The grief of relatives and friends may also attract the attention of one who has passed to the astral plane, and tend to draw him down into touch with earth life again. This downward tendency grows with use and the man is likely to exert his will to keep in touch with the physical world. For a time his power of seeing earthly things will increase ; but presently it will diminish, and then he will probably suffer mentally as he feels his power slipping from him.

A P 47-48.
H S I 340.
O S D 16-18 :
43-45.
A W 137-138.
T P 129-130.
D A 31. In many cases people not only cause themselves an immense amount of wholly unnecessary pain, but often also do serious injury to those for whom they mourn with intense and uncontrolled grief.

During the whole period of the astral plane life, whether it be long or short, the man is within the reach of earth influences. In the cases just mentioned the

passionate sorrow and desires of friends on earth would
set up vibrations in the astral body of the man who had
died, and so reach and rouse his mind or lower manas.
Thus aroused from his dreamy state to vivid remembrance of earth life, he may endeavour to communicate
with his earth friends, possibly through a medium. Such
an awakening is often accompanied by acute suffering,
and in any event the natural process of the ego's withdrawal is delayed.

Occult teaching does not for a moment counsel
forgetfulness of the dead : but it does suggest that
affectionate remembrance of the dead is a force which,
if properly directed towards helping his progress
towards the heaven-world, and his passage through
the intermediate state, might be of real value to him,
whereas mourning is not only useless but harmful.   It
is with a true instinct that the Hindu religion prescribes
its Shrâddha ceremonies and the Catholic Church its
prayers for the dead.

Prayers, with their accompanying ceremonies, create
elementals which strike against the Kâmalokic entity's
astral body, and hasten its disintegration, thus speeding
him on towards the heaven-world.

When, for example, a Mass is offered with a definite *H S I* 261 :
intention of helping a dead person, that person will 340.
undoubtedly benefit by the downpouring of force : *H S II* 245.
the strong thought about him inevitably attracts his *O S D* 17.
attention, and when he is drawn to the Church he takes
part in the ceremony and enjoys a large share in its
results.   Even if he be still unconscious, the priest's
will and prayer directs the stream of force towards the
person concerned.

Even the earnest general prayer or wish for the good *O S D* 17.
of the dead as a whole, though likely to be vague and
therefore less efficient than a more definite thought, has
yet in the aggregate produced an effect whose importance it would be difficult to exaggerate.   Europe
little knows how much it owes to those great religious
orders who devote themselves night and day to ceaseless prayer for the faithful departed.

CHAPTER XV

THE AFTER-DEATH LIFE: SPECIAL CASES

I L II 5. THERE is practically no difference between the consciousness of a psychic after death and that of an ordinary person, except that the psychic, being probably more familiar with astral matter, will feel more at home in his new environment. To be psychic means to possess a physical body in some ways more sensitive than those of most people: consequently, when the physical body is dropped, this inequality no longer exists.

I L II 15–16.
O S D 36–37. A sudden death, such as from an accident, need not necessarily affect the astral life in any way for the worse. At the same time, for most people, a more natural death is preferable, because the slow wasting away of the aged or the ravages of a long-continued illness are almost invariably accompanied by a considerable loosening and breaking up of the astral particles, so that when the man recovers consciousness upon the astral plane, he finds some, at any rate, of his principal work there already done for him.

S P 20. In most cases, when earth life is suddenly cut short by accident or suicide, the link between kâma (desire) and prâna (vitality) is not easily broken, and the astral body is consequently strongly vivified.

A P 55. The withdrawal of the principles from their physical encasement, owing to sudden death of any kind, has been aptly compared to the tearing of the stone out of an unripe fruit. A great deal of the grossest kind of astral matter still clings around the personality, which is consequently held in the seventh or lowest astral sub-plane.

I L II 16.
A W 115–117. The mental terror and disturbance which sometimes accompany accidental death are, of course, a

very unfavourable preparation for astral life. In certain rare cases the agitation and terror may persist for some time after death.

The victims of capital punishment, apart from the injury done to them by suddenly wrenching from the physical the astral body, throbbing with feelings of hatred, passion, revenge, and so forth, constitute a peculiarly dangerous element in the astral world. Unpleasant to society as a murderer in his physical body may be, he is clearly far more dangerous when suddenly expelled from the body: and, whilst society may protect itself from murderers in the physical body, it is at present defenceless against murderers suddenly projected on to the astral plane in the full flush of their passions. *D A* 38. *T N P* 90–91.

Such men may well act as the instigators of other murders. It is well known that murders of a particular kind are sometimes repeated over and over again in the same community. *C W* 96.

The position of the suicide is further complicated by the fact that his rash act has enormously diminished the power of the higher ego to withdraw its lower portion into itself, and therefore has exposed him to other and great dangers. Nevertheless it must be remembered, as already said, that the guilt of suicide differs considerably according to circumstances, from the morally blameless act of Socrates through all degrees down to that of a wretch who commits suicide in order to escape the physical results of his own crimes, and, of course, the position after death varies accordingly. *A P* 57.

The karmic consequences of suicide are usually momentous: they are certain to affect the next life, and probably more lives than one. It is a crime against Nature to interfere with the prescribed period appointed for living on the physical life. For every man has an appointed life-term, determined by an intricate web of prior causes—*i.e.*, by karma—and that term must run out its appointed sands, before the dissolution of the personality. *I L II* 12–14. *D A* 76–77: 34–38.

The attitude of mind at the time of death determines the subsequent position of the person. Thus, there is a profound difference between one who *lays down* his life from altruistic motives and one who deliberately destroys his life from selfish motives, such as fear, etc.

Pure and spiritually-minded men, who are the victims of accident, etc., sleep out happily the term of their natural life. In other cases they remain conscious —often entangled in the final scene of earth-life for a time, held in whatever region they are related to by the outermost layer of their astral body. Their normal kâmalokic life does not begin until the natural web of earth-life is out-spun, and they are vividly conscious of both their astral and physical surroundings.

I. A D 16.
O S D 48.
It must not for a moment, therefore, be supposed that because of the many superiorities of astral over physical life, a man is therefore justified in committing suicide or seeking death. Men are incarnated in physical bodies for a purpose which can be attained only in the physical world. There are lessons to be learnt in the physical world which cannot be learnt anywhere else, and the sooner we learn them the sooner we shall be free from the need to return to the lower and more limited life. The ego has to take much trouble in order to incarnate in a physical body, and also to live through the wearisome period of early childhood, during which he is gradually and with much effort gaining some control over his new vehicles, and therefore his efforts should not be foolishly wasted. In this respect the natural instinct of self-preservation is one which should be obeyed, it being a man's duty to make the most of his earthly life and to retain it as long as circumstances permit.

A P 55-56.
If a man, who has been killed suddenly, has led a low, brutal, selfish and sensual life, he will be fully conscious on the seventh astral sub-plane, and is liable to develop into a terribly evil entity. Inflamed with appetites which he can no longer satisfy, he may endeavour to gratify his passions through a medium or any sensitive person whom he can obsess. Such

entities take a devilish delight in using all the arts of
astral delusion to lead others into the same excesses
in which they themselves indulged. From this class
and from the vitalised shells (see p. 172) are drawn
the tempters—the devils of ecclesiastical literature.

The following is a strongly worded account of the D A 35.
victims of sudden death, whether suicides or killed by
accident, when such victims are depraved and gross.
" Unhappy shades, if sinful and sensual, they wander
about . . . until their death-hour comes. Cut off in
the full flush of earthly passions, which bind them to
familiar scenes, they are enticed by opportunities which
mediums afford to gratify them vicariously. They are
the Pishâchas, the Incubi and Succubæ of mediæval
times : the demons of thirst, gluttony, lust and avarice :
elementaries of intensified craft, wickedness and
cruelty : provoking their victims to horrid crimes, and
revelling in their commission ! "

Soldiers killed in battle do not quite come under this O S D 36.
category, because, whether the cause for which they
are fighting be in the abstract right or wrong, they
think it to be right : to them it is the call of duty, and
they sacrifice their lives willingly and unselfishly. In
spite of its horrors, therefore, war may nevertheless be
a potent factor in evolution at a certain level. This,
also, is the grain of truth in the idea of the Moham-
medan fanatic that the man who dies fighting for the
faith goes straight to a very good life in the next world.

In the case of children dying young, it is unlikely I L II 17.
that they will have developed much affinity for the
lowest sub-divisions of the astral world, and as a
matter of experience they are seldom found on the
lowest astral sub-planes.

Some people cling so desperately to material exist- I L II 34-37.
ence that at death their astral bodies cannot altogether
separate from the etheric, and consequently they
awaken still surrounded by etheric matter. Such
persons are in a very unpleasant condition : they are
shut out from the astral world by the etheric shell
which surrounds them, and at the same time they are

also, of course, shut off from ordinary physical life because they have no physical sense-organs.

The result is that they drift about, lonely, dumb and terrified, unable to communicate with entities on either plane. They cannot realise that if they would only let go their frenzied grasp on matter they would slip, after a few moments of unconsciousness, into the ordinary life of the astral plane. But they cling to their grey world, with their miserable half-consciousness, rather than sink into what they think complete extinction, or even the hell in which they have been taught to believe.

In process of time the etheric shell wears out, and the ordinary course of Nature reasserts itself in spite of their struggles : sometimes in sheer desperation they recklessly let themselves go, preferring even the idea of annihilation to their present existence—with a result overwhelmingly and surprisingly pleasant.

In a few cases, another astral entity may be able to help them by persuading them to let go their hold on what to them is life and sink out of it.

In other cases, they may be so unfortunate as to discover a means of reviving to some extent their touch with physical life through a medium, though as a rule the medium's " spirit-guide " very properly forbids them access.

The " guide " is right in his action, because such entities, in their terror and need, become quite unscrupulous and would obsess and even madden a medium, fighting as a drowning man fights for life. They could succeed only if the ego of the medium had weakened his hold upon his vehicles by allowing the indulgence of undesirable thoughts or passions.

I L. II 38–39. Sometimes an entity may be able to seize upon a
T B 88. baby body, ousting the feeble personality for whom it was intended, or sometimes even to obsess the body of an animal, the fragment of the group-soul which, to an animal, stands in the place of an ego, having a hold on the body less strong than that of an ego. This obsession may be complete or partial. The obsessing

entity thus once more gets into touch with the physical plane, sees through the animal's eyes, and feels any pain inflicted upon the animal—in fact, so far as his his own consciousness is concerned, he *is* the animal for the time being.

A man who thus entangles himself with an animal *I L II* 40–41. cannot abandon the animal's body at will, but only gradually and by considerable effort, extending probably over many days. Usually he is set free only at the death of the animal, and even then there remains an astral entanglement to shake off. After the death of the animal such a soul sometimes endeavours to obsess another member of the same herd, or indeed any other creature whom he can seize in his desperation. The animals most commonly seized upon seem to be the less developed ones—cattle, sheep and swine. More intelligent creatures, such as dogs, cats and horses do not appear to be so easily dispossessed, though cases do occasionally occur.

All obsessions, whether of a human or an animal *I L II* 43. body, are an evil and a hindrance to the obsessing soul, as they temporarily strengthen his hold upon the material, and so delay his natural progress into the astral life, besides making undesirable karmic links.

In the case of a man who, by vicious appetite or *I L II* 30–33. otherwise, forms a very strong link with any type of animal, his astral body shows animal characteristics, and may resemble in appearance the animal whose qualities had been encouraged during earth life. In extreme cases the man may be linked to the astral body of the animal and thus be chained as a prisoner to the animal's physical body. The man is conscious in the astral world, has his human faculties, but cannot control the animal body nor express himself through that body on the physical plane. The animal organism serves as a jailer, rather than as a vehicle: and, further, the animal soul is not ejected, but remains as the proper tenant of its body.

Cases of this kind explain, at least partially, the belief often found in Oriental countries, that a man may under certain conditions reincarnate in an animal body.

A similar fate may befall a man as he returns to the astral plane on his way to re-birth, and is described in Chapter XXIV on *Re-birth*.

O S D 234.   The class of person who is definitely held down to earth by anxiety is often termed earth-bound: as St. Martin expressed it, such men are " remainers," not " returners," being unable thoroughly to tear themselves away from physical matter until some business is settled in which they have a special interest.

S P 45–46.
D A 42–43.
M B 79.
We have already seen that after physical death the real man is steadily withdrawing himself from his outer bodies: and that, in particular, manas, or mind, endeavours to disentangle itself from kâma, or desire. In certain rare cases, the personality, or lower man, may be so strongly controlled by kâma that lower manas is completely enslaved and cannot disentangle itself. The link between the lower and the higher mental, the " silver thread that binds it to the Master," snaps in two. This is spoken of in occultism as the " loss of the soul." It is the loss of the personal self, which has separated from its parent, the higher ego, and has thus doomed itself to perish.

In such a case, even during earth-life, the lower quaternary is wrenched away from the Triad, *i.e.*, the lower principles, headed by lower manas, are severed from the higher principles, Âtmâ, Buddhi and Higher Manas. The man is rent in twain, the brute has broken itself free, and it goes forth unbridled, carrying with it the reflections of that manasic light which should have been its guide through life. Such a creature, owing to its possession of mind, is more dangerous even than an unevolved animal: though human in form, it is brute in nature, without sense of truth, love or justice.

After physical death, such an astral body is an entity of terrible potency, and is unique in this, that under certain rare conditions it can reincarnate in the world of men. With no instincts save those of the animal, driven only by passion, never even by emotion, with a cunning that no brute can rival, a wickedness that is deliberate, it touches ideal vileness, and is the natural foe of all normal human beings. A being of this class—which is known as an *Elementary*—sinks lower with each successive incarnation, until, as the evil force gradually wears itself out, it perishes, being cut off from the source of life. It disintegrates, and thus as a separate existence is lost.

From the point of view of the ego there has been no harvest of useful experience from that personality : the " ray " has brought nothing back, the lower life has been a total and complete failure.

The word Elementary has been employed by various writers in many different senses, but it is recommended that it be confined to the entity described above.

CHAPTER XVI

THE ASTRAL PLANE

THIS chapter will be confined, so far as the complexities of the subject permit, to a description of the nature, appearance, properties, etc., of the astral plane or world. A later chapter will be devoted to an enumeration and description of the entities which live in the astral world.

A P 15. The intelligent student will recognise the extreme difficulty of giving in physical language an adequate description of the astral world. The task has been compared to that of an explorer of some unknown tropical forest being asked to give a full account of the country through which he has passed. The difficulties of describing the astral world are further complicated by two factors : (1) the difficulty of correctly translating from the astral to the physical plane the recollection of what has been seen : and (2) the inadequacy of physical plane language to express much of what has to be reported.

M B 42.
A W 76-77. One of the most prominent characteristics of the astral world is that it is full of continually changing shapes : we find there not only thought-forms, composed of elemental essence and animated by a thought, but also vast masses of elemental essence from which continually shapes emerge and into which they again disappear. The elemental essence exists in hundreds of varieties on every sub-plane, as though the air were visible and were in constant undulating motion with changing colours like mother-of-pearl. Currents of thought are continually thrilling through this astral matter, strong thoughts persisting as entities for a long time, weak ones clothing themselves in elemental essence and wavering out again.

We have already seen that astral matter exists in *A P* 17.
A W 74. seven orders of fineness, corresponding to the seven physical grades of solid, liquid, gaseous, etc. Each of these seven orders of matter is the basis of one of the seven levels, sub-divisions, or sub-planes (as they are variously called) of the astral plane.

It has become customary to speak of these seven levels as being ranged one above the other, the densest at the bottom and the finest at the top : and in many diagrams they are actually drawn in this manner. There is a basis of truth in this method of representation, but it is not the whole truth.

The matter of each sub-plane interpenetrates that of the sub-plane below it : consequently, at the surface of the earth, all seven sub-planes exist together in the same space. Nevertheless, it is also true that the higher astral sub-planes extend further away from the physical earth than the lower sub-planes.

A very fair analogy of the relation between the astral *I L I* 351–352.
I L II 52. sub-planes exists in the physical world. To a considerable extent liquids interpenetrate solids, *e.g.*, water is found in soil, gases interpenetrate liquids (water usually contains considerable volumes of air), and so on. Nevertheless it is substantially true that the bulk of the liquid matter of the earth lies in seas, rivers, etc., above the solid earth. Similarly the bulk of gaseous matter rests above the surface of the water, and reaches much further out into space than either solid or liquid.

Similarly with astral matter. By far the densest *I L I* 353.
I L II 52.
T B 72.
I L I 356.
H S I 449. aggregation of astral matter lies within the limits of the physical sphere. In this connection it should be noted that astral matter obeys the same general laws as physical matter, and gravitates towards the centre of the earth.

The seventh or lowest astral sub-plane penetrates some distance into the interior of the earth, so that the entities living on it may find themselves actually within the crust of the earth.

The sixth sub-plane is partially coincident with the surface of the earth.

I L I 355.
A P 43.

The third sub-plane, which the Spiritualists call the "Summerland," extends many miles up into the atmosphere.

I L I 353.
I L II 53–54.
T B 26–27.

The outer limit of the astral world extends nearly to the mean distance of the moon's orbit, so that at perigee the astral planes of the earth and moon usually touch one another, but not at apogee. (N.B.—The earth and moon are nearly 240,000 miles apart.) Hence the name the Greeks gave to the astral plane—the sub-lunar world.

A P 18.

The seven sub-divisions fall naturally into three groups : (*a*) the seventh or lowest : (*b*) the sixth, fifth and fourth : and (*c*) the third, second and first. The difference between members of one group may be compared to that between two solids, *e.g.*, steel and sand, the difference between the groups may be compared to that between a solid and a liquid.

A P 26.
A W 119–120.

Sub-plane 7 has the physical world as its background, though only a distorted and partial view of it is visible, since all that is light and good and beautiful seems invisible. Four thousand years ago the Scribe Ani described it in an Egyptian papyrus thus : "What manner of place is this unto which I have come ? It hath no water, it hath no air ; it is deep, unfathomable ; it is black as the blackest night, and men wander helplessly about therein ; in it a man may not live in quietness of heart."

For the unfortunate human being on that level it is indeed true that "all the earth is full of darkness and cruel habitation," but it is darkness which radiates from within himself and causes his existence to be passed in a perpetual night of evil and horror—a very real hell, though, like all other hells, entirely of man's own creation.

Most students find the investigation of this section an extremely unpleasant task, for there appears to be a sense of density and gross materiality about it which is indescribably loathsome to the liberated astral body, causing it the sense of pushing its way through some black, viscous fluid, while the inhabitants and the influences encountered there are also usually exceedingly undesirable.

The ordinary decent man would probably have little to detain him on the seventh sub-plane, the only persons who would normally awake to consciousness on that sub-plane being those whose desires are gross and brutal—drunkards, sensualists, violent criminals, and the like. *A P* 42. *A W* 121.

Sub-planes 6, 5 and 4 have for their background the physical world with which we are familiar. Life on No. 6 is like ordinary physical life, minus the physical body and its necessities. Nos. 5 and 4 are less material and more withdrawn from the lower world and its interests. *A P* 18.

As in the case of the physical, the densest astral matter is far too dense for the ordinary forms of astral life : but the astral world has other forms of its own which are quite unknown to students of the surface. *I L I* 358.

On the fifth and fourth sub-planes, merely earthly associations appear to become of less and less importance, and the people there tend more and more to mould their surroundings into agreement with the more persistent of their thoughts. *A P* 42. *A W* 129.

Sub-planes 3, 2 and 1, though occupying the same space, give the impression of being further removed from the physical world and correspondingly less material. At these levels entities lose sight of the earth and its affairs : they are usually deeply self-absorbed, and to a large extent create their own surroundings, though these are sufficiently objective to be perceptible to other entities. *A P* 26–27: 43. *O S D* 84–85. *A W* 130– 134: *T B* 80–81.

They are thus little awake to the realities of the plane, but live instead in imaginary cities of their own, partly creating them entirely by their own thoughts, and partly inheriting and adding to the structures created by their predecessors.

Here are found the happy hunting-grounds of the Red Indian, the Valhalla of the Norseman, the houri-filled paradise of the Muslim, the golden and jewelled-gated New Jerusalem of the Christian, the lyceum-filled heaven of the materialistic reformer. Here is also the "Summerland" of the Spiritualists, in which exist houses, schools, cities, etc., which, real enough as they are for a time, to a clearer sight are sometimes pitiably unlike what their delighted creators suppose them to be. Nevertheless, many of the creations are of real though temporary beauty, and a visitor who knew of nothing higher might wander contentedly among the natural scenery provided, which at any rate is much superior to anything in the physical world : or he might, of course, prefer to construct his scenery to suit his own fancies.

A P 43.
A W 132–133.

The second sub-plane is especially the habitat of the selfish or unspiritual religionist. Here he wears his golden crown and worships his own grossly material representation of the particular deity of his country and time.

A P 43.
A W 133–135.

The first sub-plane is specially appropriated to those who during earth-life have devoted themselves to materialistic but intellectual pursuits, following them not for the sake of benefiting their fellow-men, but either from motives of selfish ambition or simply for the sake of intellectual exercise. Such persons may remain on this sub-plane for many years, happy in working out their intellectual problems, but doing no good to any one, and making but little progress on their way towards the heaven-world.

O S D 86.

On this, the atomic sub-plane, men do not build themselves imaginary conceptions, as they do at lower levels. Thinkers and men of science often utilise for purposes of their study almost all the powers of the entire astral plane, for they are able to descend almost to the physical along certain limited lines. Thus they can swoop down upon the astral counterpart of a physical book and extract from it the information they require. They readily touch the mind of an author, impress their ideas upon him, and receive his in return. Sometimes they seriously delay their departure for the heaven-world by the avidity with which they prosecute lines of study and experiment on the astral plane.

Although we speak of astral matter as solid, it is *I L I* 362.
never *really*, but only relatively solid.   One of the
reasons why mediæval alchemists symbolised astral
matter by water was because of its fluidity and pene-
trability.   The particles in the densest astral matter
are further apart, relatively to their size, than even
gaseous particles.   Hence it is easier for two of the
densest astral bodies to pass through each other than
it would be for the lightest gas to diffuse itself in
the air.

People on the astral plane can and do pass through *I L I* 364–
one another constantly, and through fixed astral 365.
objects.   There can never be anything like what we
mean by a collision, and under ordinary circumstances
two bodies which interpenetrate are not even appre-
ciably affected.   If, however, the interpenetration
lasts for some time, as when two persons sit side by
side in a church or theatre, a considerable effect may
be produced.

If a man *thought* of a mountain as an obstacle, he
could not pass through it.   To learn that it is not an
obstacle is precisely the object of one part of what is
called the " test of earth."

An explosion on the astral plane might be tem- *I L I* 364.
porarily as disastrous as an explosion of gunpowder on *M* 42.
the physical plane, but the astral fragments would *O S D* 385–
quickly collect themselves again.   Thus there cannot 386.
be an accident on the astral plane in our sense of the
word, because the astral body, being fluidic, cannot be
destroyed or permanently injured, as the physical can.

A purely astral object could be moved by means of *I L I* 395–
an astral hand, if one wished, but not the astral counter- 396.
part of a physical object.   In order to move an astral
counterpart it would be necessary to materialise a
hand and move the physical object, then the astral
counterpart would, of course, accompany it.   The astral
counterpart is there because the physical object is
there, just as the scent of a rose fills a room because
the rose is there.   One could no more move a physical
object by moving its astral counterpart than one could

move the rose by moving its perfume.

I L I 363. On the astral plane one never touches the surface of anything, so as to feel it hard or soft, rough or smooth, hot or cold: but on coming into contact with the interpenetrating substance one would be conscious of a different rate of vibration, which might, of course, be pleasant or unpleasant, stimulating or depressing.

Thus if one is standing on the ground, part of one's astral body interpenetrates the ground under one's feet: but the astral body would not be conscious of the fact by anything corresponding to a sense of hardness or by any difference in the power of movement.

On the astral plane one has not the sense of jumping over a precipice, but simply of floating over it.

I L I 363-364. Although the light of all planes comes from the sun, yet the effect which it produces on the astral plane is entirely different from that on the physical. In the astral world there is a diffused luminosity, not obviously coming from any special direction. All astral matter is in itself luminous, though an astral body is not like a painted sphere, but rather a sphere of living fire. It is never dark in the astral world. The passing of a physical cloud in front of the sun makes no difference whatever to the astral plane, nor, of course, does the shadow of the earth which we call night. As astral bodies are transparent, there are no shadows.

I L I 366. Atmospheric and climatic conditions make practically no difference to work on the astral and mental planes. But being in a big city makes a great difference, on account of the masses of thought-forms.

I L. I 365. On the astral plane there are many currents which tend to carry about persons who are lacking in will, and even those who have will but do not know how to use it.

I L II 103. There is no such thing as sleep in the astral world.

I L II 104. It is possible to forget upon the astral plane just as it is on the physical. It is perhaps even easier to forget on the astral plane than on the physical because that world is so busy and so populous.

Knowledge of a person in the astral world does not necessarily mean knowledge of him in the physical world.

The astral plane has often been called the realm of illusion—not that it is itself any more illusory than the physical world, but because of the extreme unreliability of the impressions brought back from it by the untrained seer. This can be accounted for mainly by two remarkable characteristics of the astral world : (1) many of its inhabitants have a marvellous power of changing their forms with protean rapidity, and also of casting practically unlimited glamour over those with whom they choose to sport : and (2) astral sight is very different from and much more extended than physical vision.

A P 12.
I L I 103.
O S D 46.

Thus with astral vision an object is seen, as it were, from all sides at once, every particle in the interior of a solid being as plainly open to the view as those on the outside, and everything entirely free from the distortion of perspective.

A P 12 : 18–19.
C 37 : 40–41.

If one looked at a watch astrally, one would see the face and all the wheels lying separately, but nothing on the top of anything else. Looking at a closed book one would see each page, not through all the other pages before or behind it, but looking straight down upon it as though it were the only page to be seen.

C 37 : 40–41.
A W 75.

It is easy to see that under such conditions even the most familiar objects may at first be totally unrecognisable, and that an inexperienced visitor may well find considerable difficulty in understanding what he really does see, and still more in translating his vision into the very inadequate language of ordinary speech. Yet a moment's consideration will show that astral vision approximates much more closely to true perception than does physical sight, which is subject to the distortions of perspective.

In addition to these possible sources of error, matters are still further complicated by the fact that this astral sight cognises forms of matter which, while still purely physical, are nevertheless invisible under ordinary conditions. Such, for example, are the particles composing the atmosphere, all the emanations which are continuously being given out by everything that has life, and also the four grades of etheric matter.

A P 23–24.   Further, astral vision discloses to view other and entirely different colours beyond the limits of the ordinary visible spectrum, the ultra-red and ultra-violet rays known to physical science being plainly visible to astral sight.

Thus, to take a concrete example, a rock, seen with astral sight, is no mere inert mass of stone. With astral vision : (1) the whole of the physical matter is seen, instead of a very small part of it : (2) the vibrations of the physical particles are perceptible : (3) the astral counterpart, composed of various grades of astral matter, all in constant motion, is visible : (4) the universal life (prâna) is seen to be circulating through it and radiating from it : (5) an aura will be seen surrounding it : (6) its appropriate elemental essence is seen permeating it, ever active but ever fluctuating. In the case of the vegetable, animal, and human kingdoms, the complications are naturally much more numerous.

A P 12–13.   A good instance of the sort of mistake that is likely to occur on the astral plane is the frequent reversal of any number which the seer has to record, so that he is liable to render, say, 139 as 931, and so on. In the case of a student of occultism trained by a capable Master, such a mistake would be impossible, except through great hurry or carelessness, since such a pupil has to go through a long and varied course of instruction in this art of seeing correctly. A trained seer in time acquires a certainty and confidence in dealing with the phenomena of the astral plane far exceeding anything possible in physical life.

It is quite a mistaken view to speak with scorn of the astral plane and to think it unworthy of attention. It would, of course, certainly be disastrous for any student to neglect his higher development, and to rest satisfied with the attainment of astral consciousness. In

some cases it is indeed possible to develop the higher
mental faculties first, to overleap the astral plane for
the time, as it were. But this is not the ordinary
method adopted by the Masters of Wisdom with their
pupils. For most, progress by leaps and bounds is
not practicable : it is necessary therefore to proceed
slowly, step by step.

In *The Voice of the Silence* three halls are spoken of. *I L I* 102-
The first, that of ignorance, is the physical plane : 105.
the second, the Hall of Learning, is the astral plane,
and is so called because the opening of the astral
chakrams reveals so much more than is visible on the
physical plane that the man feels he is much nearer
the reality of the thing : nevertheless it is still but the
place of probationary learning. Still more real and
definite knowledge is acquired in the Hall of Wisdom,
which is the mental plane.

An important part of the scenery of the astral plane *A P* 27-28.
consists of what are often, though mistakenly, called *C* 97-98 :
the Records of the Astral Light.   These records (which 102-104.
are in truth a sort of materialisation of the Divine
memory—a living photographic representation of all
that has ever happened) are really and permanently
impressed upon a very much higher level, and are only
reflected in a more or less spasmodic manner on the
astral plane ; so that one whose power of vision does
not rise above this will be likely to obtain only
occasional and disconnected pictures of the past instead
of a coherent narrative. But nevertheless these reflected
pictures of all kinds of past events are constantly
being reproduced in the astral world, and form an
important part of the surroundings of the investigator
there.

Communication on the astral plane is limited by the *A P* 45.
knowledge of the entity, just as it is in the physical *C* 125.
world.   One who is able to use the mind-body can
communicate his thoughts to the human entities there
more readily and rapidly than on earth, by means of
mental impressions :· but the ordinary inhabitants of
the astral plane are not usually able to exercise this

power; they appear to be restricted by limitations similar to those that prevail on earth, though perhaps less rigid. Consequently (as previously mentioned) they are found associating, there as here, in groups drawn together by common sympathies, beliefs, and language.

CHAPTER XVII

MISCELLANEOUS ASTRAL PHENOMENA

THERE is reason to suppose that it may not be long A P 112-114. before some applications of one or two super-physical S G O 200. forces may come to be known to the world at large. A common experience at spiritualistic *séances* is that of the employment of practically resistless force in, for example, the instantaneous movement of enormous weights, and so on. There are several ways in which such results may be brought about. Hints may be given as to four of these.

(1) There are great *etheric currents* on the surface of the earth flowing from pole to pole in volumes which make this power as irresistible as that of the rising tide, and there are methods by which this stupendous force may be safely utilised, though unskilful attempts to control it would be fraught with the greatest danger.

(2) There is an *etheric pressure*, somewhat corresponding to, though immensely greater than, the atmospheric pressure. Practical occultism teaches how a given body of ether can be isolated from the rest, so that the tremendous force of etheric pressure can be brought into play.

(3) There is a vast store of *potential energy* which has become dormant in matter during the involution of the subtle into the gross, and by changing the condition of the matter some of this may be liberated and utilised, somewhat as latent energy in the form of heat may be liberated by a change in the condition of visible matter.

(4) Many results may be produced by what is known as *sympathetic vibration*. By sounding the keynote of the class of matter it is desired to affect,

an immense number of sympathetic vibrations can be called forth. When this is done on the physical plane, *e.g.*, by sounding a note on a harp and inducing other harps tuned in unison to respond sympathetically, no additional energy is developed. But on the astral plane the matter is far less inert, so that when called into action by sympathetic vibrations, it adds its own living force to the original impulse, which may thus be multiplied many-fold. By further rhythmic repetition of the original impulse, the vibrations may be so intensified that the result is out of all apparent proportion to the cause. There seems scarcely any limit to the conceivable achievements of this force in the hands of a great Adept who fully comprehends its possibilities : for the very building of the Universe itself was but the result of the vibrations set up by the Spoken Word.

A P 115.   The class of mantras or spells which produce their result not by controlling some elemental, but merely by the repetition of certain sounds, also depend for their efficacy upon this action of sympathetic vibration.

A P 115.
O S D 359-
361.   The phenomenon of *disintegration* also may be brought about by the action of extremely rapid vibrations, which overcome the cohesion of the molecules of the object operated upon. A still higher vibration of a somewhat different type will separate these molecules into their constituent atoms. A body thus reduced to the etheric condition can be moved from one place to another with very great rapidity ; and the moment the force which has been exerted is withdrawn it will be forced by the etheric pressure to resume its original condition.

It is necessary to explain how the shape of an object is preserved, when it is disintegrated and then rematerialised. If a metal key, for example, were raised to the vaporous condition by heat, when the heat is withdrawn the metal will solidify, but instead of being a key it will be merely a lump of metal. The reason of this is that the elemental essence which informs the key would be dissipated by the alteration in its condition : not that the elemental essence can be affected by heat, but that when its temporary body is destroyed as a solid, the elemental essence pours back into the great reservoir of such essence, much as the higher principles of man, though entirely unaffected by heat or cold, are yet forced out of a physical body when the latter is destroyed by fire.

Consequently, when the metal of the key cooled into the solid condition again, the " earth " elemental essence which poured back into it would not be the same as that which it contained before, and there would therefore be no reason why the key shape should be retained.

But a man who disintegrated a key in order to move it from one place to another, would be careful to hold the elemental essence in exactly the same shape until the transfer was completed, and then when his will-force was removed it would act as a mould into which the solidifying particles would flow, or rather round which they would be re-aggregated. Thus, unless the operator's power of concentration failed, the shape would be accurately preserved.

Apports, or the bringing of objects almost instantaneously from great distances to spiritualistic *séances* are sometimes produced in this way : for it is obvious that when disintegrated they could be passed with perfect ease through any solid substance, such as the wall of a house or the side of a locked box. The passage of matter through matter is thus, when understood, as simple as the passage of water through a sieve or of a gas through a liquid. *A P* 116–117. *O S D* 359–360.

Materialisation or the change of an object from the etheric to the solid state, can be produced by a reversal of the above process. In this case also a continued effort of will is necessary to prevent the materialised matter from relapsing into the etheric condition. The various kinds of materialisation will be described in Chapter XXVIII on *Invisible Helpers*.

Electrical disturbances of any sort present diffi- *O S D* 370.

culties in either materialisation or disintegration, presumably for the same reason that bright light renders them almost impossible—the destructive effect of strong vibration.

A P 119.
O S D 371–372.
Reduplication is produced by forming a perfect mental image of the object to be copied, and then gathering about that mould the necessary astral and physical matter. The phenomenon requires considerable power of concentration to perform, because every particle, interior as well as exterior, of the object to be duplicated must be held accurately in view simultaneously. A person who is unable to extract the matter required directly from the surrounding ether may sometimes borrow it from the material of the original article, which would then be correspondingly reduced in weight.

A P 119–120.
O S D 357.
Precipitation of letters, etc., may be produced in several ways. An Adept might place a sheet of paper before him, form a mental image of the writing he wished to appear upon it, and draw from the ether the matter wherewith to objectivise the image. Or he could with equal ease produce the same result upon a sheet of paper lying before his correspondent, whatever might be the distance between them.

A third method, quicker and therefore more often adopted, is to impress the whole substance of the letter on the mind of some pupil and leave him to do the mechanical work of precipitation. The pupil would then imagine he saw the letter written on the paper in his Master's hand, and objectivise the writing as just described. If he found it difficult to draw the material from the ether and precipitate the writing on the paper simultaneously, he might have ink or coloured powder at hand on which he could draw more readily.

It is just as easy to imitate one man's hand-writing as another's, and it would be impossible to detect by any ordinary means a forgery committed in this manner. A pupil of a Master has an infallible test which he can apply, but for others the proof of origin must lie solely in the contents of the letter and the spirit breathing through it, as the hand-writing, however cleverly imitated, is valueless as evidence.

A pupil new to the work would probably be able to imagine a few words at a time only, but one with more experience could visualise a whole page or even an entire letter at once. In this manner quite long letters are sometimes produced in a few seconds at spiritualistic *séances*.

Pictures are precipitated in the same manner, except that here it is necessary to visualise the entire scene at once : and if many colours are needed they have to be manufactured, kept separate, and applied correctly. Evidently there is here scope for artistic faculty, and those with experience as artists will be more successful than those without such experience. *A P* 120 ·122. *O S D* 357.

Slate-writing is sometimes produced by precipitation, though more frequently tiny points of spirit hands are materialised just sufficiently to grasp the fragment of pencil. *A P* 121.

Levitation, that is the floating of a human body in the air, is often performed at *séances* by " spirit hands " which support the body of the medium. It may also be achieved by the aid of the elementals of air and water. In the East, however, always, and here occasionally, another method is employed. There is known to occult science a method of neutralising or even reversing the force of gravity, which is in fact of a magnetic nature, by means of which levitation may be easily produced. Doubtless this method was used in raising some of the air-ships of ancient India and Atlantis, and it is not improbable that a similar method was employed in constructing the Pyramids and Stonehenge. *A P* 121–122. *O S D* 344-345. *A W* 86.

Levitation also happens to some ascetics in India, and some of the greatest of Christian Saints have in deep meditation been thus raised from the ground— for example, S. Teresa and S. Joseph of Cupertino. *I L II* 182-183.

Since light consists of ether vibrations, it is obvious that any one who understands how to set up these vibrations can produce " *spirit lights*," either the *A P* 122.

mildly phosphorescent or the dazzling electrical variety, or those dancing globules of light into which a certain class of fire elementals so readily transform themselves.

A P 122.
O S D 372–373.
The feat of *handling fire* without injury may be performed by covering the hand with the thinnest layer of etheric substance, so manipulated as to be impervious to heat.   There are also other ways in which it may be done.

O S D 373–374.
The *production of fire* is also within the resources of the astral plane, as well as to counteract its effect. There seem to be at least three ways in which this could be done: (1) to set up and maintain the requisite rate of vibration, when combustion must ensue: (2) to introduce fourth-dimensionally a tiny fragment of glowing matter and then blow upon it until it bursts into flame: (3) to introduce chemical constituents which would produce combustion.

A P 122–123.
The *transmutation of metals* can be achieved by reducing a piece of metal to the atomic condition and rearranging the atoms in another form.

A P 123.
Repercussion, which will be dealt with in the Chapter on *Invisible Helpers*, is also due to the principle of sympathetic vibration, described above.

CHAPTER XVIII

THE FOURTH DIMENSION

THERE are many characteristics of the astral world which agree with remarkable exactitude with a world of four dimensions, as conceived by geometry and mathematics. So close, in fact, is this agreement, that cases are known where a purely intellectual study of the geometry of the fourth dimension has opened up astral sight in the student. *O S D* 109–110 : 467–468.

The classic books on the subject are those of C. H. Hinton : *Scientific Romances*, Vols. I and II : *A New Era of Thought : The Fourth Dimension.* These are strongly recommended by Bishop C. W. Leadbeater, who states that the study of the fourth dimension is the best method he knows to obtain a conception of the conditions which prevail on the astral plane, and that C. H. Hinton's exposition of the fourth dimension is the only one which gives any kind of explanation down here of the constantly observed facts of astral vision. *H S I* 28–29. *M V I* 24. *O S D* 108–109. *C* 39.

Other, and later books are several by Claude Bragdon: *The Beautiful Necessity : A Primer of Higher Space : Fourth Dimensional Vistas ;* etc., *Tertium Organum* (a most illuminating work) by P. D. Ouspensky, and no doubt many others.

For those who have made no study of this subject we may give here the very barest outline of some of the main features underlying the fourth dimension.

A *point*, which has " position but no magnitude," has no dimensions : a *line*, created by the movement of a point, has one dimension, length : a *surface*, created by the movement of a line, at right angles to itself, has two dimensions, length and breadth : a *solid*, created by the movement of a surface at right angles to itself, has three dimensions, length, breadth and thickness.

A *tesseract* is a hypothetical object, created by the movement of a solid, in a new direction at right angles to itself, having four dimensions, length, breadth, thickness and another, at right angles to these three, but incapable of being represented in our world of three dimensions.

Many of the properties of a tesseract can be deduced, according to the following table:—

O S D 114.

	Points	Lines	Surfaces	Solids
A Point has	1	–	–	–
A Line has	2	1	–	–
A Four-sided Surface has ...	4	4	1	–
A Cube has	8	12	6	1
A Tesseract has	16	32	24	8

C 39.

S O E 59.

The tesseract, as described by C. H. Hinton, is stated by Bishop C. W. Leadbeater to be a reality, being quite a familiar figure on the astral plane. In *Some Occult Experiences* by J. Van Manen, an attempt is made to represent a 4-dimensional globe graphically.

There is a close and suggestive parallel between phenomena which could be produced by means of a three-dimensional object in a hypothetical world of two dimensions inhabited by a being conscious only of two dimensions, and many astral phenomena as they appear to us living in the physical or three-dimensional world. Thus:

O S D 112–
114 : 122.

(1) Objects, by being lifted through ·.e third dimension, could be made to appear in or disappear from the two-dimensional world at will.

(2) An object completely surrounded by a line could be lifted out of the enclosed space through the third dimension.

(3) By bending a two-dimensional world, represented by a sheet of paper, two distant points could be brought together, or even made to coincide, thus destroying the two-dimensional conception of distance.

(4) A right-handed object could be turned over through the third dimension and made to re-appear as a left-handed object.

(5) By looking down, from the third dimension, on to a two-dimensional object, every point of the

latter could be seen at once, and free from the distortion of perspective.

To a being limited to a conception of two dimensions, the above would appear " miraculous," and completely incomprehensible.

It is curious that precisely similar tricks can be and are constantly being played upon us, as is well known to spiritualists : (1) entities and objects appear and disappear : (2) " apports " of articles from great distances are made : (3) articles are removed from closed boxes : (4) space appears to be practically annihilated ; (5) an object can be reversed, *i.e.*, a right hand turned into a left hand : (6) all parts of an object, *e.g.*, of a cube, are seen simultaneously and free from all distortion of perspective : similarly the whole of the matter of a closed book can be seen at once.

O S D 114.
H S I 164.

A P 19-111

The explanation of the welling-up of force, *e.g.*, in Chakrams, apparently from nowhere, is of course that it comes from the fourth dimension.

C 17-18.

A liquid, poured on to a surface, tends to spread itself out in two dimensions, becoming very thin in the third dimension. Similarly a gas tends to spread itself in three dimensions, and it may be that in so doing it becomes smaller in the fourth dimension : *i.e.*, the density of a gas may be a measure of its relative thickness in the fourth dimension.

O S D 122-123.

It is clear that there is no need to stop at four dimensions : for all we know, there may be infinite dimensions of space. At any rate, it seems certain that the astral world is four-dimensional, the mental five-dimensional, and the buddhic six-dimensional.

C 108.
M 27.

It should be clear that if there are, say, seven dimensions at all, there are seven dimensions always and everywhere : *i.e.*, there is no such thing as a third or fourth-dimensional being. The apparent difference is due to the limited power of perception of the entity concerned, not to any change in the objects perceived. This idea is very well worked out in *Tertium Organum* by Ouspensky.

I L II 118-120.
H S I 27.
O S D 107.

I L II 121-
122.   Nevertheless a man may develop astral consciousness and still be unable to perceive or appreciate the fourth dimension. In fact it is certain that the average man does not perceive the fourth dimension at all when he enters the astral plane. He realises it only as a certain blurring, and most men go through their astral lives without discovering the reality of the fourth dimension in the matter surrounding them.

Entities, such as nature-spirits, which belong to the astral plane, have by nature the faculty of seeing the four-dimensional aspect of all objects, but even they do not see them perfectly, since they perceive only the astral matter in them and not the physical, just as we perceive the physical and not the astral.

I L II 122-
123.   The passage of an object through another does not raise the question of the fourth dimension, but may be brought about by disintegration—a purely three-dimensional method.

C 138-139.   Time is not in reality the fourth dimension at all: yet to regard the problem from the point of view of time is some slight help towards understanding it. The passage of a cone through a sheet of paper would appear to an entity living on the sheet of paper as a circle altering in size : the entity would of course be incapable of perceiving all the stages of the circle as existing together as parts of one cone. Similarly for us the growth of a solid object viewed from the buddhic plane corresponds to the view of the cone as a whole, and thus throws some light on our own delusion of past, present and future, and on the faculty of prevision.

The transcendental view of time is very well treated in C. H. Hinton's story *Stella*, which is included in *Scientific Romances*, Vol. II. There are also two interesting references to this conception in *The Secret Doctrine*, Vol. I, page 69, and Vol. II, page 466.

H S II 352-
353.   It is an interesting and significant observation that geometry as we have it now is but a fragment, an exoteric preparation for the esoteric reality. Having lost the true sense of space, the first step towards that knowledge is the cognition of the fourth dimension.

We may conceive the Monad at the beginning of its *M 27-28.*
evolution to be able to move and to see in infinite *H S I 27-28.*
dimensions, one of these being cut off at each downward step, until for the physical brain-consciousness
only three are left.   Thus by involution into matter we
are cut off from the knowledge of all but a minute part
of the worlds which surround us, and even what is left
is but imperfectly seen.

With four-dimensional sight it may be observed that *I L I 219-*
the planets which are isolated in our three-dimensions *220.*
are four-dimensionally joined, these globes being in
fact the points of petals which are part of one great
flower : hence the Hindu conception of the solar system
as a lotus.

There is also, *viâ* a higher dimension, a direct con- *I L I 357-*
nection between the heart of the sun and the centre *359.*
of the earth, so that elements appear in the earth
without passing through what we call the surface.

A study of the fourth dimension seems to lead the *O S D 123-*
way direct to mysticism.   Thus C. H. Hinton con- *124.*
stantly uses the phrase " casting out the self," pointing
out that in order to appreciate a solid four-dimensionally it is necessary to regard it not from any one point
of view but from all points of view simultaneously :
i.e., the " self " or particular, isolated point of view must
be transcended and replaced by the general and unselfish view.

One is also reminded of the famous saying of St.
Paul (Ephesians iii, 17-18) : " That ye, being rooted
and grounded in love, may be able to comprehend
with all saints what is the breadth, and length, and
depth and height."

CHAPTER XIX

ASTRAL ENTITIES: HUMAN

A P 29 : 63. To enumerate and describe every kind of astral entity would be a task as formidable as that of enumerating and describing every kind of physical entity. All we can attempt here is to tabulate the chief classes and give a very brief description of each.

ASTRAL ENTITIES

Human.		Non-Human.	Artificial.
Physically Alive.	Physically Dead.		
1. Ordinary Person	1. Ordinary Person	1. Elemental Essence	1. Elementals formed unconsciously
2. Psychic	2. Shade	2. Astral Bodies of Animals	2. Elementals formed consciously
3. Adept or his pupil	3. Shell	3. Nature-Spirits	3. Human Artificials
4. Black Magician or his pupil	4. Vitalised Shell	4. Devas	
	5. Suicide and Victim of Sudden Death		
	6. Vampire and Were-wolf		
	7. Black Magician or his pupil		
	8. Pupil awaiting Reincarnation		
	9. Nirmânakaya		

In order to make the classification quite complete, *A P* 64-65. it is necessary to state that, in addition to the above, very high Adepts from other planets of the solar system, and even more august Visitors from a still greater distance, occasionally appear, but although it is possible, it is almost inconceivable, that such Beings would ever manifest themselves on a plane as low as the astral. If they wished to do so they would create a temporary body of astral matter of this planet.

Secondly, there are also two other great evolutions evolving on this planet, though it appears not to be intended that they or man should ordinarily be conscious of each other. If we did come into contact with them it would probably be physically, their connection with our astral plane being very slight. The only possibility of their appearance depends upon an extremely improbable accident in ceremonial magic, which only a few of the most advanced sorcerers know how to perform : nevertheless this has actually happened at least once.

THE HUMAN CLASS. (*a*) Physically Alive.

1. *The Ordinary Person.*—This class consists of *A P* 31-34. persons, whose physical bodies are asleep, and who float about on the astral plane, in various degrees of consciousness, as already fully described in Chapter IX on *Sleep Life.*

2. *The Psychic.*—A psychically-developed person will *A P* 31. usually be perfectly conscious when out of the physical body, but, for want of proper training, he is liable to be deceived as to what he sees. Often he may be able to range through all the astral sub-planes, but sometimes he is especially attracted to some one sub-plane, and rarely travels beyond its influences. His recollection of what he has seen may of course vary from perfect clearness to utter distortion or black oblivion. As he is assumed not to be under the guidance of a Master, he will appear always in his astral body, since he does not know how to function in his mental vehicle.

3. *The Adept and His pupils.*—This class usually *A P* 29 30.

employs, not the astral body, but the mind body, which is composed of matter of the four lower levels of the mental plane. The advantage of this vehicle is that it permits of instant passage from the mental to the astral and back, and also allows of the use at all times of the greater power and keener sense of its own plane.

The mind body not being visible to astral sight, the pupil who works in it learns to gather round himself a temporary veil of astral matter, when he wishes to become perceptible to astral entities. Such a vehicle, though an exact reproduction of the man in appearance, contains none of the matter of his own astral body, but corresponds to it in the same way as a materialisation corresponds to a physical body.

At an earlier stage of his development, the pupil may be found functioning in his astral body like any one else: but, whichever vehicle he is employing, a pupil under a competent teacher is always fully conscious and can function easily upon all the sub-planes.

A P 34-35.   4. *The Black Magician and his pupils.*—This class corresponds somewhat to that of the Adept and His pupils, except that the development has been for evil instead of good, the powers acquired being used for selfish instead of for altruistic purposes. Among its lower ranks are those who practise the rites of the Obeah and Voodoo schools, and the medicine-men of various tribes. Higher in intellect, and therefore more blameworthy, are the Tibetan black magicians.

THE HUMAN CLASS. (*b*) Physically Dead.

A P 38-49.   1. *The Ordinary Person after Death.*—This class, obviously a very large one, consists of all grades of persons, in varying conditions of consciousness, as already fully described in Chapters XII to XV on *After-Death Life*.

A P 49-52.   2. *The Shade.*—In Chapter XXIII we shall see that
D A 39-42.   when the astral life of a person is over, he dies on the
A W 136-   astral plane and leaves behind him his disintegrating
137.   astral body, precisely as when he dies physically he
1 B 85-86.   leaves behind him a decaying physical corpse.

In most cases the higher ego is unable to withdraw from his lower principles the whole of his mânasic (mental) principle: consequently, a portion of his lower mental matter remains entangled with the astral corpse. The portion of mental matter thus remaining behind consists of the grosser kinds of each sub-plane, which the astral body has succeeded in wrenching from the mental body.

This astral corpse, known as a Shade, is an entity which is not in any sense the real individual at all: nevertheless it bears his exact personal appearance, possesses his memory, and all his little idiosyncrasies. It may therefore very readily be mistaken for him, as indeed it frequently is at *séances*. It is not conscious of any act of impersonation, for as far as its intellect goes it must necessarily suppose itself to be the individual: it is in reality merely a soulless bundle of all his lowest qualities.

The length of life of a shade varies according to the amount of the lower mental matter which animates it: but as this is steadily fading out, its intellect is a diminishing quantity, though it may possess a great deal of a certain sort of animal cunning, and even quite towards the end of its career it is still able to communicate by borrowing temporary intelligence from the medium. From its very nature it is exceedingly liable to be swayed by all kinds of evil influences, and, being separated from its higher ego, it has nothing in its constitution capable of responding to good ones. It therefore lends itself readily to various minor purposes of some of the baser sort of black magicians. The mental matter it possesses gradually disintegrates and returns to the general matter of its own plane.

3. *The Shell.*—A shell is a man's astral corpse in the later stages of its disintegration, every particle of mind having left it. It is consequently without any sort of consciousness or intelligence, and drifts passively about upon the astral currents. Even yet it may be galvanised for a few moments into a ghastly burlesque of life if it happens to come within reach of a medium's

A P 52-53.
D A 39-42.
A W 130-137.
T B 86.

aura. Under such circumstances it will still exactly resemble its departed personality in appearance and may even reproduce to some extent his familiar expressions or handwriting.

It has also the quality of being still blindly responsive to such vibrations, usually of the lowest order, as were frequently set up in it during its last stage of existence as a shade.

A P 54-55.   4. *The Vitalised Shell.*—This entity is not, strictly speaking, human : nevertheless, it is classified here because its outer vesture, the passive, senseless shell, was once an appanage of humanity. Such life, intelligence, desire, and will as it may possess are those of the artificial elemental (see page 45) animating it, this elemental being itself a creation of man's evil thought.

A vitalised shell is always malevolent : it is a true tempting demon, whose evil influence is limited only by the extent of its power. Like the shade, it is frequently used in Voodoo and Obeah forms of magic. It is referred to by some writers as an " elementary."

A P 55-57.   5. *The Suicide and Victim of Sudden Death.*—These have already been described in Chapter XV on *After-Death Life.* It may be noted that this class, as well as Shades and Vitalised Shells, are what may be called minor vampires, because when they have an opportunity they prolong their existence by draining away the vitality from human beings whom they are able to influence.

A P 57-60.   6. *The Vampire and Werewolf.*—These two classes are to-day extremely rare ; examples are occasionally found.

It is just possible for a man to live such a degraded, selfish and brutal life that the whole of the lower mind becomes immeshed in his desires and finally separates from the higher ego. This is possible only where every gleam of unselfishness or spirituality has been stifled, and where there is no redeeming feature whatever.

Such a lost entity very soon after death finds himself unable to stay in the astral world, and is irresistibly drawn in full consciousness into " his own place," the mysterious eighth sphere, there slowly to disintegrate after experiences best left undescribed. If, however, he perishes by suicide or sudden death, he may under certain circumstances, especially if he knows something of black magic, hold himself back from that fate by the ghastly existence of a vampire.

Since the eighth sphere cannot claim him until after the death of the body, he preserves it in a kind of cataleptic trance by transfusing into it blood drawn from other human beings by his semi-materialised astral body, thus postponing his final destiny by the commission of wholesale murder. The most effective remedy in such a case, as popular " superstition " rightly supposes, is to cremate the body, thus depriving the entity of his *point d'appui*.

When the grave is opened, the body usually appears quite fresh and healthy, and the coffin is not unusually filled with blood. Cremation obviously makes this sort of vampirism impossible.

The Werewolf can first manifest only during a man's A P 60-61. physical life, and it invariably implies some knowledge of magical arts—sufficient at any rate to enable him to project the astral body.

When a perfectly cruel and brutal man does this, under certain circumstances the astral body may be seized upon by other astral entities and materialised, not into the human form, but into that of some wild animal, usually the wolf. In that condition it will range the surrounding country, killing other animals, and even human beings, thus satisfying not only its own craving for blood, but also that of the fiends who drive it on.

In this case, as so often with ordinary materialisations, a wound inflicted upon the astral form will be reproduced upon the human physical body by the curious phenomenon of repercussion (see page 241). But after the death of the physical body, the astral body, which will probably continue to appear in the same form, will be less vulnerable.

It will then, however, be also less dangerous, as unless it can find a suitable medium, it will be unable to materialise fully. In such manifestations, there is probably a great deal of the matter of the etheric double, and perhaps even some of liquid and gaseous constituents of the physical body, as in the case of some materialisations. In both cases this fluidic body seems able to pass to much greater distances from the physical than is otherwise possible, so far as is known, for a vehicle containing etheric matter.

The manifestations of both vampires and were-wolves are usually restricted to the immediate neighbourhood of their physical bodies.

A P 61–62.   7. *The Black Magician and his Pupil.*—This class corresponds, *mutatis mutandis*, to the pupil awaiting reincarnation, but in this case the man is defying the natural process of evolution by maintaining himself in astral life by magical arts—sometimes of the most horrible nature.

It is considered undesirable to enumerate or describe the various sub-divisions of this class, as an occult student wishes only to avoid them. All these entities, who prolong their life thus on the astral plane beyond its natural limit, do so at the expense of others and by the absorption of their life in some form or another.

A P 36–38.   8. *The Pupil awaiting Reincarnation.*—This is also *A W* 93.   at present a rare class. A pupil who has decided not to " take his devachan," *i.e.*, not to pass into the heaven-world, but to continue to work on the physical plane, is sometimes, by permission only of a very high authority, allowed to do so, a suitable reincarnation being arranged for him by his Master. Even when permission is granted, it is said that the pupil must confine himself strictly to the astral plane while the matter is being arranged, because if he touched the mental plane even for a moment he might be swept as by an irresistible current into the line of normal evolution again and so pass into the heaven-world.

Occasionally, though rarely, the pupil may be placed directly in an adult body whose previous tenant has no further use for it : but it is seldom that a suitable body is available.

Meanwhile the pupil is of course fully conscious on the astral plane and able to go on with the work given to him by his Master, even more effectively than when hampered by a physical body.

9. *The Nirmânakaya.*—It is very rarely indeed that a being so exalted as a Nirmânakaya manifests himself on the astral plane. A Nirmânakaya is one who, having won the right to untold ages of rest in bliss unspeakable, yet has chosen to remain within touch of earth, suspended as it were between this world and Nirvana, in order to generate streams of spiritual force which may be employed for the helping of evolution. If He wished to appear on the astral plane he would probably create for himself a temporary astral body from the atomic matter of the plane. This is possible because a Nirmânakaya retains His causal body, and also the permanent atoms which He has carried all through His evolution, so that at any moment He can materialise round them mental, astral or physical bodies, if He so desires.

A P 36.
H S I 480-481.
I L I 5 6.
M P 237

CHAPTER XX

ASTRAL ENTITIES: NON-HUMAN

A P 65. 1. *Elemental Essence.*—The word "elemental" has been used by various writers to mean many different kinds of entities. It is here employed to denote, during certain stages of its existence, monadic essence, which in its turn may be defined as the outpouring of spirit or divine force into matter.

A P 70-71. It is most important that the student should realise that the evolution of this elemental essence is taking place on the downward curve of the arc, as it is often called : *i.e.*, it is progressing *towards* the complete entanglement in matter which we see in the mineral kingdom, instead of *away* from it ; consequently for it progress means *descent* into matter instead of *ascent* towards higher planes.

A P 65. Before the "outpouring" arrives at the stage of individualisation at which it ensouls man, it has already passed through and ensouled six earlier phases of evolution, viz., the first elemental kingdom (on the higher mental plane), the second elemental kingdom (on the lower mental plane), the third elemental kingdom (on the astral plane), the mineral, vegetable and animal kingdoms. It has sometimes been called the animal, vegetable or mineral monad, though this is distinctly misleading, as long before it arrives at any of these kingdoms it has become not *one* but *many* monads.

A P 66-67. We are here dealing, of course, only with the astral elemental essence. This essence consists of the divine outpouring which has already veiled itself in matter down to the atomic level of the mental plane, and then plunged down directly into the astral plane, aggregating round itself a body of *atomic* astral matter

Such a combination is the elemental essence of the astral plane, belonging to the third elemental kingdom, the one immediately preceding the mineral.

In the course of its 2,401 differentiations on the astral plane, it draws to itself many and various combinations of the matter of the various sub-planes. Nevertheless these are only temporary, and it still remains essentially one kingdom. *A P 67.*

Strictly speaking, there is no such thing as *an* elemental in connection with the group we are considering. What we find is a vast store of elemental essence, wonderfully sensitive to the most fleeting human thought, responding with inconceivable delicacy, in an infinitesimal fraction of a second, to a vibration set up in it by an entirely unconscious exercise of human will or desire.

But the moment that by the influence of such thought or will it is moulded into a living force, it becomes *an* elemental, and belongs to the " artificial " class, to which we shall come in our next chapter. Even then its separate existence is usually evanescent, for as soon as its impulse has worked itself out, it sinks back into the undifferentiated mass of elemental essence from which it came.

A visitor to the astral world will inevitably be impressed by the protean forms of the ceaseless tide of elemental essence, ever swirling around him, menacing often, yet always retiring before a determined effort of the will ; and he will marvel at the enormous army of entities temporarily called out of this ocean into separate existence by the thoughts and feelings of man, whether good or evil. *C 44.*

Broadly, the elemental essence may be classified according to the kind of matter it inhabits : *i.e.*, solid, liquid, gaseous, etc. These are the " elementals " of the mediæval alchemists. They held, correctly, that an " elemental," *i.e.*, a portion of the appropriate living elemental essence, inhered in each " element," or *constituent part*, of every physical substance. *A P 68–69.*

Each of these seven main classes of elemental

essence may also be sub-divided into seven sub-divisions, making 49 sub-divisions.

A P 69-70. In addition to, and quite separate from, these *horizontal* divisions, there are also seven perfectly distinct types of elemental essence, the difference between them having nothing to do with degree of materiality, but rather with character and affinities. The student will be familiar with this classification as the " perpendicular " one, having to do with the seven " rays."

There are also seven sub-divisions in each ray-type, making 49 perpendicular sub-divisions: The total number of kinds of elemental essence is thus 49×49 or 2,401.

The perpendicular division is clearly far more permanent and fundamental than the horizontal division : for the elemental essence in the slow course of evolution passes through the various horizontal classes in succession, but remains in its own perpendicular sub-division all the way through.

A P 71. When any portion of the elemental essence remains for a few moments entirely unaffected by any outside influence—a condition hardly ever realised—it has no definite form of its own : but on the slightest disturbance it flashes into a bewildering confusion of restless, ever-changing shapes, which form, rush about, and disappear with the rapidity of the bubbles on the surface of boiling water.

These evanescent shapes, though generally those of living creatures of some sort, human or otherwise, no more express the existence of separate entities in the essence than do the equally changeful and multiform waves raised in a few moments on a previously smooth lake by a sudden squall. They seem to be mere reflections from the vast storehouse of the astral light, yet they have usually a certain appropriateness to the character of the thought-stream which calls them into existence, though nearly always with some grotesque distortion, some terrifying or unpleasant aspect about them.

When the elemental essence is thrown into shapes *A P* 72. appropriate to the stream of half-conscious, involuntary thoughts which the majority of men allow to flow idly through their brains, the intelligence which selects the appropriate shape is clearly not derived from the mind of the thinker : neither can it derive from the elemental essence itself, for this belongs to a kingdom further from individualisation even than the mineral, entirely devoid of awakened mental power.

Nevertheless, the essence possesses a marvellous adaptability which often seems to come very near to intelligence : it is no doubt this property that caused elementals to be spoken of in early books as " the semi-intelligent creatures of the astral light."

The elemental kingdoms proper do not admit of such conceptions as good or evil. Nevertheless there is a sort of bias or tendency permeating nearly all their sub-divisions which renders them hostile rather than friendly towards man. Hence the usual experience of the neophyte on the astral plane, where vast hosts of protean spectres advance threateningly upon him, but always retire or dissipate harmlessly when boldly faced. As stated by mediæval writers, this bias or tendency is *A P* 73. due entirely to man's own fault, and is caused by his *I Y* 127. indifference to, and want of sympathy with, other *T N P* 66 living beings. In the " golden age " of the past it was not so, any more than it will be so in the future when, owing to the changed attitude of man, both the elemental essence and also the animal kingdom will once again become docile and helpful to man instead of the reverse.

It is thus clear that the elemental kingdom as a whole is very much what the collective thought of humanity makes it.

There are many uses to which the forces inherent *A P* 74. in the manifold varieties of the elemental essence can be put by one trained in their management. The vast majority of magical ceremonies depend almost entirely upon its manipulation, either directly by the will of the magician, or by some more definite astral entity evoked by him for the purpose.

By its means nearly all the physical phenomena of the *séance* room are produced, and it is also the agent in most cases of stone-throwing or bell-ringing in haunted houses, these latter being the results of blundering efforts to attract attention made by some earth-bound human entity, or by the mere mischievous pranks of some of the minor nature-spirits belonging to our third class (see p. 181). But the " elemental " must never be thought of as a prime mover : it is simply a latent force, which needs an external power to set it in motion.

A P 75 : 106–107.

2. *The Astral Bodies of Animals.*—This is an extremely large class, yet it does not occupy a particularly important position on the astral plane, since its members usually stay there but a very short time. The vast majority of animals have not as yet permanently individualised, and when one of them dies, the monadic essence which has been manifesting through it flows back again into the group-soul whence it came, bearing with it such advancement or experience as has been attained during earth life. It is not, however, able to do this immediately ; the astral body of the animal rearranges itself just as in man's case, and the animal has a real existence on the astral plane, the length of which, though never great, varies according o the intelligence which it has developed. In most cases it does not seem to be more than dreamily conscious, but appears perfectly happy.

A P 76.
M V I 42–43.

The comparatively few domestic animals who have already attained individuality, and will therefore be re-born no more as animals in this world, have a much longer and more vivid life on the astral plane than their less advanced fellows.

I·L II 44.

Such an individualised animal usually remains near his earthly home and in close touch with his especial friend and protector. This period will be followed by a still happier period of what has been called dozing consciousness, which will last until in some future world the human form is assumed. During all that time he is in a condition analogous to that of a human being in the heaven-world, though at a somewhat lower level.

One interesting sub-division of this class consists of *A P* 76. the astral bodies of those anthropoid apes mentioned in *The Secret Doctrine* (Vol. I, p. 184) who are already individualised, and will be ready to take human incarnation in the next round, or perhaps some of them even sooner.

In " civilised " countries these animal astral bodies *A W* 90-91 add much to the general feeling of hostility on the astral plane, for the organised butchery of animals in slaughter-houses and for " sport " sends millions into the astral world, full of horror, terror and shrinking from man. Of late years these feelings have been much intensified by the practice of vivisection.

3. *Nature-Spirits of all Kinds.*—This class is so large *A P* 76-77. and so varied that it is possible here to give only some idea of the characteristics common to all of them.

The nature-spirits belong to an evolution quite distinct from our own : they neither have been nor ever will be members of a humanity such as ours. Their only connection with us is that we temporarily occupy the same planet. They appear to correspond to the animals of a higher evolution. They are divided into seven great classes, inhabiting the same seven states of matter permeated by the corresponding varieties of elemental essence. Thus, there are nature- *A P* 78. spirits of the earth, water, air, fire (or ether)—definite, *L A D* 41. intelligent astral entities residing and functioning in *S G O* 198. each of those media. *T B* 84.

Only the members of the air class normally reside in the astral world, but their numbers are so prodigious that they are everywhere present in it.

In mediæval literature earth-spirits are often called gnomes, water-spirits undines, air-spirits sylphs, and ether-spirits salamanders. In popular language they have been variously called fairies, pixies, elves, brownies, peris, djinns, trolls, satyrs, fauns, kobolds, imps, goblins, good people, etc.

Their forms are many and various, but most frequently human in shape and somewhat diminutive in size. Like almost all astral entities they are able to assume any appearance at will, though they undoubtedly have favourite forms which they wear when they have no special object in taking any other. Usually they are invisible to physical sight, but they have the power of making themselves visible by materialisation when they wish to be seen.

A W 85. At the head of each of these classes is a great Being, the directing and guiding intelligence of the whole department of nature which is administered and energised by the class of entities under his control. These are known by the Hindus as (1) *Indra*, lord of the Akasha, or ether : (2) *Agni*, lord of fire : (3) *Pavana*, lord of air : (4) *Varuna*, lord of water : (5) *Kshiti*, lord of earth.

C 33. The vast kingdom of nature-spirits, as stated above, is in the main an astral kingdom, though a large section of it appertains to the etheric levels of the physical plane.

A P 69.
L A D 41.
H S I 143-
145.
S G O 198-
199.
There is an immense number of sub-divisions or races among them, individuals varying in intelligence and disposition just as human beings do. Most of them avoid man altogether : his habits and emanations are distasteful to them, and the constant rush of astral currents set up by his restless, ill-regulated desires disturbs and annoys them. Occasionally, however, they will make friends with human beings and even help them.

The helpful attitude is rare : in most cases they exhibit either indifference or dislike, or take an impish delight in deceiving and tricking men. Many instances of this may be found in lonely mountainous districts and in the *séance* room.

They are greatly assisted in their tricks by the wonderful power of glamour they possess, so that their victims see and hear only what these fairies impress upon them, exactly as with mesmerised

A P 80.
H S I 146-
148.
S G O 221.
subjects. The nature-spirits, however, cannot dominate the human will, except in the case of very weak-minded people, or of those who allow terror to paralyse

their will. They can deceive the senses only, and they have been known to cast their glamour over a considerable number of people at the same time. Some of the most wonderful feats of Indian jugglers are performed by invoking their aid in producing collective hallucination.

They seem usually to have little sense of responsibility, and the will is generally less developed than in the average man. They can, therefore, readily be dominated mesmerically and employed to carry out the will of the magician. They may be utilised for many purposes, and will carry out tasks within their power faithfully and surely.

S G O 199.

They are also responsible, in certain mountainous regions, for throwing a glamour over a belated traveller, so that he sees, for example, houses and people where he knows none really exist. These delusions are frequently not merely momentary, but may be maintained for quite a considerable time, the man going through quite a long series of imaginary but striking adventures and then suddenly finding that all his brilliant surroundings have vanished, and that he is left standing in a lonely valley or on a wind-swept plain.

A P 107.
H S I 145-146.

In order to cultivate their acquaintance and friendship, a man must be free from physical emanations which they detest, such as those of meat, alcohol, tobacco, and general uncleanliness, as well as from lust, anger, envy, jealousy, avarice and depression, *i.e.*, he must be clean and unobjectionable both physically and astrally. High and pure feelings which burn steadily and without wild surgings create an atmosphere in which nature-spirits delight to bathe. Almost all nature-spirits delight also in music : they may even enter a house in order to enjoy it, bathing in the sound-waves, pulsating and swaying in harmony with them.

H S II 324-326.

To nature-spirits must also be attributed a large portion of what are called physical phenomena at spiritualistic *séances* : indeed, many a *séance* has been

A P 107-108: 75.
H S I 148-149.

given entirely by these mischievous creatures. They
are capable of answering questions, delivering pretended
messages by raps or tilts, exhibiting " spirit " lights,
the *apport* of objects from a distance, the reading of
thoughts in the mind of any person present, the
precipitation of writing or drawings, and even materialisations. They could, of course, also employ their
power of glamour to supplement their other tricks.

H S I 163-
164
They may not in the least mean to harm or deceive,
but naïvely rejoice in their success in playing their
part, and in the awe-stricken devotion and affection
lavished upon them as " dear spirits " and " angel-
helpers." They share the delight of the sitters and
feel themselves to be doing a good work in thus comforting the afflicted.

H S I 162-
163.
They will also sometimes masquerade in thought-
forms that men have made, and think it a great joke
to flourish horns, to lash a forked tail, and to breathe
out flame as they rush about. Occasionally an
impressionable child may be terrified by such appearances, but in fairness to the nature-spirit it must be
remembered that he himself is incapable of fear and
so does not understand the gravity of the result,
probably thinking that the child's terror is simulated
and a part of the game.

None of the nature-spirits possess a permanent
reincarnating individuality. It seems, therefore, that
in their evolution a much greater proportion of intelligence is developed before individualisation takes place.

The life periods of the various classes vary greatly,
some being quite short, others much longer than our
human lifetime. Their existence on the whole appears
to be simple, joyous, irresponsible, such as a party
of happy children might lead among exceptionally
favourable physical surroundings.

H S I 139.
There is no sex among nature-spirits, there is no
disease, and there is no struggle for existence. They
have keen affections and can form close and lasting
friendships. Jealousy and anger are possible to them,
but seem quickly to fade away before the overwhelming

delight in all the operations of nature which is their
most prominent characteristic.

Their bodies have no internal structure, so that *II S I* 141.
they cannot be torn asunder or injured, neither has
heat or cold any effect upon them. They appear to
be entirely free from fear.

Though tricky and mischievous, they are rarely
malicious, unless definitely provoked. As a body they
distrust man, and generally resent the appearance of *A P* 81.
a newcomer on the astral plane, so that he usually
meets them in an unpleasant or terrifying form. If,
however, he declines to be frightened by them they
soon accept him as a necessary evil and take no further
notice of him, while some may even become friendly.

One of their keenest delights is to play with and to *II S I* 163.
entertain in a hundred different ways children on the
astral plane who are what we call " dead."

Some of the less childlike and more dignified have
sometimes been reverenced as wood-gods or local
village gods. These would appreciate the flattery
paid them, and would no doubt be willing to do any
small service they could in return.

The Adept knows how to use the services of the *A P* 81.
nature-spirits, and frequently entrusts them with *H S I* 158-160.
pieces of work, but the ordinary magician can do so
only by invocation, that is, by attracting their attention
as a suppliant and making some kind of a bargain with
them, or by evocation, that is, by compelling their
obedience. Both methods are extremely undesirable :
evocation is also exceedingly dangerous, as the operator
would arouse a hostility which might prove fatal to
him. No pupil of a Master would ever be permitted
to attempt anything of the kind.

The highest type of nature-spirits consists of the *H S I* 156
sylphs or the spirits of the air, which have the astral 158.
body as their lowest vehicle. They have intelligence
equal to that of the average man. The normal method
for them to attain to individualisation is to associate
with and love the members of the next stage above
them—the astral angels.

I L I 480.   A nature-spirit who desires experience of human life may obsess a person living in the physical world.

H S I 150.   There have been times when a certain class of nature-spirits have physically materialised themselves and so entered into undesirable relationships with men and women. Perhaps from this fact have come the stories of fauns and satyrs, though these sometimes also refer to quite a different sub-human evolution.

H S I 168–169.   In passing, it is worth noting that although the kingdom of the nature-spirits is radically dissimilar from the human—being without sex, fear, or the struggle for existence—yet the eventual result of its unfoldment is in every respect equal to that attained by humanity.

A P 82–83.   4. *The Devas.*—The beings called by the Hindus devas are elsewhere spoken of as angels, sons of God, etc. They belong to an evolution distinct from that of humanity, an evolution in which they may be regarded as a kingdom next above humanity.

In Oriental literature the word deva is also used vaguely to mean any kind of non-human entity. It is used here in the restricted sense stated above.

I L II 245.   They will never be human, because most of them are already beyond that stage, but there are some of them who have been human beings in the past.

I L II 246–253.   The bodies of devas are more fluidic than those of men, the texture of the aura being, so to speak, looser; they are capable of far greater expansion and contraction, and have a certain fiery quality which is clearly distinguishable from that of an ordinary human being. The form inside the aura of a deva, which is nearly always a human form, is much less defined than in a man : the deva lives more in the circumference, more all over his aura than a man does. Devas usually appear as human beings of gigantic size. They have a colour language, which is probably not as definite as our speech, though in certain ways it may express more.

Devas are often near at hand and willing to expound and exemplify subjects along their own line to any human being sufficiently developed to appreciate them.

Though connected with the earth, the devas evolve *A P* 83. through a grand system of seven chains, the whole of our seven worlds being as one world to them. Very few of our humanity have reached the level at which it is possible to join the deva evolution. Most of the recruits of the deva kingdom have been derived from other humanities in the solar system, some lower and some higher than ours.

The object of the deva evolution is to raise their *A P* 84. foremost rank to a much higher level than that intended for humanity in the corresponding period.

The three lower great divisions of the devas are: *A P* 84-85. (1) Kâmadevas, whose lowest body is the astral: *I L II* 245. (2) Rûpadevas, whose lowest body is the lower mental: (3) Arûpadevas, whose lowest body is the higher mental or causal.

For Rûpadevas and Arûpadevas to manifest on the astral plane is at least as rare as for an astral entity to materialise on the physical plane.

Above these classes are four other great divisions, and above and beyond the deva kingdom are the great hosts of the Planetary Spirits.

We are concerned here principally with the Kâma- *A P* 85. devas. The general average among them is much higher than among us, for all that is definitely evil has long ago been eliminated from them. They differ widely in disposition, and a really spiritual man may well stand higher in evolution than some of them.

Their attention can be attracted by certain magical evocations, but the only human will which can dominate theirs is that of a certain high class of Adepts.

As a rule they seem scarcely conscious of our physical world, though occasionally one of them may render assistance, much as any of us would help an animal in trouble. They understand, however, that at the present stage, any interference with human affairs is likely to do far more harm than good.

It is desirable to mention here the four *Devarâjas*, *A P* 85-86. though they do not strictly belong to any of our classes.

These four have passed through an evolution which

is certainly not anything corresponding to our humanity.

They are spoken of as the Regents of the Earth, the Angels of the four Cardinal Points, or the Chatur Mahârâjas. They rule, not over devas, but over the four " elements " of earth, water, air and fire, with their indwelling nature-spirits and essences. Other items of information concerning them are for convenience tabulated below :—

Name	Appropriate Point of Compass	Elemental Hosts	Symbolical Colour
Dhritarâshtra	East	Gandharvas	White
Virûdhaka	South	Kumbhandas	Blue
Virûpaksha	West	Nâgas	Red
Vâishrâvana	North	Yakshas	Gold

The Secret Doctrine mentions them as " winged globes and fiery wheels," and in the Christian Bible Ezekiel attempts to describe them in very similar words. References to them are made in the symbology of every religion, and they are always held in the highest reverence as the protectors of mankind.

They are the agents of man's Karma during his earth life, and they thus play an extremely important part in human destiny. The great Karmic deities of the Kosmos, the Lipika, weigh the deeds of each personality when the final separation of the principles takes place at the end of its astral life, and give as it were the mould of an etheric double exactly suitable to its Karma for the man's next birth. But it is the Devarâjas, who, having command of the " elements " of which that etheric double must be composed, arrange their proportion so as to fulfil accurately the intention of the Lipika.

A P 87.

All through life they constantly counterbalance the changes introduced into man's condition by his own free will and that of those around him, so that Karma may be accurately and justly worked out. A learned dissertation on these beings will be found in *The Secret Doctrine*, Vol. I, pp. 122–126. They are able to take human material forms at will, and cases are recorded where they have done so.

All the higher nature-spirits and hosts of artificial elementals act as their agents in their stupendous work : but all the threads are in their own hands and they assume the whole responsibility. They seldom manifest on the astral plane, but when they do they are certainly the most remarkable of its non-human inhabitants.

There must really be seven, not four, Devarâjas, but outside the circle of Initiation little is known and less may be said concerning the higher three.

CHAPTER XXI

ASTRAL ENTITIES: ARTIFICIAL

A P 87. THE artificial entities form the largest class and are also much the most important to man. They consist of an enormous inchoate mass of semi-intelligent entities, differing among themselves as human thoughts differ, and practically incapable of detailed classification and arrangement. Being entirely man's own creation, they are related to him by close karmic bonds, and their action upon him is direct and incessant.

A P 88. 1. *Elementals formed Unconsciously.*—The way in which these desire- and thought-forms are called into being has already been described in Chapter VII. The desire and thought of a man seize upon the plastic elemental essence and mould it instantly into a living being of appropriate form. The form is in no way under the control of its creator, but lives out a life of its own, the length of which is proportional to the intensity of the thought which created it, and which may be anything from a few minutes to many days. For further particulars the student is referred back to Chapter VII.

A P 95 96. 2. *Elementals formed Consciously.*—It is clear that elementals formed. consciously, by those who are acting deliberately and know precisely what they are doing, may be enormously more powerful than those formed unconsciously. Occultists of both white and dark schools frequently use artificial elementals in their work, and few tasks are beyond the powers of such creatures when scientifically prepared and directed with knowledge and skill. One who knows how to do so can maintain a connection with his elemental and guide it, so that it will act practically as though endowed with the full intelligence of its master.

It is unnecessary to repeat here descriptions of this class of elemental, which have already been given in Chapter VII.

3. *Human Artificials.*—This is a very peculiar class, A P 98. containing but few individuals, but possessing an importance quite out of proportion to its numbers, owing to its intimate connection with the spiritualistic movement.

In order to explain its genesis it is necessary to go A P 99. back to ancient Atlantis. Among the lodges for occult study, preliminary to Initiation, formed by Adepts of the Good Law, there is one which still observes the same old-world ritual, and teaches the same Atlantean tongue as a sacred and hidden language, as in the days of Atlantis.

The teachers in this lodge do not stand at the Adept A P 100. level, and the lodge is not directly a part of the Brotherhood of the Himâlayas, though there are some of the Himâlayan Adepts who were connected with it in former incarnations.

About the middle of the nineteenth century, the chiefs ·of this lodge, in despair at the rampant materialism of Europe and America, determined to combat it by novel methods, and to offer opportunities by which any reasonable man could acquire proof of a life apart from the physical body.

The movement thus set on foot grew into the vast fabric of modern spiritualism, numbering its adherents by millions. Whatever other results may have followed, it is unquestionable that by means of spiritualism vast numbers of people have acquired a belief in at any rate some kind of future life. This A P 101. is a magnificent achievement, though some think that it has been attained at too great a cost.

The method adopted was to take some ordinary person after death, arouse him thoroughly upon the astral plane, instruct him to a certain extent in the powers and possibilities belonging to it, and then put him in charge of a spiritualistic circle. He in his turn " developed " other departed personalities along the same lines, they all acted upon those who sat at their *séances*, and "developed" them as mediums. The leaders of the movement no doubt occasionally manifested themselves in astral form at the circles, but in most cases they merely directed and guided as they considered necessary. There is little doubt that the movement increased so much that it soon got quite beyond their control; for many of the later developments, therefore, they can be held only indirectly responsible.

The intensification of the astral life of the "controls" who were put in charge of circles distinctly delayed their natural progress, and although it was thought that full compensation for such loss would result from the good karma of leading others to truth, it was soon found that it was impossible to make use of a "spirit-guide" for any length of time without doing him serious and permanent injury.

In some cases such "guides" were withdrawn, and others substituted for them. In others, however, it was considered undesirable to make such a change, and then a remarkable expedient was adopted which gave rise to the curious class of creatures we have called "human artificials."

A P 102. The higher principles of the original "guide" were allowed to pass on to their long-delayed evolution into the heaven-world, but the shade (see p. 170) which he left behind was taken possession of, sustained, and operated upon so that it might appear to the circle practically just as before.

At first this seems to have been done by members of the lodge, but eventually it was decided that the departed person who would have been appointed to succeed the late "spirit-guide" should still do so, but should take possession of the latter's shade or shell, and, in fact, simply wear his appearance. This is what is termed a "human artificial" entity.

In some cases more than one change seems to have been made without arousing suspicion, but, on the other hand, some investigators of spiritualism have observed that after a considerable time differences suddenly appeared in the manner and disposition of a " spirit."

None of the members of the Himâlayan Brotherhood have ever undertaken the formation of an artificial entity of this sort, though they could not interfere with any one who thought it right to take such a course.

Apart from the deception involved, a weak point in the arrangement is that others besides the original lodge may adopt the plan, and there is nothing to *A P* 103. prevent black magicians from supplying communicating spirits, as, indeed, they have been known to do.

CHAPTER XXII

SPIRITUALISM

THE term "spiritualism" is used nowadays to denote communication of many different kinds with the astral world by means of a medium.

The origin and history of the spiritualistic movement have already been described in Chapter XXI.

The etheric mechanism which makes spiritualistic phenomena possible has been fully described in *The Etheric Double*, to which work the student is referred.

There remains now for us to consider the value, if any, of this method of communicating with the unseen world, and the nature of the sources from which the communications may come.

I L I 209.   In the early days of the Theosophical Society, H. P. Blavatsky wrote with considerable vehemence on the subject of spiritualism, and laid great stress on the uncertainty of the whole thing, and the preponderance of personations over real appearances.

A E P.   There seems little doubt that these views have largely coloured and determined the unfavourable attitude which most members of the Theosophical Society take towards spiritualism as a whole.

I L I 209-210.   Bishop Leadbeater, on the other hand, affirms that his own personal experience has been more favourable. He spent some years experimenting with spiritualism, and believes that he has himself repeatedly seen practically all the phenomena which may be read about in the literature of the subject.

In his experience, he found that a distinct majority of the apparitions were genuine. The messages they give are often uninteresting, and their religious teaching he describes as being usually "Christianity and water": nevertheless, as far as

it goes, it is liberal, and in advance of the bigoted
orthodox position.

Bishop Leadbeater points out that Spiritualists and
Theosophists have much important ground in common,
e.g., (1) that life after death is an actual, vivid, ever-
present certainty ; and (2) that eternal progress and
ultimate happiness, for every one, good and bad alike,
is also a certainty. These two items are of such
tremendous and paramount importance, constituting
as they do so enormous an advance from the ordinary
orthodox position, that it seems somewhat regrettable
that Spiritualists and Theosophists cannot join hands
on these broad issues and agree, for the present, to
differ upon minor points, until at least the world at
large is converted to that much of the truth. In this
work there is ample room for the two bodies of seekers
after truth.

I L I 208–
209.
O S D 399–
401.

Those who wish to see phenomena, and those who
cannot believe anything without ocular demonstration,
will naturally gravitate towards spiritualism. On the
other hand, those who want more philosophy than
spiritualism usually provides, will naturally turn to
Theosophy. Both movements thus cater for the
liberal and open-minded, but for quite different types
of them. Meanwhile, harmony and agreement between
the two movements seems desirable, in view of the
great ends at stake.

It must be said to the credit of spiritualism that it
has achieved its purpose to the extent of converting
vast numbers of people from a belief in nothing in
particular to a firm faith in at any rate some kind of
future life. This, as we said in the last chapter, is
undoubtedly a magnificent result, though there are
those who think that it has been attained at too great
a cost.

A P 100–
101.

There is undoubtedly danger in spiritualism for
emotional, nervous and easily influenced natures, and
it is advisable not to carry the investigations too far,
for reasons which by now must be apparent to the
student. But there is no readier way of breaking

S P 77.

down the unbelief in anything outside the physical plane than trying a few experiments, and it is perhaps worth while to run some risk in order to effect this.

L A D 3-4.
O S D 25.
Bishop Leadbeater fearlessly asserts that, in spite of the fraud and deception which undoubtedly have occurred in some instances, there are great truths behind spiritualism which may be discovered by anyone willing to devote the necessary time and patience to their investigation. There is, of course, a vast and growing literature on the subject.

I H 83-84.
A P 48.
O S D 408, 409.
Furthermore, good work, similar to that done by Invisible Helpers (see Chapter XXVIII), has sometimes been done through the agency of a medium, or of some one present at a *séance*. Thus, though spiritualism has too often detained souls, who but for it would have attained speedy liberation, yet it has also furnished the means of escape to others, and thus opened up the path of advancement for them. There have been instances in which the deceased person has been able to appear, without the assistance of a medium, to his relatives and friends, and explain his wishes to them. But such cases are rare, and in most cases earth-bound souls can relieve themselves of their anxieties only by means of the services of a medium, or of a conscious " Invisible Helper."

L A D 50.
It is thus an error to look only at the dark side of spiritualism : it must not be forgotten that it has done an enormous amount of good in this kind of work, by giving to the dead an opportunity to arrange their affairs after a sudden and unexpected departure.

I L I 210-211.
The student of these pages should not be surprised that amongst spiritualists are some who know nothing, for example, of reincarnation, though there are schools of spiritualism which do teach it. We have already seen that when a man dies, he usually resorts to the company of those whom he has known on earth : he moves among exactly the same kind of people as during physical life. Hence such a man is little more likely

to know or recognise the fact of reincarnation after death than before it. Most men are shut in from all new ideas by a host of prejudices: they carry those prejudices into the astral world with them, and are no more amenable to reason and common-sense there than in the physical world.

Of course a man who is really open-minded can learn a great deal on the astral plane : he may speedily acquaint himself with the whole of the Theosophical teaching, and there are dead men who do this. Hence it often happens that portions of that teaching are found among spirit-communications.

It must also be borne in mind that there is a higher *I L I* 211– spiritualism of which the public knows nothing, and *212.* which never publishes any account of its results. The *H S I* 355– best circles of all are strictly private, restricted to a *357.* small number of sitters. In such circles the same people meet over and over again, and no outsider is ever admitted to make any change in the magnetism. The conditions set up are thus singularly perfect, and the results obtained are often of the most surprising character. Often the so-called dead are just as much part of the daily life of the family as the living. The hidden side of such *séances* is magnificent : the thought-forms surrounding them are good, and calculated to raise the mental and spiritual level of the district.

At public *séances* an altogether lower class of dead people appear, because of the promiscuous jumble of magnetism.

One of the most serious objections to the general *A P* 46–47. practice of spiritualism, is that in the ordinary man after death the consciousness is steadily rising from the lower part of the nature towards the higher : the ego, as we have repeatedly said, is steadily withdrawing himself away from the lower worlds : obviously, therefore, it cannot be helpful to his evolution that the lower part should be re-awakened from the natural and desirable unconsciousness into which it is passing, and dragged back into touch with earth in order to communicate through a medium.

D A 33.   It is thus a cruel kindness to draw back to the earth-sphere one whose lower manas still yearns after kâmic gratifications, because it delays his forward evolution and interrupts what should be an orderly progression. The period in kâmaloka is thus lengthened, the astral body is fed, and its hold on the ego is maintained ; thus the freedom of the soul is deferred, " the immortal Swallow being still held by the birdlime of earth."

D A 36.   Especially in cases of suicide or sudden death is it most undesirable to re-awaken Trishnâ, or the desire for sentient existence.

A P 47.   The peculiar danger of this will appear when it is recollected that since the ego is withdrawing into himself, he becomes less and less able to influence or guide the lower portion of his consciousness, which, nevertheless, until the separation is complete, has the power to generate karma, and under the circumstances is far more likely to add evil than good to its record.

D A 34.
O S D 402.
A W 122–
123.   Furthermore, people who have led an evil life and are filled with yearnings for the earth life they have left, and for the animal delights they can no longer directly taste, tend to gather round mediums or sensitives, endeavouring to utilise them for their own gratification. These are among the more dangerous of the forces so rashly confronted in their ignorance by the thoughtless and the curious.

H S I 358.
O S D 402–
403.
S G O 232.   A desperate astral entity may seize upon a sensitive sitter and obsess him, or he may even follow him home and seize upon his wife or daughter. There have been many such cases, and usually it is almost impossible to get rid of such an obsessing entity.

D A 31.   We have already seen that passionate sorrow and desires of friends on earth also tend to draw departed entities down to the earth-sphere again, thus often causing acute suffering to the deceased as well as interfering with the normal course of evolution.

Turning now to the kinds of entities who may communicate through a medium, we may classify them as follows :—

Deceased human beings on the astral plane.
Deceased human beings in devachan.
Shades.
Shells.
Vitalised shells.
Nature-Spirits.
The medium's ego.
Adepts.
Nirmânakâyas.

As most of these have already been described in Chapter XIV on *Astral Entities*, little more need be said about them here.

It is theoretically possible for any deceased person *D A* 66. on the astral plane to communicate through a medium, *A P* 108. though this is far easier from the lower levels, becoming more and more difficult as the entity rises to the higher-sub-planes. Hence, other things being equal, it is natural to expect that a majority of the communications received at *séances* will be from the lower levels and therefore from relatively undeveloped entities.

The student will recollect (see page 138) that suicides, *D A* 36–37. and other victims of sudden death, including executed criminals, having been cut off in the full flush of physical life, are especially likely to be drawn to a medium, in the hope of satisfying their Trishnâ, or thirst for life.

Consequently, the medium is the cause of developing in them a new set of *Skandhas* (see page 208), a new body with far worse tendencies and passions than the one they lost. This would be productive of untold evils for the ego, and cause him to be re-born into a far worse existence than before.

Communication with an entity in devachan, *i.e.*, in the heaven-world, needs a little further explanation. Where a sensitive, or medium, is of a pure and lofty nature, his freed ego may rise to the devachanic plane and there contact the entity in devachan. The impression is often given that the entity from devachan has come to the medium, but the truth is the reverse of this : it is the ego of the medium who has risen to the level of the entity in devachan.

D A 69–70   Owing to the peculiar conditions of the consciousness of entities in devachan (into which we cannot enter in this book), messages thus obtained cannot altogether be relied upon : at best the medium or sensitive can know, see and feel only what the particular entity in devachan knows, sees and feels.   Hence, if generalisations are indulged in, there is much possibility of error, since each entity in devachan lives in his own particular department of the heaven-world.

In addition to this source of error,whilstthethoughts, knowledge and sentiments of the devachanic entity form the substance, it is likely that the medium's own personality and pre-existing ideas will govern the form of the communication.

A P 49–52.   A *shade* (see page 170) may frequently appear and
D A 39–40.   communicate at *séances;* bearing the exact appearance of the departed entity, possessing his memory, idiosyncrasies, etc., it is often mistaken for the entity himself, though it is not itself conscious of any impersonation.   It is in reality a " soulless bundle of the lowest qualities " of the entity.

A P 52–53.   A *shell* (see page 171) also exactly resembles the
D A 39–40.   departed entity, though it is nothing more than the astral corpse of the entity, every particle of mind having left it.   By coming within reach of a medium's aura it may be galvanised for a few moments into a burlesque of the real entity.

S P 43.   Such " spooks " are conscienceless, devoid of good impulses, tending towards disintegration, and consequently can work for evil only, whether we regard them as prolonging their vitality by vampirising at *séances,* or polluting the medium and sitters with astral connections of an altogether undesirable kind.

A P 54.   A *vitalised shell* (see page 172) may also communicate through a medium.   As we have seen, it consists of an astral corpse animated by an artificial elemental, and is always malevolent.   Obviously it constitutes a source of great danger at spiritualistic *séances.*

Suicides, shades and vitalised shells, being minor *A P 57.*
vampires, drain away vitality from human beings whom
they can influence.   Hence both medium and sitters
are often weak and exhausted after a physical *séance.*
A student of occultism is taught how to guard himself
from their attempts, but without that knowledge it is
difficult for one who puts himself in their way to avoid
being laid more or less under contribution by them.

It is the use of shades and shells at *séances* which *D A 40.*
brands so many of spiritualistic communications with
intellectual sterility.   Their apparent intellectuality
will give out only reproductions : the mark of non-
originality will be present, there being no sign of new
and independent thought.

Nature-Spirits.   The part which these creatures so
often play at *séances* has already been described on
pages 182 *et sqq.*

Many of the phenomena of the *séance*-room are *D A 41.*
clearly more rationally accounted for as the tricky
vagaries of sub-human forces, than as the act of
" spirits " who, while in the body, were certainly
incapable of such inanities.

The medium's ego.   If the medium be pure and *D A 73.*
earnest and striving after the light, such upward
striving is met by a down-reaching of the higher
nature, light from the higher streaming down and
illuminating the lower consciousness.   Then the lower
mind is, for the time, united with its parent the higher
mind, and transmits as much of the knowledge of the
higher mind as it is able to retain.   Thus some communications through a medium may come from the
medium's own higher ego.

The class of entity drawn to *séances* depends of *S P 20.*
course very much on the type of medium.   Mediums
of low type inevitably attract eminently undesirable
visitors, whose fading vitality is reinforced in the
séance-room.   Nor is this all : if at such *séances* there
be present a man or woman of correspondingly low
development, the spook will be attracted to that
person and may attach itself to him or her, thus setting

up currents between the astral body of the living person and the dying astral body of the dead person, and generating results of a deplorable kind.

D A 73.   An *Adept* or *Master* often communicates with His disciples, without using the ordinary methods of communication. If a medium were a pupil of a Master, it is possible that a message from the Master might " come through," and be mistaken for a message from a more ordinary " spirit."

D A 72.   A *Nirmânakâya* is a perfected man, who has cast aside his physical body but retains his other lower principles, remaining in touch with the earth for the sake of helping the evolution of mankind. These great entities can and do on rare occasions communicate through a medium, but only through one of a very pure and lofty nature. (See also page 175.)

I L I 61–65.   Unless a man has had very wide experience with
O S D 325–   mediumship, he would find it difficult to believe how
326.   many quite ordinary people on the astral plane are burning with the desire to pose as great world-teachers. Usually they are honest in their intentions, and really think they have teaching to give which will save the world. Having realised the worthlessness of merely worldly objects, they feel, quite rightly, that if they could impress upon mankind their own ideas the whole world would immediately become a very different place.

Having flattered the medium into believing that he or she is the sole channel for some exclusive and transcendent teaching, and having modestly disclaimed any special greatness for himself, one of these communicating entities is often imagined by the sitters to be at least an archangel, or even some more direct manifestation of the Deity. Unfortunately, however, it is usually forgotten by such an entity that when he was alive in the physical world, other people were making similar communications through various mediums, and that he paid not the slightest attention to them. He does not realise that others also, still immersed in the affairs of the world, will pay no more attention to him and will decline to be moved by his communications.

Sometimes such entities will assume distinguished names, such as George Washington, Julius Cæsar, or the Archangel Michael, from the questionably pardonable motive that the teachings they give will so be more likely to be accepted than if they emanate from plain John Smith or Thomas Brown.

Sometimes also, such entities, seeing the minds of others full of reverence for the Masters, will personate these very Masters in order to command more ready acceptance for the ideas they wish to promulgate.

Also there are some who attempt to injure the work of the Master by assuming His form and so influencing His pupil. Although they might be able to produce an almost perfect physical appearance, it is quite impossible for them to imitate a Master's causal body, and consequently one with causal sight could not possibly be deceived by such an impersonation.

In a few instances the members of the lodge of *A P* 109. occultists who originated the spiritualistic movement (see page 191) have themselves given valuable teachings on deeply interesting subjects, through a medium. But this has invariably been at strictly private family *séances*, never at public performances for which money has been paid.

The Voice of the Silence wisely enjoins: " Seek not *I L I* 65. thy Guru in these mâyâvic regions." No teaching from a self-appointed preceptor on the astral plane should be blindly accepted: all communications and advice which comes thence should be received precisely as one would receive similar advice on the physical plane. Teaching should be taken for what it is worth, after examination by conscience and intellect.

A man is no more infallible because he happens to *M* 101. be dead than when he was physically alive. A man may spend many years on the astral plane and yet know no more than when he left the physical world. Accordingly we should attach no more importance to communications from the astral world, or from any higher plane, than we should to a suggestion made on the physical plane.

A P 108-109.
O S D 25:
404 : 406.
A manifesting " spirit " is often exactly what it professes to be : but often also it is nothing of the kind. For the ordinary sitter there is no means of distinguishing the true from the false, since the resources of the astral plane can be used to delude persons on the physical plane to such an extent that no reliance can be placed even on what seems the most convincing proof. It is not for a moment denied that important communications have been made at *séances* by genuine entities : but it is claimed that it is practically impossible for an ordinary sitter to be quite certain that he is not being deceived in half a dozen different ways.

D A 73-74.
From. the above it will be seen how varied may be the sources from which communications from the astral world may be received. As said by H. P. Blavatsky : " The variety of the causes of phenomena is great, and we need to be an Adept, and actually look into and examine what transpires, in order to be able to explain in each case what really underlies it."

To complete the statement, it may be said that what the average person can do on the astral plane after death he can do in physical life : communications may be as readily obtained by writing, in trance, or by utilising the developed and trained powers of the astral body, from embodied as from disembodied persons. It would therefore seem to be more prudent to develop within oneself the powers of one's own soul, instead of ignorantly plunging into dangerous experiments. In this manner knowledge may be safely accumulated and evolution accelerated. Man must learn that death has no real power over him : the key of the prison-house of the body is in his own hands, and he may learn how to use it if he wills.

A E P.
From a careful weighing of all the evidence available, both for and against spiritualism, it would seem that, if employed with care and discretion, it may be justifiable, purely in order to break down

materialism. Once this purpose is achieved, its use seems too beset with dangers, both to the living and the dead, to make it advisable, as a general rule, though in exceptional cases it may be practised with safety and benefit.

CHAPTER XXIII

ASTRAL DEATH

WE have now reached the end of the life-history of the astral body, and little remains to be said regarding its death and final dissolution.

The steady withdrawal of the ego, as we have seen, causes, in a time which varies within very wide limits, the particles of the astral body gradually to cease to function, this process taking place, in most cases, in layers arranged according to degree of density, the densest being on the outside.

I L II 24–25. The astral body thus slowly wears away and disintegrates as the consciousness is gradually withdrawn from it by the half-unconscious effort of the ego, and thus the man by degrees gets rid of whatever holds him back from the heaven-world.

D A 30.
S P 41. During the stay on the astral plane, in kâmaloka, the mind, woven with the passions, emotions and desires, has purified them, and assimilated their pure part, and has absorbed into itself all that is fit for the higher ego, so that the remaining portion of Kâma is a mere residue, from which the ego, the Immortal Triad of Âtmâ-Buddhi-Manas (as it is often called), can readily free itself. Slowly the Triad or ego draws into itself the memories of the earth-life just ended, its loves, hopes, aspirations, etc., and prepares to pass out of kâmaloka into the blissful state of devachan, the " abode of the gods," the " heaven-world."

Into the history of the man when he has reached the heaven-world we cannot enter here, as it lies beyond the scope of this treatise : it is hoped, however, to deal with it in the third volume of this series.

S P 41. For the moment, however, it may be said, in brief, that the period spent in devachan is the time for the

assimilation of life experiences, the regaining of
equilibrium, ere a new descent into incarnation is
undertaken.   It is thus the day that succeeds the
night of earth-life, the subjective as contrasted with
the objective period of manifestation.

When the man passes out of kâmaloka into devachan,   *M B* 59: 78.
he cannot carry thither with him thought-forms of an
evil type ; astral matter cannot exist on the devachanic
level, and devachanic matter cannot answer to the
coarse vibrations of evil passions and desires.   Consequently all that the man can carry with him when
he finally shakes off the remnants of his astral body
will be the latent germs or tendencies which, when
they can find nutriment or outlet, manifest as evil
desires and passions in the astral world.   But these he
does take with him, and they lie latent throughout his
devachanic life, in the astral permanent atom.   At   *S C* 105: 93:
the end of the kâmalokic life, the golden life-web (see   107–108.
A Study in Consciousness, pages 91–93) withdraws
from the astral body, leaving it to disintegrate, and
enwraps the astral permanent atom, which then retreats
within the causal body.

The final struggle with the desire-elemental (see   *I L I* 407–
pp. 6 & 108) takes place at the conclusion of the astral   408.
life, for the ego is then endeavouring to draw back into
himself all that he put down into incarnation at the
beginning of the life which has just ended.   When he
attempts to do this he is met with determined opposition from the desire-elemental, which he himself has
created and fed.

In the case of all ordinary people, some of their
mental matter has become so entangled with their
astral matter that it is impossible for it to be entirely
freed.   The result of the struggle is therefore that some
portion of the mental matter, and even of causal
(higher mental) matter is retained in the astral body
after the ego has completely broken away from it.
If, on the other hand, a man has during life completely
conquered his lower desires and succeeded in absolutely
freeing the lower mind from desire, there is practically

no struggle, and the ego is able to withdraw not only all that he " invested " in that particular incarnation, but also all the " interest," *i.e.*, the experiences, faculties, etc., that have been acquired. There are also extreme cases where the ego loses both the " capital " invested and the " interest," these being known as " lost-souls " or elementaries (see page 145).

The full treatment of the method in which the ego puts a portion of himself down into incarnation and then endeavours to withdraw it again, must clearly be reserved for the third and fourth volumes of this series, which will deal with the mental and causal bodies.

D A 31.
M B 107.

The exit from the astral body and the astral plane is thus a second death, the man leaving behind him an astral corpse which, in its turn, disintegrates, its materials being restored to the astral world, just as the materials of the physical body are returned to the physical world.

This astral corpse, and the various possibilities which may happen to it, have already been dealt with in Chapter XIX on *Astral Entities*, under the headings Shades (page 170), Shells (page 171), Vitalised Shells (page 172), etc.

CHAPTER XXIV

RE-BIRTH

AFTER the causes that carried the ego into devachan are exhausted, the experiences gathered having been wholly assimilated, the ego begins to feel again the thirst for sentient material life, that can be gratified only on the physical plane. That thirst is known by the Hindus as *trishnâ*. D A 61. M V I 68. O S D 90.

It may be considered, first, as a desire to express himself: and second, as a desire to receive those impressions from without which alone enable him to feel himself alive. For this is the law of evolution. O S D 90.

Trishnâ appears to operate through kâma, which, for the individual as for the Cosmos, is the primary cause of reincarnation. R 36–38 : 41.

During the devachanic rest the ego has been free from all pain and sorrow, but the evil he did in his past life has been in a state, not of death, but of suspended animation. The seeds of past evil tendencies commence to germinate as soon as the new personality begins to form itself for the new incarnation. The ego has to take up the burden of the past, the germs or seeds coming over as the harvest of the past life being called by the Buddhists *skandhas*. D A 62–63. K T 95.

Kâma, with its army of skandhas, thus waits at the threshold of devachan, whence the ego re-emerges to assume a new incarnation. The skandhas consist of material qualities, sensations, abstract ideas, tendencies of mind, mental powers.

The process is brought about by the ego turning his attention, first to the mental unit, which immediately resumes its activity, and then to the astral permanent atom, into which he puts his will. I L II 436–437.

The tendencies, which we have seen are in a condition M B 59–60 : 78 : 109.

O S D 92–93.
A W 208 :
266–267.
T N P 37–39.

of suspended animation, are thrown outwards by the ego as he returns to re-birth, and draw around themselves, first, matter of the mental plane, and also elemental essence of the second great kingdom, these expressing exactly the mental development which the man had gained at the end of his last heaven-life. He thus begins in this respect exactly where he left off.

Next, he draws round himself matter from the astral world, and elemental essence of the third kingdom, thus obtaining the materials out of which his new astral body will be built, and causing to re-appear the appetites, emotions, and passions which he brought over from his past lives.

D 11.
A P 22.

The astral matter is gathered by the ego descending to re-birth, not of course consciously, but automatically.

I L I 404.
O'S D 93.
H S II 283.

This material is, moreover, an exact reproduction of the matter in the man's astral body at the end of his last astral life. The man thus resumes his life in each world just where he left it last time.

M B 59–60 :
109.
K 44.

The student will recognise in the above a part of the workings of karmic law, into which we need not enter in this present volume. Each incarnation is inevitably, automatically, and justly linked with the preceding lives, so that the whole series forms a continuous, unbroken chain.

I L I 390–391.

The astral matter thus drawn round the man is not yet formed into a definite astral body. It takes, in the first place, the shape of that ovoid which is the nearest expression that we can realise of the true shape of the causal body. As soon as the baby physical body is formed, the physical matter exerts a violent attraction for the astral matter, which previously was fairly evenly distributed over the ovoid, and so concentrates the great bulk of it within the periphery of the physical body.

As the physical body grows, the astral matter follows its every change, 99 per cent. of it being concentrated within the periphery of the physical body, and only about 1 per cent. filling the rest of the ovoid and constituting the aura, as we saw in an earlier chapter (see page 7).

The process of gathering matter round the astral *K* 44-45. nucleus sometimes takes place rapidly, and sometimes causes long delay; when it is completed the ego stands in the karmic vesture he has prepared for himself, ready to receive from the agents of the Lords of Karma the etheric double, into which, as into a mould, the new physical body will be built (see *The Etheric Double*, page 67).

The man's qualities are thus not at first in action: *H S II* 283- they are simply the germs of qualities, which have 284. secured for themselves a possible field of manifestation *I L II* 438-439. in the matter of the new bodies. Whether they *O S D* 94-95. develop in this life into the same tendencies as in the last one will depend largely upon the encouragement, or otherwise, given to them by the surroundings of the child during his early years. Any one of them, good or bad, may be readily stimulated into activity by encouragement, or, on the other hand, may be starved out for lack of that encouragement. If stimulated, it becomes a more powerful factor in the man's life this time than it was in his previous existence; if starved out, it remains merely as an unfructified germ, which presently atrophies and dies out, and does not make its appearance in the succeeding incarnation at all.

The child cannot thus be said to have as yet a definite mind-body or a definite astral body, but he has around and within him the matter out of which these are to be builded.

Thus, for example, suppose a man was a drunkard *O S D* 15-16. in his past life: in kâmaloka he would have burnt out the desire for drink and be definitely freed from it. But although the desire itself is dead, there still remains the same weakness of character which made it possible for him to be subjugated by it. In his next life his astral body will contain matter capable of giving expression to the same desire; but he is in no way bound to employ such matter in the same way as before. In the hands of careful and capable parents, in fact, being trained to regard such desires as evil, he would gain control over them, repress them as they appear, and thus the astral matter will remain unvivified and become atrophied from want of use. It will be recollected that the matter of the astral body is slowly but constantly wearing away and being replaced, precisely as is that of the physical body, and as atrophied matter disappears it will be replaced by matter of a more refined order. Thus are vices finally conquered and made virtually impossible for the future, the opposite virtue of self-control having been established.

During the first few years of the man's life the ego has but little hold over his vehicles, and he therefore looks to his parents to help him to obtain a firmer grasp and to provide him with suitable conditions.

H S II 285–286. It is impossible to exaggerate the plasticity of these unformed vehicles. Much as can be done with the physical body in its early years, as in the case of children trained as acrobats, for example, far more can be done with the astral and mental vehicles. They thrill in response to every vibration which they encounter, and are eagerly receptive of all influences, good or evil, emanating from those around them. Moreover, though in early youth they are so susceptible and so easily moulded, they soon set and stiffen and acquire habits which, once firmly established, can be altered only with great difficulty. Thus to a far larger extent than is realised by even the fondest parents, the child's future is under their control.

S G O 378. It is only the clairvoyant who knows how enormously and how rapidly child-characters would improve if only adult characters were better.

M P 85–86. A very striking instance is recorded where the brutality of a teacher irreparably injured the bodies of a child so as to make it impossible for the child in this life to make the full progress that was hoped for it.

M P 88. So vitally important is the early environment of a child that the life in which Adeptship is attained must have absolutely perfect surroundings in childhood.

I L II 437. In the case of lower-class monads with unusually strong astral bodies, who reincarnate after a very short interval, it sometimes happens that the shade or shell left over from the last astral life still persists, and in that case it is likely to be attracted to the new personality. When that happens it brings with it strongly the old habits and modes of thought, and sometimes even the actual memory of that past life.

In the case of a man who has led such an evil life *I Y* 129-130. that his astral and mental bodies are torn away from the ego after death, the ego, having no bodies in which to live in the astral and mental worlds, must quickly form new ones. When the new astral and mental bodies are formed, the affinity between them and the old ones, not yet disintegrated, asserts itself, and the old mental and astral bodies become the most terrible form of what is known as the " dweller on the threshold."

In the extreme case of a man, returning to re-birth, *I L II* 30-33. who by vicious appetite or otherwise, has formed a very strong link with any type of animal, he may be linked by magnetic affinity to the astral body of the animal whose qualities he has encouraged, and be chained as a prisoner to the animal's physical body. Thus chained he cannot go onward to re-birth : he is conscious in the astral world, has his human faculties, but cannot control the brute body with which he is connected, nor express himself through that body on the physical plane. The animal organism is thus a jailor, rather than a vehicle. The animal soul is not ejected, but remains as the proper tenant and controller of its own body.

Such an imprisonment is not reincarnation, though it is easy to see that cases of this nature explain at least partially the belief often found in Oriental countries that man may under certain circumstances reincarnate in an animal body.

In cases where the ego is not degraded enough for absolute imprisonment, but in which the astral body is strongly animalised, it may pass on normally to human re-birth, but the animal characteristics will be largely reproduced in the physical body—as witness the people who in appearance are sometimes pig-faced, dog-faced, etc. The suffering entailed on the conscious human entity, thus temporarily cut off from progress and from self-expression, is very great, though, of course, reformatory in its action. It is somewhat similar to that endured by other egos, who are linked to human bodies with unhealthy brains, *i.e.*, idiots, lunatics, etc., though idiocy and lunacy are the results of other vices.

CHAPTER XXV

THE MASTERY OF EMOTION

THIS book will have been compiled in vain if the student has not become impressed with the necessity, first, of controlling the astral body: secondly, of gradually training it into a vehicle of consciousness, completely subservient to the will of the real man, the ego: and thirdly, in due time, of steadily developing and perfecting its various powers.

The average worldly person knows little and cares less about such matters: but to the student of occultism it is clearly of fundamental importance that he should attain full mastery over all his vehicles—physical, astral and mental. And although for purposes of analysis and study it is necessary to separate these three bodies and study them individually, yet, in practical life, it will be found that to a great extent the training of all of them can be carried on simultaneously, any power gained in one helping to some extent in the training of the other two.

We have already seen (page 64) the desirability of purifying the physical body, by means of food, drink, hygiene, etc., in order to make slightly less difficult the control of the astral body. The same principle applies with even greater force to the mental body, for it is in the last analysis only by the use of mind and will that the desires, emotions and passions of the astral body can be brought into perfect subjection.

For many temperaments, at least, a careful study of the psychology of emotion is of very great assistance, as it is clearly much easier to bring under control a force the genesis and nature of which is thoroughly understood.

For this purpose, the present writer very strongly recommends a thorough study of the principles laid down in that masterly treatise *The Science of the Emotions*, by Bhagavan Das. (An admirable epitome of this work has been written by Miss K. Browning, M.A., under the title *An Epitome of the Science of the Emotions*.) The main thesis may be very briefly set out as follows.

S E 19–21. All manifested existence may be analysed into the Self, the Not-Self, and the Relationship between these two.

S E 23–24. That Relationship may be divided into (1) Cognition (Gnyânam) : (2) Desire (Ichchâ) : (3) Action (Kriyâ). To know, to desire, and to endeavour or act—those three comprise the whole of conscious life.

S E 21–22 : Feeling or emotion is of two kinds—pleasurable or
27 : 30.   painful. Pleasure, fundamentally a sense of moreness,
I V 89–90.   produces attraction, love (râga) : pain, fundamentally
S C 311.   a sense of lessness, produces repulsion, hate (dvesha).

From attraction proceed all love-emotions : from repulsion proceed all hate-emotions. All emotions arise from love or hate, or from both, in varying degrees of intensity.

The precise nature of a particular emotion is also determined by the relationship between the one who experiences the emotion and the object which is the occasion of the emotion. The one who experiences the

S E 29. emotion may be, *so far as the circumstances connected with the particular emotion are concerned*, (1) Greater

S E 35–38. than : (2) Equal to : or (3) Less than the object.

Pursuing this analysis, we arrive at the six possible types of emotion-elements given in column three of the table appended. Column four gives sub-divisions of the primary elements in varying degrees of intensity, the strongest being at the head and the weakest at the foot of each group.

S E 39. All human emotions consist of one of these six emotion-elements, or, more frequently, of two or more of them combined together. The student must now be referred to the treatise mentioned above for a detailed elaboration of the fundamental principles set forth above. His labour will be amply rewarded.

GENESIS OF EMOTIONS

Relation towards the object		Primary Emotion-Element 3	Degrees of the Emotion 4
Qualitative 1	Quantitative 2		
LOVE (for)	Superior	Reverence	Worship Adoration Reverence Esteem Respect Admiration
	Equal	Affection	Affection Comradeship Friendliness Politeness
	Inferior	Benevolence	Compassion Tenderness Kindness Pity
HATE (for)	Superior	Fear	Horror Dread Fear Apprehension
	Equal	Anger	Hostility Rudeness Aversion Coldness Aloofness
	Inferior	Pride or Tyranny (a)	Scorn Disdain Contempt Superciliousness

(a) The English language appears to possess no one word which accurately describes this emotion-element.

Another valuable line of study, for the student who is aiming at self-knowledge in order to attain self-mastery, is that of collective or crowd-consciousness. By far the best book, with which the present writer is acquainted, on this interesting subject is *The Crowd in Peace and War*, by Sir Martin Conway.

With wonderful lucidity and richness of illustration, Sir Martin demonstrates the following fundamental facts.

C P W 4-8. (1) The great majority of men are brought up in, and all their lives belong to, certain psychological " crowds," *i.e.*, groups of people who think, and above all, feel similarly. Such crowds are those of the home, friends and associates, schools and universities, professions, religious sects, political parties, schools of thought, nations, races, and so on. Even those who read the same newspapers or belong to the same club form a psychological " crowd."

C P W 26-27 : 33. H S I 294-295. (2) Such crowds are in the main formed by, nourished on, and dominated by feeling or emotion—*not by thought*. A crowd has all the emotions, but no intellect : it can feel, but it cannot think. The opinions of crowds are seldom or never reached by reason, but are merely infectious passions which sweep through the whole body like an electric current, these frequently originating from a single brain. Once caught up in the crowd, the individual rapidly loses his power of individual thought and feeling, and becomes one with the crowd, sharing its life, its opinions, its attitudes, prejudices, and the like.

(3) Very few ever have the courage or the strength to break away from the various crowds to which they belong ; the vast majority remain all their lives under the sway of the crowds which have absorbed them.

C P W 27-32. Our author then proceeds to enumerate and describe the various crowd virtues and to show that they differ from the virtues of the individual, being on the whole at a much lower and more primitive level.

C P W 88-89. Every crowd, being unable to lead itself, needs and finds a leader. Of such leaders there are three main types.

(a) The *Crowd-Compeller*. He is one who dominates and leads the crowd by imposing upon it his own ideas by the sheer force of his own personality. Examples of this type are Napoleon, Disraeli, Cæsar, Charlemagne.

(b) The *Crowd-Exponent*. This type, totally dis- C P W 101-
tinct from the Crowd-Compeller, is one which feels by 102.
natural sensitiveness what the crowd feels, or is going
to feel, and which expresses in clear and usually
graphic language the emotions of the crowd, which on
its own account is inarticulate. Such men seldom
think out problems for themselves and then proclaim
their gospel.   Rather they wait for the emotions of the
crowd to take form : then they plunge into the thick
of the fray and say with eloquence, power and en-
thusiasm that which people about them are dimly and
vaguely feeling. Examples of this type are very
common, especially in the field of politics.

(c) The *Crowd-Representative*. Crowd leaders of C P W 114-
this type are picturesque figureheads rather than 118.
individual forces. Typical examples are a constitu-
tional king, a consul, an ambassador, a judge (at any
rate in England). These men are merely the people,
" public opinion," personified : they speak with the
voice of the people, act for them, and stand for them in
the sight of the world.   They must suppress or conceal
their own individual opinions, and appear to feel as
the public feels, to act in conformity with the public
wishes and sentiments.

The above is the merest sketch of the leading
principles enunciated in the extremely able book
mentioned, and the student is urged to make a careful
study of that work for himself. It will help him not
only to appreciate more justly the forces by which
" the public " is swayed, but also to assess at their true
value many of his own beliefs, opinions and attitudes
towards many questions of the day.

It is clearly of the utmost importance that, in all H S I 298.
his feelings and thoughts, the student of occultism
should act deliberately and consciously. The Greek
saying *Gnothi seauton*, Know Thyself, is a fine piece of I L I 260.
advice, for self-knowledge is absolutely necessary to
any candidate for progress. The student should not A W 81-83.
allow himself to be swept off his feet by becoming K 20.
submerged in a collective emotion—or thought-form,

which forms a kind of atmosphere through which every
thing is seen and by which everything is coloured, and
which so manifestly dominates and sways the many
H S I 292. crowds amongst which he moves.   It is no easy matter
to stand against a strong popular bias, owing to the
ceaseless beating upon us of the thought-forms and
currents of thought which fill the atmosphere : yet
the student of occultism must learn to do so.

A E P. He should, moreover, be able to recognise the various
types of crowd-leaders and to refuse to allow himself
to be dominated, persuaded or cajoled into accepting
ideas or following lines of action unless he does so quite
deliberately, and with all his own faculties alert.

The influence of psychological crowds and crowd-
leaders in the world to-day, as well probably as in
every age, is very great indeed, and the forces they
wield subtle and far-reaching, so that the student who
aims at self-mastery and who wishes to lead his own
emotional and intellectual life, must be continuously
on his guard against these insidious influences.

The present writer is of opinion that a study of
The Science of the Emotions and *The Crowd in Peace and
War* is an invaluable preliminary to the task of training
and developing the astral body till it becomes a useful
and obedient servant of the sovereign will of the ego.

One other line of study is also strongly urged upon
the student, viz., that of the sub-conscious mind,
to-day often called the "unconscious." For this
purpose, as an introduction to the subject, *The Law
of Psychic Phenomena* by T. J. Hudson, is recommended.

In studying this book, the student should recollect
that it was written in 1892.   In the light of present
day knowledge it is not necessary to subscribe wholly
to Hudson's analysis, classification, or terminology.
Moreover, in the opinion of the present writer, Hudson
builds a great deal too much on his premises, straining
his theories far beyond breaking-point.   Nevertheless,
the book is still of great value, first as encouraging a
healthy scientific scepticism towards accepting too
readily plausible and glib explanations of many psychic

phenomena, and secondly, in bringing home with great force the tremendous potentialities latent in the sub-conscious part of man's nature, which may be utilised by the careful and discreet student to considerable effect in bringing his own astral nature under control and, in general, purifying and building up his own character. There are, of course, hosts of other and more modern books which will also help towards this end.

Briefly, Hudson states :—

(1) That the mentality of man is clearly divisible *L P P 29* into two parts, each with its own separate powers and functions. These he calls the *objective* and the *subjective minds*.

(2) That the objective mind is that which takes cognisance of the objective world, using as its medium of observation the physical senses, and having as its highest function the reason.

(3) That the subjective mind takes cognisance of its environment by means independent of the physical senses. It is the seat of the emotions and the store-house of memory. It performs its highest functions when the objective senses are in abeyance, *e.g.*, in a state of hypnotism or somnambulism. Many of the other faculties attributed by Hudson to the subjective mind are clearly those of the astral body, *e.g.*, the ability to travel to distant places, to read thoughts, etc.

Furthermore, whilst the objective mind is not *L P P 3c.* controllable by " suggestion," against reason, positive knowledge, or the evidence of the senses, the subjective mind is constantly amenable to the power of suggestion, whether from other people, or *from the objective mind of its owner*.

With the help of modern knowledge regarding our astral and mental bodies, and the nature and use of thought- and-emotion-forms, the student will recognise here many interesting and independent confirmations of what he has learnt from Theosophical authorities, and, as already said, he will be better able to realise that virtually limitless powers latent in his own psychological make-up, which he may proceed to use along lines laid down by occultists of repute : such as that of meditation, for example. He will also, perhaps, realise rather more vividly than before the way in which kâma, or desire, and manas, or mind, are entangled, and how they may be disentangled, to the great benefit and strengthening of both.

S C 318-319, 322.

It must ever be remembered that it is by thought that desire can be changed, and finally mastered. As mind learns to assert control, desire becomes transmuted into will, the governance then not being by external objects that attract or repel, but by the spirit of the man, the ego, the inner ruler.

We shall now return to our more specific " Theosophical " authorities, and proceed to consider certain other factors in the development and training of the astral body.

I L I 89-91.

It is obvious that the student should aim at mastering and eliminating certain minor defects, such as emotional weaknesses or vices. In this task it is important to recollect that such a vice as irritability, for example, which has become a habit through repeated indulgence, is stored up, not in the ego as an inherent quality, but in the astral permanent atom (see page 207). However great the force that is there piled up, it is a scientific certainty that perseverance will in due time lead to victory. On the side of the ego, there is the force of his own will, and behind that the infinite force of the Logos Himself, because progress by means of evolution is His will. A grasp of the idea of unity thus gives the man an adequate motive for the undoubtedly hard, and at times distasteful, work of character-building. However great the struggle, the forces of infinity being on his side, he is bound ultimately to overcome the finite forces for evil which he has stored up in his past lives.

I L I 110-111.

A man who seeks to kill out desire, in order to balance his karma perfectly and so obtain liberation for himself, may achieve his object. He cannot, however, escape from the law of evolution, and sooner or later he will be swept forward again into the stream by its resistless pressure, and so be forced into re-birth. Killing out desire is not the path of the true occultist.

Personal loves are not to be killed out, but are to be expanded till they become universal : loves are to be levelled up, not down.   The failure to realise this, and the tremendous difficulty of the task, when realised, have led in some cases to the stifling of love instead of its growth.   But overflowing love, not lovelessness, will save the world.   The Mahâtmâ is the Ocean of Compassion : not an iceberg.   To try to kill out love is the way of the left-hand path.   *R 40.* *I Y 102.*

It is, however, necessary to kill out completely the lower and coarser desires ;   the remainder must be purified and transmuted into aspirations, and resolution.   It is waste of force to desire or wish : the occultist *wills* instead.   Will is a higher aspect of desire.   *I L I 292–293.*

It has also been said that we should slay the " lunar form," *i.e.*, the astral body.   This does not mean that all feelings and emotions should be destroyed, but rather that the astral body should be completely under control, that we should be able to slay the lunar form *at will*.   As the man develops, he makes his will one with the will of the Logos, and the Logos wills evolution.   Needless to say, such an at-one-ment *ipso facto* eliminates such desires as ambition, desire for progress, and the like.   *I L I 293.*

The Voice of the Silence warns us that beneath each flower in the astral world, however beautiful it may be, lies coiled the serpent of desire.   In the case of affection, for example, everything of a grasping nature must be altogether transcended : but high, pure and unselfish affection can never be transcended, since it is a characteristic of the Logos Himself, and is a necessary qualification for progress upon the Path which leads to the Masters and to Initiation.   *I L I 103.*

CHAPTER XXVI

DEVELOPMENT OF ASTRAL POWERS

I L II 171.
A P 31.
O S D 465.

THE possession of psychic powers does not necessarily involve high moral character, any more than does the possession of physical strength, neither are psychic powers in themselves a sign of great development in any other direction, *e.g.*, that of intellect.

L L 3-4.

While, therefore, it is not true that the great psychic is necessarily a spiritual person, it is true, on the other hand, that a great spiritual person is inevitably psychic.

I L II 171.

Psychic powers can be developed by anyone who will take the trouble, and a man may learn clairvoyance or mesmerism just as he may learn the piano, if he is willing to go through the necessary hard work.

S P 73.

Astral senses exist in all men, but are latent in most, and generally need to be artificially forced if they are to be used in the present stage of evolution. In a few they become active without any artificial impulse ; in very many they can be artificially awakened and developed. The condition, in all cases, of the activity of the astral senses is the passivity of the physical, and the more complete the physical passivity the greater the possibility of astral activity.

G 21-23.
C W 230.
T N P 80-82.

Clairvoyance is often possessed by simple peoples. This is sometimes called the lower psychism, and is by no means the same thing as the faculty possessed by a properly trained and more advanced man, nor is it arrived at in the same way.

The occasional appearance of psychism in an undeveloped person is a kind of massive sensation vaguely belonging to the whole vehicle rather than an exact and definite perception coming through specialised organs. This was especially characteristic of the Atlantean

(Fourth) Root Race. It works not through the astral Chakrams, but through the astral centres connected with the physical senses. These are not distinctively *T N P* 80–82. *S C* 251. astral, although they are aggregations of astral matter in the astral body. They are of the nature of connecting bridges between the astral and physical planes, and are not developed astral senses in the proper sense of the term. " Second sight " belongs to this type of sensitiveness, and is often symbolical, the perceiver transmitting his knowledge in this curious symbolical way. To stimulate the centres which are *T N P* 125. bridges, instead of evolving the Chakrams, which are the astral organs, is a complete blunder. This lower psychism is also associated with the sympathetic nervous system, whereas the higher psychism is associated with the cerebro-spinal system. To revive control of the sym- *S C* 431. pathetic system is a retrograde and not a forward step.

In course of time the lower psychism disappears, to re-open at a later stage when it will be brought under the control of the will.

Hysterical and highly nervous people may occasion- *C* 53. ally become clairvoyant, the fact being a symptom of their disease, and due to the weakening of the physical vehicle to such a degree that it no longer presents any obstacle to a measure of etheric or astral vision. Delirium tremens is an extreme example of this class of psychism, victims of the disease often being able temporarily to perceive certain loathsome elemental and etheric entities.

For those who have not yet developed astral vision, *M B* 39. it is desirable to appreciate intellectually the reality of the astral world, and to realise that its phenomena are open to competent observation just as are those of the physical world.

There exist definite methods of Yoga by which the *M B* 47–48. astral senses may be developed in a rational and healthy way. But it is not only useless, it may be dangerous, to attempt these until the preparatory stage of purification has first been passed. Both the physical and the astral body must first be purified, by breaking the bonds of evil habits in eating, drinking, giving way to hate-emotions of all kinds, etc.

M B 40.
C 166.

Speaking generally, it is not desirable to force the development of the astral body by artificial means, for until spiritual strength is attained the intrusion of astral sights, sounds, and other phenomena is apt to be disturbing and even alarming.

Sooner or later, according to the karma of the past, one who follows the " ancient and royal " path will find knowledge of astral phenomena gradually coming to him : his keener vision will awaken, and new vistas of a wider universe will be unfolded to him on every side.   It is an illustration of the saying : " Seek ye first the Kingdom of Heaven, and all these things shall be added unto you."

A P 125.
I L II 172-174.
C 24 : 52-53 :
163-164.
O S D 457-464.
L L 12-14.
H S II 361.
T N P 127.

The attainment of astral powers as an end in itself inevitably leads to what is called in the East the *laukika* method of development : the powers obtained are only for the present personality and, there being no safeguards, the student is extremely likely to misuse them.   To this class belong the practices of Hatha Yoga, prânayama or breath-control, invocation of elementals, and all systems which involve deadening the physical senses in some way, *actively* by drugs (*e.g.*, bhang, haschish, etc.), by self-hypnotisation, or, as among the dervishes, by whirling in a mad dance of religious fervour until vertigo and insensibility supervene : or *passively* by being mesmerised—so that the astral senses may come to the surface.   Other methods are crystal-gazing (which leads to nothing but the lowest type of clairvoyance), the repetition of invocations, or the use of charms or ceremonies.

A man who entrances himself by the repetition of words or charms may probably return in his next life as a medium or at any rate be mediumistic.   Medium-

S G O 232.

ship should not be regarded as a psychic power at all : for a medium, so far from exercising power, on the contrary abdicates control over his own bodies in favour of another entity.   Mediumship is thus not a power but a condition.

There are many stories of some mysterious ointment *C* 33-34. or drug which, when applied to the eyes, enables a man to see fairies, etc. Anointing of the eyes might stimulate etheric sight but could not by any possibility open astral vision, though certain ointments rubbed over the whole body will greatly assist the astral body to leave the physical in full consciousness—a fact, the knowledge of which seems to have survived to mediæval times, as can be seen from the evidence given at some of the trials for witchcraft.

The *lokottara* method consists of Râja Yoga or *A P* 125- spiritual progress, and this is unquestionably the best 126: 14. method. Though slower, the powers gained by it *I L II* 172- belong to the permanent individuality, and are never 173. again lost, while the guiding of a Master ensures perfect *C*165-167: 20. *O S D* 464- safety so long as His orders are scrupulously obeyed. 465. *L L* 12-14.

Another great advantage of being trained by a *C* 21. Master is that whatever faculties the pupil may achieve are definitely under his command and can be used fully and constantly when needed : whereas in the case of the untrained man such powers often manifest themselves only very partially and spasmodically, and appear to come and go, as it were, of their own sweet will.

The temporary method is like learning to ride by *I L II* 173. stupefying the horse : the permanent method is like learning to ride properly, so that any horse can be ridden. The permanent method means real evolution, the other does not necessarily involve anything of the sort, as the powers gained by it may perish with the death of the body.

The wider sight of the astral plane is not an unmixed *A P* 126. blessing, as it reveals the sorrow and misery, the evil *C* 169-170. and greed of the world. The words of Schiller spring to mind : " Why hast thou cast me thus into the town of the ever-blind, to proclaim thine oracle with the opened sense ? Take back this sad clear-sightedness ; take from mine eyes this cruel light ! Give me back my blindness—the happy darkness of my senses ; take back thy dreadful gift ! "

I L II 185–
188.   Clairvoyant power, if properly and sensibly used,
may be a blessing and a help : misused, it may be a
hindrance and a curse. The principal dangers attend-
ant upon it arise from pride, ignorance, and impurity.
It is obviously foolish for a clairvoyant to imagine
that he or she is the only one thus endowed, and the
one person specially selected under angelic guidance
to found a new dispensation : and so on. Moreover,
there are always plenty of sportive and mischievous
astral entities ready and anxious to foster such delusions
and to fulfil any *rôle* that may be assigned to them.

It is useful for a clairvoyant to know something
of the history of the subject and to understand something of the conditions of the higher planes, as well,
if possible, as to possess some knowledge of scientific
subjects.

Further, a man of impure life or motive inevitably
attracts to himself the worst elements in the invisible
world. A man who is pure in thought and life, on the
other hand, is by that very fact guarded from the
influence of undesirable entities from other planes.

C 19–20.   In many cases a man may have occasional flashes of
astral consciousness without any awakening of etheric
vision at all. This irregularity of development is one
of the principal causes of the extreme liability of error
in matters of clairvoyance in at any rate its earlier
stages.

I L I 104–
105.   In the normal course of things people awake to the
realities of the astral plane very slowly, just as a
baby awakes to the realities of the physical plane.
Those who are deliberately and, as it were, prematurely
entering upon the Path, are developing such knowledge
abnormally, and are consequently more liable to err at
first.

Danger and injury might easily come were it not
that all pupils under proper training are assisted and
guided by competent teachers who are already accustomed to the astral plane. That is the reason why
all sorts of horrible sights, etc., are shown to the
neophyte, as tests, so that he may understand them and

become accustomed to them. Unless this were done, he might receive a shock which might not only prevent his doing useful work but might also be positively dangerous to his physical body.

The first introduction to the astral world may come *A P* 14. in various ways. Some people only once in their *C* 26. whole lives become sensitive enough to experience the presence of an astral entity or some astral phenomenon. Others find themselves with increasing frequency seeing and hearing things to which others are blind and deaf : others again begin to recollect their sleep-experiences.

When a person is beginning to become sensitive to *A W* 83–84. astral influences, he will occasionally find himself *S G O* 284– suddenly overpowered by inexplicable dread. This *T N P* 66–67. arises partly from the natural hostility of the elemental world against the human, on account of man's many destructive agencies on the physical plane, which react upon the astral, and partly to the many unfriendly artificial elementals, bred by human minds.

Some people begin by becoming intermittently *C* 26. conscious of the brilliant colours of the human aura : others may see faces, landscapes, or coloured clouds floating before their eyes in the dark before they sink to rest. Perhaps the most common experience is to begin to recollect with increasing clearness experiences of the other planes acquired during sleep.

Sometimes a person once in his whole life will *C* 54. perceive, for example, the apparition of a friend at the point of death. This may be due to two causes, in each the strong wish of the dying man being the impelling force. That force may have enabled the dying man to materialise himself for a moment, in which case, of course, no clairvoyance is needed : more probably it may have acted mesmerically upon the percipient and momentarily dulled his physical and stimulated his higher sensitiveness.

A man with developed astral vision is of course no *M B* 99. longer limited by physical matter : he sees through all physical bodies, physically opaque substances being to him as transparent as glass. At a concert, he sees glorious symphonies of colours : at a lecture, he sees the speaker's thoughts in colour and form, and is therefore in a position to understand him more fully than one without astral vision.

M B 100.
H S I 345.

A little examination will reveal that many people gain from a speaker more than the mere words convey : many will find in their memory more than the speaker uttered. Such experiences indicate that the astral body is developing and becoming more sensitive, responding to the thought-forms created by the speaker.

I L I 366.
T N P 73-74.

Some places afford greater facilities for occult work than others : thus California has a very dry climate with much electricity in the air, which is favourable for the development of clairvoyance.

Some psychics require a temperature of 80° in order to do their best work : others do not work well except at a lower temperature.

M V I 78-79.
M 38-39.
C 42.

A trained clairvoyant being able to see a man's astral body, it follows that on the astral plane no man can hide or disguise himself : what he truly is, that he is seen to be by any unprejudiced observer. It is necessary to say unprejudiced, because a man sees another through the medium of his own vehicles, which is somewhat like seeing a landscape through coloured glass. Until he has learnt to allow for this influence, a man is liable to consider as most prominent in another man those characteristics to which he himself most readily responds. Practice is needed to free oneself from the distortion produced by this personal equation so as to be able to observe clearly and accurately.

A P 24-25.

Most of the psychics who occasionally get glimpses of the astral world, as well as most of the communicating entities at spiritualistic *séances*, fail to report many of the complexities of the astral plane which are described in this book. The reason is that few people see things as they really are on the astral plane until after very long experience. Even those who do see fully are often too dazed and confused to understand or to remember, and hardly any one can translate the recollection into physical plane language. Many untrained psychics never examine their visions scientifically : they simply obtain an impression, which may be quite correct, but may also be half false, or even wholly misleading.

Also, as we have seen, frequent tricks are played by sportive denizens of the astral world, against which the untrained person is usually defenceless.

In the case of an astral entity who constantly works through a medium, his finer astral senses may even become so coarsened as to become insensitive to the higher grades of astral matter.

Only the trained visitor from the physical plane, who is fully conscious on both planes, can depend upon seeing both astral and physical planes clearly and simultaneously.

True, trained, and absolutely reliable clairvoyance *A P* III. demands faculties belonging to a plane higher than the astral. The faculty of accurate prevision also belongs to that higher plane : yet flashes or reflections of it frequently show themselves to purely astral sight, more especially among simple-minded people who live under suitable conditions—what is called second-sight among the Highlanders of Scotland being a well-known example.

There are astrally, as well as physically, blind *M B* 39-40. persons, so that many astral phenomena escape *I L I* 103-ordinary astral vision. At first, in fact, many mistakes 104. may be made in using astral vision, just as a child makes mistakes when it first begins to use its physical senses, though after a time it becomes possible to see and hear as accurately on the astral as on the physical plane.

Another method of developing clairvoyance, which *C* 167. is advised by all the religions alike, and which if *O S D* 469-adopted carefully and reverently can do no harm to 476. any human being, is that of meditation, by means of which a very pure type of clairvoyance may sometimes be developed. A succinct account of the processes involved in meditation is given in *The Other Side of*

Death, by Bishop C. W. Leadbeater, pages 469–476, as well of course as in many other books.

C W 223.
By means of meditation extreme sensitiveness can be developed, and at the same time perfect balance, sanity and health.

I L I 328–
329; 348.
The student will readily recognise that the practice of determined meditation builds higher types of matter into the bodies. Grand emotions may be felt, which come from the buddhic level, *i.e.*, from the plane next above the higher mental, and are reflected in the astral body. It is, however, necessary also to develop the mental and causal bodies in order to give balance. A man cannot leap from the astral consciousness to the buddhic without developing the intervening vehicles. With feeling alone we can never obtain perfect balance or steadiness : grand emotions that have swayed us in the right direction may very readily become a little twisted and sway us along less desirable lines. Emotions provide motive force, but directing power comes from wisdom and steadiness.

I L I 348.
C W 213.
There is a close connection between the astral and the buddhic planes, the astral body being in some ways a reflection of the buddhic.

H S I 226–
230.
An example of the close relationship between the astral and buddhic planes is found in the Christian Mass. At the moment of Consecration of the Host a force rays out which is strongest in the buddhic world, though also powerful in the higher mental world : in addition, its activity is marked in the first, second and third astral sub-planes, though this may be a reflection of the mental or an effect of sympathetic vibration. The effect may be felt by people even far away from the church, a great wave of spiritual peace and strength passing over the whole countryside, though many would never connect it with the Mass being celebrated.

In addition to the above, another effect is produced as a result of, and in proportion to, the intensity of the conscious feeling of devotion of each individual during the celebration. A ray, as of fire, darts from the uplifted Host and sets the higher part of the astral body glowing intensely. Through the astral body, by reason of its close relation with it, the buddhic vehicle is also strongly affected. Thus both buddhic and astral vehicles act and react on one another.

A similar effect occurs when the Benediction is *H S I* 231. given with the blessed Sacrament.

CHAPTER XXVII

CLAIRVOYANCE IN SPACE AND TIME

C 59 : 61.   THERE are four methods by which it is possible to observe events taking place at a distance.

C 62-66.   1. *By means of an astral current.* This method is somewhat analogous to the magnetisation of a bar of steel, and consists of what may be called polarisation, by an effort of the will, of a number of parallel lines of astral atoms from the observer to the scene he wishes to observe. All the atoms are held with their axes rigidly parallel to one another, forming a kind of temporary tube, along which the clairvoyant may look. The line is liable to be disarranged or even destroyed by any sufficiently strong astral current which happens to cross its path : this, however, seldom happens.

The line is formed either by the transmission of energy from particle to particle, or by the use of force from a higher plane, which acts upon the whole line simultaneously : the latter method implies far greater development, involving the knowledge of, and power to use, forces of a considerably higher level. A man who could make a line in this way would not, for his own use, need such a line at all, because he could see far more easily and completely by means of a higher faculty.

C 88 : 90 : 92.   The current or tube may be formed even quite unconsciously and unintentionally, and is often the result of a strong thought or emotion projected from one end or the other—either from the seer or from the person who is seen. If two persons are united by strong affection, it is probable that a fairly steady stream of mutual thought is constantly flowing between them, and some sudden need or dire extremity on the part of one of them may endue this stream temporarily with the polarising power which is needful to create the astral telescope.

The view obtained by this means is not unlike that seen through a telescope. Human figures, for example, would usually appear very small, but perfectly clear : sometimes, but not usually, it is possible to hear as well as to see by this method.

The method has distinct limitations, as by it the astral telescope reveals the scene from one direction only, and has a limited and particular field of view. In fact, astral sight directed along such a tube is limited much as physical sight would be under similar circumstances.

This type of clairvoyance may be greatly facilitated C 66 : 86. by using a physical object as a starting point—a focus for the will power. A ball of crystal is the most common and effective of such foci, as, owing to its peculiar arrangement of elemental essence, it also possesses within itself qualities which stimulate psychic faculty. Other objects are also used for the same purpose, such as a cup, a mirror, a pool of ink, a drop of blood, a bowl of water, a pond, water in a glass bowl or almost any polished surface, or, on the other hand, a dead black one, produced by a handful of powdered charcoal in a saucer.

There are some who can determine what they C 85. see by their will, that is to say they can point their telescope as they wish : but the great majority form a fortuitous tube and see whatever happens to present itself at the end of it.

Some psychics are able to use the tube method only C 66-67. when under the influence of mesmerism. There are two varieties of such psychics : (1) those who are able to make the tube for themselves : (2) those who look through a tube made by the mesmeriser.

Occasionally, though rarely, magnification is also possible by means of the tube, though in these cases it is probable that an altogether new power is beginning to dawn.

2. *By the projection of a thought-form.* This method C 67-69. consists of the projection of a mental image of oneself, O S D 166.

round which astral matter is also drawn, such connection with the image being retained as will render it possible to receive impressions by means of it : the form thus acts as a kind of outpost of the consciousness of the seer. Such impressions would be transmitted to the thinker by sympathetic vibration. In a perfect case, the seer is able to see almost as well as he would if he himself stood in the place of the thought-form. In this method it is possible also to shift the point of view, if desired. Clairaudience is perhaps less frequently associated with this type of clairvoyance than with the first type. The moment that the intentness of the thought fails the whole vision is gone, and it will be necessary to construct a fresh thought-form before it can be resumed. This type of clairvoyance is rarer than the first type because of the mental control required and the finer nature of the forces employed. It is tedious except for quite short distances.

C 71.

C 69–71.   3. *By travelling in the astral body*, either in sleep or trance. This process has already been described in previous chapters.

C 78–79.   4. *By travelling in the mental body.* In this case, the astral body is left behind with the physical, and, if it is desired to show oneself on the astral plane, a temporary astral body, or mâyâvirûpa is formed, as described on p. 255.

C 61–62.   It is possible also to obtain information regarding events at a distance by invoking or evoking an astral entity, such as a nature-spirit, and inducing or compelling him to undertake the investigation. This, of course, is not clairvoyance, but magic.

C 79·81.   In order to find a person on the astral plane, it is necessary to put oneself *en rapport* with him, a very slight clue being usually sufficient, such as a photograph, a letter written by him, an object which belonged to him, etc. The operator then sounds out the man's keynote when, if the man sought is on the astral plane, an immediate response will be forthcoming.

I L II 204–208.
C 80–81.   This keynote of the man on the astral plane is a sort of average tone which emerges from all the different

vibrations which are habitual to his astral body. There is also a similar average tone for each man's mental and other bodies, all the keynotes together forming the man's chord—or mystic chord as it is often called.

The trained seer attunes his own vehicles for the moment exactly to the man's note, and then by an effort of will sends forth its sound.   Wherever in the three worlds the man sought may be, an instant response is evoked from him ; this response is at once visible to the seer, so that he is able to form a magnetic line of connection with the man.

Another form of clairvoyance enables the seer to *C* 126. perceive events that have happened in the past.   There are many degrees of this power, from the trained man who can consult the Akâshic Records for himself at will, down to the person who gets occasional glimpses only. The ordinary psychometer needs an object physically connected with the scene in the past that he wishes to see, or, of course, he may use a crystal or other object as his focus.

The Akâshic Records represent the Divine memory, which is briefly mentioned on p. 155.   The records seen on the astral plane, being but a reflection of a reflection from a much higher plane, are exceedingly imperfect, fragmentary in the extreme, and often seriously distorted.   They have been compared to the reflections in the surface of water ruffled by wind. On the mental plane the records are full and accurate and can be read with exactitude : but this, of course, demands faculties pertaining to the mental plane.

CHAPTER XXVIII

INVISIBLE HELPERS

THE student of the preceding pages will by now have perceived that the instances of "intervention" in human affairs by invisible agents, which occur from time to time, and which are, of course, quite inexplicable from the materialistic standpoint, may readily be explained, rationally and simply, by one who understands something of the astral plane and its possibilities.

I H 8.
L A D 38.
In the East the existence of "invisible helpers" has always been recognised; even in Europe we have had the old Greek stories of the interference of gods in human affairs, and the Roman legend that Castor and Pollux led the legions of the infant republic in the Battle of Lake Regillus. In mediæval times there were many stories of saints who appeared at critical moments and turned the fortune of war in favour of the Christian hosts—such as that of St. James having led the Spanish troops—and of guardian angels who sometimes saved a traveller from serious danger or even death.

I H 23.
Help may be given to men by several of the classes of inhabitants of the astral plane. It may come from nature-spirits, from devas, from those who are physically dead, or from those who, whilst still alive physically, are able to function freely on the astral plane.

I H 29-30.
L A D 41.
The cases in which help is given to men by nature-spirits are few. Nature-spirits (see Chapter XX) mostly shun the haunts of man, disliking his emanations, his bustle and his unrest. Also, excepting some of their higher orders, they are generally inconsequent and thoughtless, more like happy children at play than like grave and responsible entities. As a rule they cannot be relied upon for anything like steady co-operation in

this class of work, though occasionally one of them will become attached to a human being and do him many a good turn.

The work of the Adept, or Master, lies chiefly upon the arûpa levels of the mental plane, where He may influence the true individualities of men, and not the mere personality, which is all that can be reached in the astral or physical world. It is seldom, therefore, that He finds it necessary or desirable to work on a plane so low as the astral.   *I H 24.*

The same consideration applies to devas, those of this class of entity, who sometimes respond to man's higher yearnings or appeals, working on the mental plane rather than on the astral or physical, and more frequently in the periods between incarnations than during physical existence.

Help is sometimes given by those who have recently died physically and who remain still in close touch with earthly affairs. The student will readily perceive, however, that the amount of such help must in the nature of things be exceedingly limited, because the more unselfish and helpful a person is, the less likely is he to be found after death lingering in full consciousness on the lower levels of the astral plane, from which the earth is most readily accessible.   *I H 30.*
L A D 43.

Furthermore, in order that a dead person may be able to influence one still living physically, either the latter must be unusually sensitive, or the would-be helper must possess a certain amount of knowledge and skill. These conditions are of course fulfilled only very rarely.   *I H 31.*

It follows, then, that at present the work of helping on the astral and lower mental planes is chiefly in the hands of pupils of the Masters, and any others who are sufficiently evolved to function consciously upon these two planes.   *I H 27, 31.*
L A D 44.

Varied as is this class of work on the astral plane, it is all, of course, directed to the one great end of furthering evolution. Occasionally it is connected with the development of the lower kingdoms, elemental as well as vegetable and animal, which it is possible   *I H 37.*
M V I 45 :
61.

to accelerate under certain conditions. It is, in fact, in some cases only through connection with or use by man that the progress of these lower kingdoms takes place. Thus, for example, an animal can individualise only through certain classes of animals which have been domesticated by man.

By far the largest and most important part of the work is connected with humanity in some way or other, chiefly with his spiritual development, though very rarely even purely physical assistance may be given.

I H 38-39. In the classic book on the subject, *Invisible Helpers*, by Bishop C. W. Leadbeater, a number of typical examples of physical intervention are given. Sometimes an invisible helper, with his wider vision, is able to perceive a danger which is threatening some one, and to impress the idea upon the person threatened,

I H 69. or upon a friend who will go to his assistance. In
I H 12-13: this way, shipwrecks have sometimes been prevented.
13-14: 15: At other times the helper may materialise himself,
16-18: 47 or be materialised by a more experienced helper,
-51. sufficiently to lead some one out of danger, *e.g.*, to take a child out of a burning building, to save some one from falling over a precipice, to bring home children

I H 41-42. who have lost their way, and so on. One instance is given where a helper, finding a boy who had fallen over a cliff and cut an artery, was materialised in order that he might tie a bandage and so stop the bleeding, which otherwise would have proved fatal, another helper meanwhile impressing the idea of danger upon the boy's mother and leading her to the spot.

I L I 442. It may be asked how it is that an astral entity becomes aware of a physical cry, or an accident. The answer is that any cry which has in it a strong feeling or emotion would produce an effect upon the astral plane, and would convey exactly the same idea there as on the physical plane. In the case of an accident the rush of emotion caused by pain or fright would flame out like a great light, and could not fail to attract the attention of an astral entity if he were anywhere near.

In order to bring about the necessary materialisation of an astral body, so that a means of performing purely physical acts may be obtained, a knowledge of the method of doing this is clearly essential.

There are three well-defined varieties of materialisation : (1) that which is tangible, though not visible to ordinary physical sight ; at *séances*, this is the commonest kind ; it is used for moving small objects and for the " direct voice." An order of matter is used which can neither reflect nor obstruct light, but which under certain conditions can be used to produce sound. A variety of this class is one which is able to affect some of the ultra-violet rays, thus enabling " spirit-photographs " to be taken. (2) That which is visible, but not tangible. (3) The perfect materialisation, which is both visible and tangible. Many spiritualists are familiar with all these three types. *I H* 54-55. *A P* 118.

Such materialisations as we are here considering, are brought about by an effort of will. This effort, directed towards changing matter from its natural state into another, is temporarily opposing the cosmic will, as it were. The effort must be maintained the whole time, for if the mind be taken off it for one half-second, the matter flies back to its original condition like a flash of lightning. *I H* 42-43.

At spiritualistic *séances*, a full materialisation is usually brought about by utilising matter from the etheric and the physical bodies of the medium, and also from those of the sitters. In such cases, it is clear that the very closest connection is thus set up between the medium and the materialised body. The significance of this we shall consider in a moment. *I H* 55.

In the case of a trained helper, who finds it necessary to produce a temporary materialisation, quite another method is employed. No pupil of a master would ever be permitted to put such a strain on anyone else's body as would occur were matter from that body to be used for the materialisation : nor, indeed, would such a plan be necessary. A far less dangerous method is to condense from the circumambient ether, or even from *I H* 57.

the physical air, such amount of matter as may be required. This feat, though no doubt beyond the power of the average entity manifesting at a *séance*, presents no difficulty to a student of occult chemistry.

In a case of this kind, whilst we have an exact reproduction of the physical body, it is created by a mental effort, out of matter entirely foreign to that body. Consequently, the phenomenon known as repercussion could not possibly take place, as it could happen where a form is materialised with matter drawn from a medium's body.

I H 56 -57.   Repercussion occurs where an injury inflicted upon a materialised form is reproduced, with faithful accuracy, upon the corresponding part of the medium's body. Or it may occur, as is very common at spiritualistic *séances*, where chalk is rubbed, say, on a materialised hand ; after the materialised hand has vanished, the chalk is found upon the hand of the medium.

An injury to a form materialised by a helper from the ether or air could no more affect the helper's physical body by repercussion than a man could be

I Y 131-132.   affected by an injury to a marble statue of himself.

But if on the astral plane one is unwise enough to think that a danger which belongs to the physical, *e.g.*, a falling object, can injure one, an injury to the physical body through repercussion is possible.

I H 53.   The subject of repercussion is abstruse and difficult, and as yet by no means fully understood. In order to understand it perfectly, it would probably be necessary to comprehend the laws of sympathetic vibration on more planes than one.

I H 58.   There is no doubt whatever as to the stupendous power of will over matter of all planes, so that if only the power be strong enough, practically *any* result may be produced by its direct action, without any knowledge or even thought on the part of the man exercising the will as to *how* it is to do its work.

I L I 327.   There is no limit to the degree to which will may be developed.

This power holds good in the case of materialisation, *I H 58-59.*
although ordinarily it is an art which must be learnt
just like any other.   An average man on the astral
plane would no more be able to materialise himself
without having previously learnt how to do it, than an
average man on this plane would be able to play the
violin without having previously learnt to do so.

There are, however, exceptional cases where intense *I H 62.*
sympathy and firm deliberation enable a person to
effect a temporary materialisation even though he does
not consciously know how to do it.

It is worth noting that these rare cases of physical *I H 46.*
intervention by an astral helper are often made
possible by the existence of a karmic tie between the
helper and the one to be helped.   In this way, old
services are acknowledged and a kindness rendered in
one life is repaid in a future life, even by such unusual
methods as those described.

Or, in great catastrophes, where many people are *L A D 48.*
killed, it is sometimes permitted for one or two persons
to be " miraculously " saved, because it so happens that
it is not their " karma " to die just then, *i.e.*, they owe
to the Divine law no debt that can be paid in that
particular fashion.

Very occasionally, physical assistance is given to
human beings even by a Master.

Bishop Leadbeater describes a case which happened *I H 18-19.*
to himself.   Walking along a road, he suddenly heard
in his ear the voice of his Indian teacher, who at the
time was physically 7,000 miles away, cry " Spring
back ! "   He started violently back just as a heavy
metal chimney pot crashed upon the pavement less
than a yard in front of his face.

Another remarkable case is recorded where a lady, *I H 20-21.*
who found herself in serious physical peril in the middle
of a dangerous street *fracas*, was suddenly whirled
out of the crowd and placed quite uninjured in an
adjoining and empty by-street.   Her body must have
been lifted right over the intervening houses, and set
down in the next street, a veil, probably of etheric

matter, being thrown round her whilst in transit so that she should not be visible as she passed through the air.

I H 75-77.
L A D 48:
49.

From a perusal of the chapters on *After-Death Life*, it will be evident that there is ample scope for the work of invisible helpers among people who have died. Most of these being in a condition of complete ignorance regarding life after death, and many, in western countries at least, being also terrified at the prospect of " hell," and " eternal damnation," there is much to be done in enlightening people as to their true state and the nature of the astral world in which they find themselves.

I H 86-87.
I L II 25.
H S II 233.
O S D 38.

The main work done by the invisible helper is that of soothing and comforting the newly dead, of delivering them, where possible, from the terrible though unnecessary fear which but too often seizes them, and not only causes them much suffering, but retards their progress to higher spheres, and of enabling them, so far as may be, to comprehend the future that lies before them.

O S D 38.

It is stated that this work was in earlier periods attended to exclusively by a high class of non-human entities ; but for some time past those human beings who are able to function consciously upon the astral plane have been privileged to render assistance in this labour of love.

I L II 51.

In cases where the rearrangement by the desire-elemental of the astral body has taken place, an astral helper may break up that arrangement and restore the astral body to its previous condition, so that the dead man can perceive the whole of the astral plane instead of only one sub-plane of it.

I H 87.

Others who have been longer on the astral plane may also receive help from explanations and advice as to their course through its different stages.   Thus they may be warned of the danger and delay caused by attempting to communicate with the living through a medium, and sometimes, though rarely, an entity already drawn into a spiritualistic circle may be guided into higher and healthier life.   The memory of such

teaching cannot, of course, be directly carried over to
the next incarnation, but there always remains the
real inner knowledge, and therefore the strong pre-
disposition to accept it immediately when heard again
in the new life.

Some of the newly-dead see themselves on the astral *L A D* 50.
plane as they really are, and are therefore filled with
remorse.   Here the helper is able to explain that the
past is past, that the only repentance worth while is
the resolve to do better in future, that each man must
take himself as he is and steadily work to improve
himself and lead a truer life in the future.

Others, again, are troubled by their desire to make *O S D* 128 :
reparation for some injury they did whilst on earth, 220.
to ease their conscience by disclosing a discreditable
secret they have jealously guarded, to reveal the hiding
place of important papers or money, and so forth.
In some cases it is possible for the helper to intervene
in some way on the physical plane and so satisfy the
dead man ; but in most cases the best he can do is to
explain that it is now too late to make reparation and
therefore useless to grieve over the trouble, and to
persuade the man to abandon his thoughts of earth
which hold him down in close touch with earth-life,
and to make the best of his new life.

An immense amount of work is also done for the *I H* 88 -89.
living by putting good thoughts into the minds of those
who are ready to receive them.

It would be perfectly easy—easy to a degree quite
incredible to those who do not understand the subject
practically—for a helper to dominate the mind of an
average man and make him think just as the helper
pleased, without arousing any suspicion of outside
influence in the mind of the subject. Such a proceeding,
however, would be entirely inadmissible.   All that may
be done is to throw the good thought into the person's
mind among the thousands that are constantly surging
through it, and hope that the person will take it up,
make it his own, and act upon it.

Very varied assistance can be given in this manner. *I H* 89.
                                                      L A D 47.

Consolation is often given to those in sorrow or sickness ; reconciliations are attempted between those who have been separated by conflict of opinions or interests ; earnest truth-seekers are guided towards the truth ; it is often possible to put the solution of some spiritual or metaphysical problem into the mind of one who is *H S I* 346– spending anxious thought upon it. Lecturers may be 347. helped by suggestions or illustrations either materialised *M* 99. in subtler matter before the speaker or impressed upon his brain.

I L II 95–96.   A regular invisible helper soon acquires a number of " patients," whom he visits every night, just as a doctor upon earth makes a regular round among his patients. Each worker thus usually becomes the centre of a small group, the leader of a band of helpers for whom he is always able to find constant employment. Work can be found in the astral world for any number of workers, and every one who wishes—man, woman or child—may be one of them.

I H 89–90.   A pupil may often be employed as an agent in what *I L I* 195.   practically amounts to the answering of prayer. Although it is true that any earnest spiritual desire, such as may be expressed in prayer, is a force which automatically brings about certain results, it is also a fact that such a spiritual effort offers an opportunity of influence to the Powers of Good. A willing helper may thus be made the channel through which energy is poured forth. This is true of meditation to an even greater extent.

I L I 195–   In some cases such a helper is taken to be the saint, 196.   etc., to whom the petitioner prayed, and there are many stories to illustrate this.

I H 90–91.   Pupils who are fitted for the work are also employed *L A D* 48.   to suggest true and beautiful thoughts to authors, *H S I* 234.   poets, artists and musicians.

Sometimes, though more rarely, it is possible to warn people of the danger to their moral development of some course that they are pursuing, to clear away evil influence from about some person or place, or to counteract the machinations of black magicians.

There is so much work for invisible helpers on the *I L I* 37.
astral plane that it is clearly emphatically the duty of
the student to fit himself by every means in his power
to assist in its performance. The work of the invisible
helpers would not be done unless there were pupils at
the stage where it is the best work that they can do.
As soon as they pass beyond that stage and can do
higher work, the higher work will certainly be given
to them.

It should be borne in mind that when power and *L A D* 44-45.
training are given to a helper, they are given to him *C* 172.
under restrictions. He must never use them selfishly,
never display them to gratify curiosity, never employ
them to pry into the business of others, never give what
at spiritualistic *séances* are called tests, *i.e.*, he must
never do anything which can be proved as a phenomenon on the physical plane. He might take a message
to a dead man, but not, unless under direct instructions
from his Master, bring back a reply from the dead
to the living. Thus the band of invisible helpers is
neither a detective office nor an astral information
bureau, but is intended simply and quietly to do such
work as is given to it to do or as comes in its way.

As an occult student progresses, instead of assisting
individuals only, he learns to deal with classes, nations,
and races. As he acquires the requisite powers and
knowledge, he begins to wield the greater forces of the
âkâsha and the astral light, and is shown how to make
the utmost possible use of each favourable cyclic
influence. He is brought into relationship with the
great Nirmânakâyas, and becomes one of their almoners,
learning how to dispense the forces which are the fruit
of their sublime self-sacrifice.

There is no mystery as to the qualifications needed *I H* 93.
by one who aspires to be a helper : to some extent *H S II* 235.
these have already been incidentally described, but it
may be useful also to set them out fully and
categorically.

(1) *Single-mindedness*, sometimes called one-pointed- *I H* 93-94.
ness ; the would-be helper must make the work of *L A D* 51.

helping others his first and highest duty: the work which the Master would have him do must be the one great interest of his life.

Furthermore, intelligent discrimination is needed not only between useful and useless work, but also between the different kinds of useful work. Economy of effort is a prime law of occultism, and every student should devote himself to the very highest work of which he is capable. It is also essential that the student should on the physical plane do the utmost that lies in his power to further the same great ends of helping his fellows.

I L I 38-40:
57 : 58.
H S II 180:
200-201.
M P 53.

(2) *Self-Control.*—This comprises complete control of temper, so that nothing seen or heard can cause real irritation, for the consequences of such irritation would be far more serious on the astral than on the physical plane. If a man with fully awakened faculty on the astral plane were to feel anger against a person on that plane, he would do him serious and perhaps fatal injury. Any manifestation of irritability, excitement or impatience in the astral world would at once make a helper a fearsome object, so that those whom he wished to help would fly from him in terror.

I H 94-95.
L A D 51.

H S II 236.

A case is recorded where an invisible helper keyed herself up to such a state of excitement that her astral body greatly increased in size, vibrating violently and flashing forth fiery colours. The newly-dead person she was hoping to help was horrified to see the huge, flaming, flashing sphere rushing at him, took it for the theological devil *in propriâ personâ*, and fled in terror, his terror being increased by the would-be helper persistently following him.

I L II 89.

In addition, control of nerve is essential, so that none of the fantastic or terrible sights that may be encountered may be able to shake the student's dauntless courage. As previously stated, it is to make sure of this control of nerve, and to fit him for the work that has to be done, that candidates are always made, now as in days of old, to pass what are called the tests of earth, water, air and fire

I H 95-96.
L A D 51.

The student has to realise that in the astral body the densest rock offers no impediment to his freedom of movement, that he may leap with impunity from the highest cliffs, and plunge with absolute confidence into the heart of a raging volcano or the deepest abyss of the fathomless ocean. These things have to be sufficiently realised for the student to act upon them instinctively and confidently.

Further, control of mind and desire are needed : of mind, because without the power of concentration it would be impossible to do good work amid all the distracting currents of the astral plane ; of desire, because in the astral world to desire is very often to have, and, unless desire were well controlled, the student might find himself faced with creations of his own of which he should be heartily ashamed. *I H 96-97. L A D 51.*

(3) *Calmness.*—This means the absence of worry and depression. Much of the work consisting of soothing those who are disturbed and cheering those in sorrow, it is clear that a helper could not do such work if his own aura were vibrating with continual fuss and worry, or grey with the gloom of depression. Nothing is more fatal to occult progress or usefulness than worrying over trifles. The optimistic view of everything is always nearest to the divine view, and therefore to the truth, because only the good and beautiful can be permanent, while evil by its very nature is temporary ; unruffled calm leads to a serenity which is joyous, making depression impossible. *I H 97-98. L A D 51. M V I 112.*

As stated previously, depression is exceedingly contagious, and must be entirely eliminated by one who aims at becoming an invisible helper. Such an one would be characterised by his absolute serenity under all possible difficulties, and by his radiant joy in helping others.

(4) *Knowledge.*—The more knowledge a man has in any and every direction, the more useful he will be. He should fit himself by careful study of everything that has been written about the astral plane and astral work in occult literature, for he cannot *I H 98. L A D 51. I L II 83. C 125.*

expect others, whose time is already fully occupied, to
expend some of it in explaining to him what he might
have learnt for himself in the physical world by taking
the trouble to read books.

C 125.

There is perhaps no kind of knowledge of which a
use cannot be found in the work of the occultist.

I H 99.
L A D 51.

(5) *Love.*—This, the last and greatest of the qualifications, is also the most misunderstood. Emphatically it is not backboneless sentimentalism, overflowing
with vague and gushing generalities, which fears to
stand firm for the right lest it should be stigmatised
by the ignorant as " unbrotherly." What is wanted
is love strong enough to act without talking about
it ; the intense desire for service whicn is ever on the
watch for an opportunity to render it, even though it
prefers to do so anonymously ; the feeling which
springs up in the heart of him who has realised the
great work of the Logos, and, having once seen it,
knows that for him there can be in the three worlds
no other course but to identify himself with it to the
utmost limit of his power—to become, in however
humble a way, and at however great a distance, a
tiny channel of that wondrous love of God which, like
the peace of God, passeth man's understanding.

I L II 99.
C 125.

It will be recollected that for two persons on the
astral plane to communicate with one another astrally,
it is necessary that they should have a language in
common ; therefore the more languages an astral
plane helper knows, the more useful he is.

I H 99–101.
L A D 51–52.

The standard set for an Invisible Helper is not an
impossible one ; on the contrary it is attainable by
every man, though it may take him time to reach it.
Every one knows of some case of sorrow or distress,
whether among the living or the dead does not matter.
On going to sleep a resolution should be made to do
what is possible, whilst asleep and in the astral body, to
help that person. Whether the memory of what has
been done penetrates into the waking consciousness or
not is of no consequence ; it may be taken as a certainty
that something has been achieved, and some day,

sooner or later, evidence will be forthcoming that success has been attained.

With a person who is fully awakened to the astral plane the last thought before going to sleep would matter less, because he would have the power of turning readily from one thought to another in the astral world. In his case, the general trend of his thought would be the important factor, for equally during day and night his mind would be likely to move in its accustomed fashion.

O S D 35.

CHAPTER XXIX

CONCLUSION

ALTHOUGH there are at present relatively few who possess direct, personal knowledge of the astral world, its life and its phenomena, yet there are many reasons for believing that this small group, of those who know these things from their own experience, is rapidly growing and is likely to be very largely increased in the near future.

Psychic faculty, especially among children, is becoming less and less rare : as it gradually becomes accepted, and ceases to be regarded as unhealthy or " tabu," it is likely to increase both in extent and in intensity. Thus, for example, books have recently been published, and widely read, dealing with nature-spirits, better known as fairies, and showing even photographs of these dainty creatures and their work in the economy of nature : whilst any open-minded enquirer will experience little difficulty in finding people, young and old, who frequently see fairies, at work and at play, as well as many other entities and phenomena of the astral world.

Again, the enormous vogue of spiritualism has made the astral world and many of its phenomena objectively real and thoroughly familiar to many millions of persons in every part of the globe.

Physical science, with its ions and electrons, is on the threshold of the astral world, while the researches of Einstein and others are rapidly making acceptable the conception of the fourth dimension, which for so long has been familiar to students of the astral world.

In the realm of psychology, modern analytical methods give promise of being able to reveal the true nature of, at any rate, the lower fraction of man's psychic mechanism, confirming incidentally some of the statements and teachings put forward by ancient Eastern books and by Theosophists and occultists of to-day. Thus, for example, a well-known author of books on psychology and psycho-analysis, recently informed the present writer that in his view the " complex " was identical with the " skandhâra " of the Buddhist system, while another psychologist of world-wide repute told a friend of the present writer that his psychological—*not* psychic—researches had led him irresistibly to the fact of re-incarnation.

These are some of the indications that the methods of orthodox Western science are leading to results identical with those which have for ages been common knowledge in certain parts of the East, and which have, during approximately the last half-century, been re-discovered by a small group of individuals who, guided by Eastern teachings, have developed within themselves the faculties necessary for the direct observation and investigation of the astral (as well as higher) worlds.

It would be a platitude to remark that the acceptance by the world in general of the existence of the astral plane and its phenomena—which cannot be much longer deferred—will inevitably and immeasurably enlarge and deepen man's conception of himself and his own destiny, as well as revolutionise his attitude towards the outer world, including the other kingdoms of nature, physically visible and invisible. Once a man succeeds in establishing to his own satisfaction the reality of the astral world, he is compelled to re-orient himself, and to make for himself a new set of values for the factors which affect his life and determine his activities.

Sooner or later, but inevitably, the broad conception that merely physical things play a very small part in the life of the human soul and spirit, and that man is essentially a spiritual being, unfolding his latent powers with the help of the various vehicles, physical, astral, and other, which from time to time he assumes—will displace all other viewpoints and lead men to a complete re-alignment of their lives.

A realisation of his own true nature, of the fact that through life after life on earth, with interludes in other and subtler worlds, he is steadily evolving and becoming more and more spiritual, logically and inevitably leads man to see that, if and when he chooses, he may cease from dallying with life and with drifting on the broad current of the evolutionary stream, and may instead assume the helm of his own life-voyage. From this point in the growth of his " awareness " of things, and of his own inherent possibilities, he will pass to the next stage, where he approaches the " ancient and narrow " Path, upon which he will find Those Who, outstripping Their fellows, have achieved the maximum possible in purely *human* development. These are They Who, eagerly, yet with limitless patience, wait for Their younger brothers to come out of the nursery of ordinary worldly life into Their higher life where, with Their guidance and assisted by Their compassion and power, man may rise to the stupendous heights of spirituality to which They have attained, and become in his turn a saviour and helper of mankind, thus speeding the mighty plan of evolution towards its goal.

INDEX

QUEST BOOKS
are published by
The Theosophical Society in America,
Wheaton, Illinois 60189-0270,
a branch of a world organization
dedicated to the promotion of the unity of
humanity and the encouragement of the study of
religion, philosophy, and science, to the end that
we may better understand ourselves and our place in
the universe. The Society stands for complete
freedom of individual search and belief.
For further information about its activities,
write or call 1-800-669-1571.

*The Theosophical Publishing House
is aided by the generous support of
THE KERN FOUNDATION,
a trust established by Herbert A. Kern
and dedicated to Theosophical education.*